TONE MANUAL
DISCOVERING YOUR ULTIMATE
ELECTRIC GUITAR SOUND

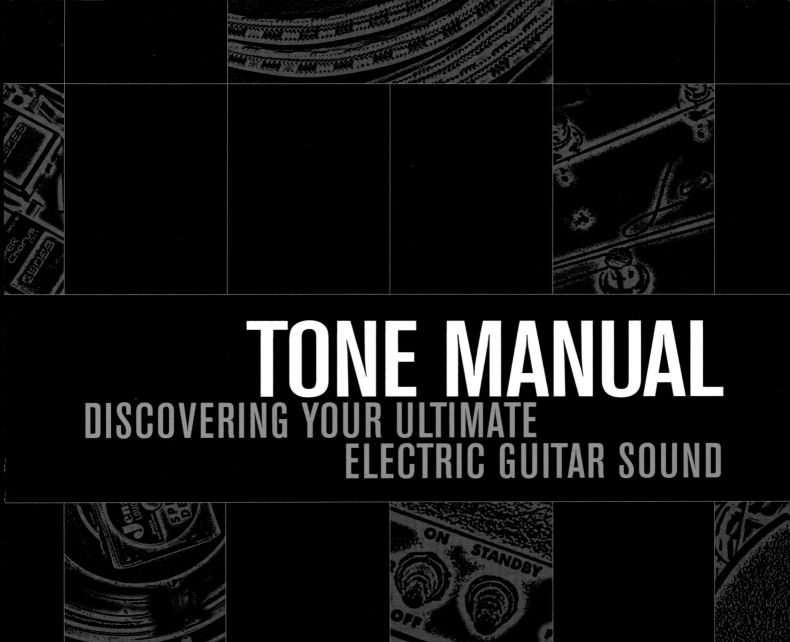

TONE MANUAL
DISCOVERING YOUR ULTIMATE
ELECTRIC GUITAR SOUND

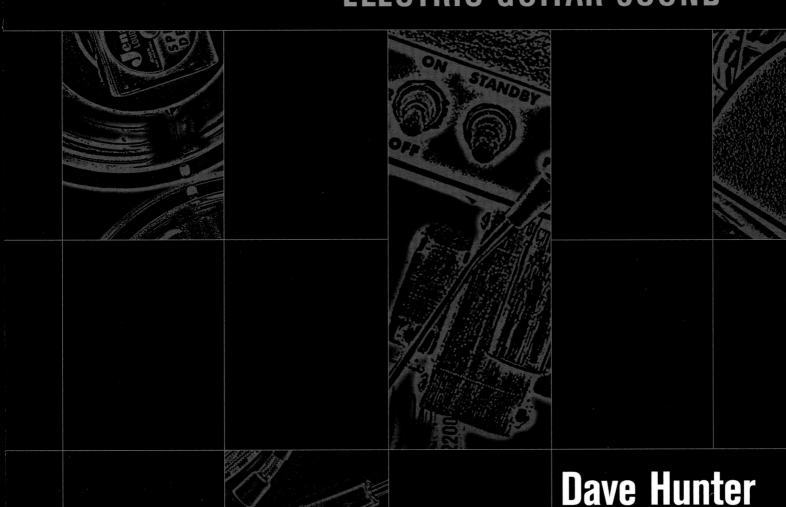

Dave Hunter

TONE MANUAL
Discovering your ultimate electric guitar sound
Dave Hunter

A BACKBEAT BOOK

First edition 2011

Published by Backbeat Books

An Imprint of Hal Leonard Corporation

7777 West Bluemound Road

Milwaukee, WI 53213

www.backbeatbooks.com

Devised and produced for Backbeat Books by

Outline Press Ltd

2A Union Court, 20-22 Union Road

London SW4 6JP, England

www.jawbonepress.com

ISBN 978-1-61713-004-5

A catalogue record for this book is available from the British Library.

Editor: David Sheppard

Design: Paul Cooper Design

Printed by Everbest Printing Co. Ltd, China

11 12 13 14 15 5 4 3 2 1

CONTENTS

INTRODUCTION

We might think of the quest for tone as a recent phenomenon, but guitarists have always talked tone. Hell, *musicians* have always talked tone. Jazz cats discussed it incessantly in the 30s and 40s and it's always been important to classical musicians. Renaissance lutenists probably obsessed over it now and then. If you are serious about playing, the chances are you are also serious about how that playing *sounds*.

I reckon the modern guitarists' conscious quest for tone began on July 7 1981, when Soft Cell released their cover of 'Tainted Love,' replete with its cheesy, synth-pop intro and mechanized beat. Soon, synth players and manufacturers everywhere—and even many guitar makers, it seemed—were sounding the death knell of the electric guitar, convinced that synthesized instruments would take the place of just about every traditional musical implement in existence. If you had that sterile, one-dimensional, highly synthetic 'Elec Gtr' preset on your keyboard, why bother with a troublesome plank of wood with six strings and no internal processing?

Despite this onslaught of plasticized sound, guitarists who still loved their instrument of choice quickly realized that they needed something to combat the ersatz quality of the synth, and that something was tone. The ceramic-loaded, double-locking 'superstrat' guitar of the day, fed through several rack units and a 200-watt, high-gain amp stack, just wasn't going to do it, so they started exploring the sounds, and therefore the ingredients, that made those rich, juicy cuts on original blues, jazz, country, and rock'n'roll records so great in the first place. Thus, we guitarists rediscovered the beauty of simplicity, in tonal terms, and in so doing also reaffirmed that, when played with gusto and attitude through a rig with some sonic virtue, the electric guitar was still the most expressive instrument on the planet. Ultimately, we decided that with genuine tone in our back pocket we really didn't need to sound like a string section or a brass ensemble, still less a synthesizer. We discovered, in short, the modern quest for tone, and we have never looked back since then. Or at least, that *might* be how this all got started.

Whatever brought about this state of affairs, guitarists today sure like to talk about the sound of their instruments: a basic Google search for 'guitar tone' turns up more than a million hits. This is the most-discussed concept in the guitar world today, and the majority of people who take themselves at all seriously as players put at least some thought into improving their tone, while others live in hope of achieving the nebulous phenomenon that is 'the ultimate tone.'

The dilemma about tone as a concept, as I see it, is that it is both subjective *and* objective. That might seem contradictory, but it absolutely has to be so. I firmly believe that we can define certain sounds as having empirically 'good tone'—possessing purity, depth, harmonic complexity, and so forth—while still appealing to us personally, as music, irrespective of tonal considerations. The former is objective, the latter subjective; both are valid, and what's more, somewhere the twain shall meet and work hand in hand to determine what constitutes great tone *for you*.

Whatever sound you are seeking—whether it be, in the subjective sense, clean, crunchy, heavily distorted, bluesy and warm, or country bright—certain 'universal virtues' of good tone remain. Regardless of the broad categorization of the sound you use to make your music, that sound rendered with great tone will generally be one that is harmonically rich, resonant, lively, balanced, and multi-dimensional (possessing the aural equivalent of 3D imagery); it should have good clarity and definition even amid distortion, and should not present any harsh or piercing frequencies even when bright and bold. These qualities might combine in varying proportions to define several very different sounds, but most, if not all of them, are likely to be present to some extent in anything that can be described as 'excellent tone.'

Good tone may be extremely hard to define, but we know it when we hear it. With truly outstanding guitar tone at my fingertips, I am capable of sitting for hours on end playing the same simple chords and riffs, just feeding off the way that the multidimensionality of the sound triggers whatever pleasure mechanism it is that exists within the human sense of hearing. If you haven't experienced tone like that, it is worth striving for, although that sensation alone isn't going to land you a chart-topping record.

To these ends, *The Tone Manual* is a book about guitars, amps, effects, and related gear that is written from the perspective of tone rather than from that of historical chronology, which is the path that the majority of guitar books follow. While remaining conscious of the fact that there are different sounds for different musical styles, and different tastes, it works from the premise that there are efficiencies of design and virtues of construction for all such gear—and for all component parts of any piece of musical equipment as a whole—that contribute to certain universals of good tone. Many things discussed in these pages might be most useful to newcomers to the subjects, or even to advanced players who have previously given little time to considerations of tone; but I present this material in the hope that it will enliven the imaginations of enthusiastic amateur, hardened pro, and total gearhound alike.

As obsessive and even snobbish as all of this might sound, I also want to establish right up front that you don't necessarily *need* excellent tone to make exemplary music—or creative music, or art, or whatever you want to call the good stuff. In the end, what you do with what you've got matters more than anything, and a great riff is still a great riff, a great song still a great song, irrespective of tone. Talented musicians have made outstanding recordings for years with what is really pretty mediocre tone (or worse), but we come to count it as great tone because the music has impact, and we forget that on analysis the sound of the guitar may actually be nondescript at best, or grating and harsh at worst. In the face of a standout song or performance, matters of tone can still fade to the background. In light of this, it is always going to be more important to strive for *your own* great tone than for a simulacrum of some major artist's inspirational sound. You might impress a few pals now and then by sounding 'quite a bit like' Jimi Hendrix, Eric Johnson, Brian May, or Josh Homme, but you will impress more people more of the time by sounding like yourself, and by doing so distinctively and consistently.

Ultimately, this book is not aimed at telling you what good tone is, as such. Instead, it seeks to define the many elements of tone—helping you to understand how different pieces fit together to create the overall tonal picture, and which of those elements might be best deployed to achieve the tone you seek. Thus armed, you can select your own ideal 'whole' as a sum of the parts, in the hope that, as you make it your own, it will be *more* than the sum of its parts. It will be your own creative expression, and ideally, a thing that transcends the tone that transports it to the listener. It will be music.

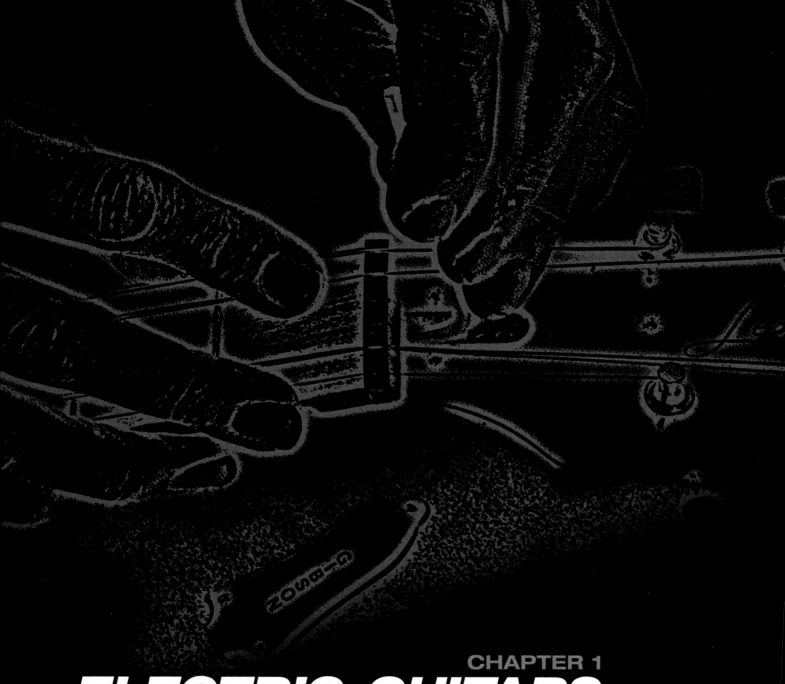

CHAPTER 1
ELECTRIC GUITARS

- Bolt-neck solidbodies
- Set-neck solidbodies
- Semi-acoustic electrics
- Hollowbody electrics
- Peripherals and extras

It will hardly be a surprise if I start talking about the electric guitar as the principal source of tone. For many players, however, taking that fact to heart is more difficult than it would seem. Or, put more precisely, digesting and understanding all of the guitar's tonal facets and implications often requires a little more concentrated thought. For, while any electric guitar can be approached as a 'whole,' it is always simultaneously both more and less than that. While it is always the sum of its parts, in the interaction of those parts tremendous variables exist, and it is within these permutations that tone really begins.

Players seem to settle periodically *en masse* on one tone 'culprit' or another, obsessing over pickups (which are back in fashion in a big way lately), bridges, frets, nuts, and, of course, wood—light, rare, resonant, etc—as the definitive key to tonal bliss. Of course, that key is found in all of these things in combination, and different combinations of even 'the best' ingredients will result in very different tones. If your dream tone emanates from a Telecaster with swamp-ash body, vintage-style pickups, brass saddles on a plain steel bridge plate, and a maple fingerboard, that tone will be a little different with 'hot blues' pickups and a stainless steel bridge plate—and different again with that combination and a rosewood fingerboard.

Whether said tone is 'superior' or 'inferior' is irrelevant, incalculable even, but it will definitely be *different*. There certainly are poor tones—base, dull, uninspiring ones—but there's no universal 'best tone.' There are countless superb tones, all of which are capable of inspiring different players and capable of proving to be an outstanding means of musical expression; but it's healthier to think in terms of a spectrum of different tones rather than a sliding scale of bad to good.

In the introduction to this book, I proposed that there are certain universal elements present within anything that we can call 'excellent tone,' and these can be present (or lacking) within the individual components of any guitar, too. As a simple example of this, consider that the bridge saddle which is cut with extreme accuracy from a type of steel that encourages string vibration is likely to enhance a guitar's tone, while the saddle that is cut rather randomly from a material that deadens or impedes vibration will impair a guitar's tone. Often, such matters are as simple as this to define, at other times they are not, and ingredients that might not appear entirely 'tone enhancing' on paper can work toward creating a lively, responsive, or in some way appealing sound nonetheless. Also, the 'enhancing' or 'impairing' factors mentioned here tend to increase exponentially as you heap one inferior or superior component upon another inferior or superior component.

Things get tough when certain components in a guitar are working for you while others are working against you. This is where serious tone-tweaking, pickup-swapping, and component-tasting comes in. These are exercises, however, that you can practice *ad infinitum* unless you can first define which elements are working for you and which against—an understanding that this chapter of *The Tone Manual* seeks to help you achieve.

To that end, let's dive in and look under the skin of several electric guitar designs and component groups, with the aim of understanding a bit more about what affects what and how.

C H A P T E R 1

THE MAJOR DESIGN TEMPLATES

In this postmodern age of guitar design, there are so many types of electric instruments on the market that just about any combination of components is available somewhere. Nevertheless, there remain a handful of significant templates whose elements still account—with a tweak here or there, perhaps—for some 90 per cent of all existing guitars, perhaps more. Therefore, any study of guitar tone really should begin with an analysis of what makes the best guitars constructed to these templates tick. And rather than simply running down the standard features of these classics (and some more original models inspired by them), let's dig a little into some of the enigmatic interactions between the components that make up each such guitar in an effort to better pin down what it is that makes them work. Many of the relevant components will be dealt with in the sections on the design templates with which they are most associated, although some other generic and universal parts will be addressed subsequently.

BOLT-NECK SOLIDBODIES

Not the first electric guitars available, bolt-neck solidbodies have nevertheless remained among the most influential types ever since Fender's Telecaster (originally known as the Esquire, then Broadcaster) and Stratocaster first carved their enduring niches in popular music, in 1950 and 1954, respectively. In tackling these guitars first, I will inevitably give them a little more attention than other types, but an understanding of these seminal bolt-neck guitars will serve as a springboard for comparing and contrasting the differences heard in set-neck solid and semi-solid electrics.

Leo Fender developed his bolt-neck design (in which the guitar's neck is actually attached to its body with wood screws, not bolts, whatever the accepted terminology) for ease and efficiency of manufacture and repair, but the template has myriad tonal consequences, too. To get to the heart of the 'bolt-neck tone' of vintage-style Telecasters and Stratocasters—a group that can include original instruments, contemporary Fender Vintage Reissue and Custom Shop reproductions, and those from other makers—we need to consider both the inherent sonic qualities of the screwed-together body and neck, and other components and design points that are coincidental to these models. For the great variety of other worthwhile bolt-neck instruments (whether a Paul Reed Smith CE 22, a Tom Anderson Drop Top "S," or a Don Grosh ElectraJet), the final voice is often more of a mix-and-match affair.

In addition to blueprinting a guitar that could be manufactured easily thanks to its slab body and one-piece, screwed-on neck, Leo Fender took advantage of the information he'd gleaned from the musicians who frequented his radio repair shop and who, in the early days of his manufacturing business, used his lap-steel guitars and amplifiers. Fender set out to create a guitar that would be bright, in order to cut through the other instruments in the band, and whose clarity would enhance that brightness while offering a lively alternative to the often woolly-sounding hollowbody arch-top electrics prevalent at the time. He also aimed to make an instrument to match the sonic weight and dynamics that horns, fiddles, and steel guitars enjoyed, while being resistant to feedback, so that guitarists could play them at the maximum volumes which available amplification would allow.

C H A P T E R   1

To bring about these ends, Fender employed variations on the narrow, single-coil pickups which the company had used successfully on steel guitars (addressing brightness and clarity in particular); used brass saddles and a steel bridge plate in place of the wood saddles that most electric Spanish guitars still favored (again enhancing brightness, clarity, and also sustain); made the neck from solid maple (brightness and clarity again) and the body from solid wood (to resist feedback); and anchored the strings in steel ferrules in the back of the body (for further sustain). In these ways, and others, several different elements of the design worked toward achieving common goals.

CLASSIC BOLT-NECK BODY WOODS

In addition to these design points—all of which are recognized as cornerstones of the Telecaster's construction—the woods themselves played a part in enhancing Fender's tonal ambitions. The swamp ash that most Telecaster and early Stratocaster bodies were made from (following prototype experiments with pine and other timbers) offered sweet highs and good clarity, along with firm lows and a certain 'airy' quality that enhanced a guitar's overall depth of tone. Swamp ash's midrange content can be slightly pronounced, although this varies from cut to cut, depending on the density and growth pattern of the wood (in some cases it can even sound rather 'scooped'). It's worth noting that swamp ash, harvested from the lower portions of ash trees grown in the wetlands of the southern USA, is very different from dense northern ash, which is harder and heavier, as is the timber taken from the upper portions of swamp ash trees. Only genuine swamp ash is considered a premium tonewood; other varieties are used in less expensive guitars by makers who are still keen to promote the advantages of an ash body.

From the late 50s and early 60s onward, several Fender Teles, Strats, and other models—those with opaque, custom color finishes in particular—were made with alder bodies. The impetus for the move to alder seems to have been twofold. As Fender's production increased, adequate supplies of light, properly-dried swamp ash became harder to find, and, obscured beneath the opaque finishes that were becoming popular, the ash's visually attractive grain was wasted anyway. Fortunately, alder is an outstanding tonewood. It lends a slightly different edge to the Fender sound, although not dramatically so. It has a good density for solidbody guitar building, offering excellent sustain along with complex, musical highs, a balanced and full-voiced midrange with beefy lower-mids, and strong lows.

Plenty of other makers have dabbled, particularly in recent years, with alternative and even exotic woods in their bolt-neck designs, which might otherwise follow the archetypal Fender patterns; but alder and ash remain far and away the most popular materials for these designs. Guitar maker Don Grosh, who is known for updated renditions of classic bolt-neck templates, believes the popularity of these woods is down to familiarity of reference. "For an alder-body Strat it's going to sound a certain way, and if you try to use mahogany or poplar instead, it just doesn't seem to work with the pickups those guitars are using," he says. "It's the same thing with a Tele. If you deviate from what the standard woods are, you usually get something that isn't that appealing. If the standard woods are working really well, the job is more about fine-tuning other aspects of the guitar."

C H A P T E R   1

Acoustic Wood Resonance in Electric Guitars

Multiple components work together to create the tone that any electric guitar produces, but however much time and consideration you have put into pickup and hardware selection, the way in which the body and neck woods resonate together remains the make-or-break factor that determines the voice of your instrument. Opinions on this subject vary widely, but I feel there are several factors you can look for to pinpoint the guitars that are really happening, resonance-wise.

The first step in determining whether or not a guitar has got it together in tonal terms is to give it a thorough acoustic check up. I'm talking purely electric solidbody or semi-solidbody instruments here, but if you play *any* guitar unamplified it will perform as an acoustic instrument, and the extent to which it excels or falls flat in this regard should tell you a lot about how it will sound when plugged in and cranked up. This is really a matter of learning how to assess the structural and resonant virtues of an instrument; you can try it with guitars you already own, or apply these techniques while perusing your local dealer.

Weight plays a part in this equation, but is generally secondary to the virtue of the build and whether the wood itself—whether heavy or light—is working with the resonance and harmonics of the guitar, or against them. While a well-built example of a finely designed guitar *should* live up to its tonal potential, occasionally, slightly inferior examples of otherwise great, even legendary, guitars do see the light of day. This isn't necessarily the result of any great 'mistake' in the manufacturing process. Sometimes, a piece of wood just doesn't want to be a guitar: it wants to be a park bench. When that occurs, you find that the acoustic tones of body and neck fight each other and just don't vibrate in harmony, or the guitar simply throws out less-than-flattering peaks, nulls, and dead spots that hinder the acoustic voice of the instrument and impede its plugged-in performance as a result.

Let's take a look at methods of discerning an electric guitar's acoustic performance. Firstly, put the guitar in question on your lap, in playing position; strum a first-position chord and feel the tip of the headstock with your right hand while still holding that chord with

CLASSIC BOLT-ON NECK AND FINGERBOARD WOODS

The all-maple neck (in which the neck and fingerboard are carved from a single plank of maple) is one of the classic ingredients of the bolt-neck guitar, although it was greeted with a certain amount of derision when Leo Fender introduced it on early Broadcasters, Telecasters, and Stratocasters. However much early detractors saw it as the sign of a cheap or poorly made instrument, that length of solid maple would help to add bite, definition, and clarity to a guitar whose tone had previously lacked those very qualities. More than just contributing the clean, clear, and bright elements that so many people attribute to maple necks, this hard, dense wood seriously upped the harmonic-sparkle factor in early Fender guitars, making them cut through the mix like nothing before. As guitar effects maker Michael Fuller, an acclaimed guitarist in his own right, notes: "What I love is, you get a good maple-neck Strat and play a complex chord on a nice, clean amp, and you get these magical overtones that make it fatter than it really is." For all the narrow pickups, solid woods, and the implicit 'thinness' of the Fender designs, these

C H A P T E R 1

your left (vice versa if you're a lefty). You should feel a significant amount of vibration there, almost a surprising amount of movement in some cases (note that set-neck guitars exhibit a bit less of this by nature, and set-neck semi-acoustics a little less still; this doesn't indicate a lack of tonal resonance, it just is characteristic of the breeds. You need to assess like against like as far as overall resonance is concerned). Now, strum again and feel the strap button at the lower end of the body, and also the treble-side lower bout (the edge of the guitar near the controls). These regions should vibrate too, a little less than the tip of the headstock perhaps, but you should feel something there. Next, pluck an open G-string and check these same locations: on really resonant guitars, you should still feel some action there. Put your ear to the bass-side bout (the upper horn or shoulder of the guitar) and play a little. You should hear a full, round, even voice, which might be surprisingly loud on a really tone-rich guitar. It should be deep and woody. Ideally, you shouldn't hear anything that's too boomy, choked, or spiky, or any harshness in treble response. Finally, just play the guitar in a range of styles, up and down the neck, and listen normally. It might not be really loud but should be full, even, and lively—and, in some cases, louder than you'd think for a solidbody electric. Play both chords and single notes and hold them; listen to how long the guitar sustains and whether the decay has a pleasing character. Does it sound good to you and make you want to play? Does it represent a quieter version of the kind of tonality that you'd like to have at the core of your sound when amplified? If so, you could be on to a winner.

First-call LA session guitarist Carl Verheyen passed one of his own guitar-buying tips to me when we were working together recently. Carl said that when he approaches an instrument hanging on the wall in a guitar store, he simply plucks the B-string, then grabs the lower treble bout of the guitar (the region around the jack socket) to feel if there's any vibration there. If there is, he takes it down and plays it further. If there isn't, he passes it up. Experiment with playing acoustically on as many electric guitars as you can, put some thought into wood resonance, and see what you discover. Often, it's the first step toward nailing a really great tone machine.

new instruments churned out a fat breed of clean (not to mention a snarling breed of dirty) tones that immediately turned on contemporary players.

Adding a rosewood fingerboard to the maple brought a little more warmth and breadth to Leo Fender's guitars, even if he—as one popular legend has it—made the change simply because he didn't like the way the worn, smudged, maple Fender fingerboards looked on television. Made with a flat underside glued to a flat-topped maple neck, Fender's rosewood 'slab board,' used between 1959 and mid 1962, is generally considered more desirable and tonally superior to the curved or 'round lam' (laminated) rosewood board that was introduced subsequently, simply, perhaps, because many players equate 'thicker' rosewood with 'better.' The fact that this is the fretboard on the late Stevie Ray Vaughan's 'Number One' Strat has hardly hurt the slab board's reputation. According to Fender Custom Shop 'Master Builder' Chris Fleming, however, the thinner curved board deserves plenty of respect in its own right. "I've made a lot of slab board rosewood fingerboards and what we call 'round lams,'" he says, "and I prefer the round lams."

Fleming has his own theories about Leo Fender's preference for round lams. "I think it was for a couple of reasons. One is that he liked the idea of the maple being more of a majority of the wood, and he liked the idea that it was kind of a custom way to do it; it was proprietary. And I'd also like to think that he liked the sound of it. I feel like the slab board was the way that they did it because they had to figure out how to do it quickly. Then they had to tool up to make the rounded board and never turned back."

However you look at it, attaching a curved rosewood fingerboard to a maple neck with a radiused top surface is a lot more work than attaching a flat slab to a flat neck; so Fender certainly didn't choose the post-1962 construction technique as some kind of 'easy option.'

WEIGHT AND TONE

A lot has been made of weight—of the tonewoods used and of the finished guitar itself. In the 70s, the belief that super-heavy guitars offered greater sustain was widespread. This was probably because guitars made in that era—when careful timber selection seemed to have fallen by the wayside—tended to be heavier, and lightweight instruments were rare. It may also have had something to do with the over-wound ceramic pickups and high-gain amps that were becoming prevalent, so that guitarists attributed what they were hearing to the deadweight instruments in their hands. In recent years, this thinking has been reversed: the received wisdom now is that the lighter the guitar, the more it will resonate and the better its tone will be.

In truth, although a body wood's weight—or, more accurately, its density—might play some part in shaping its tone, its general quality and overall resonant characteristics (which can vary wildly even between timber stocks of a similar weight) and the way the guitar has been put together will usually contribute far more to the final result. In the end, for the most versatile and consistently outstanding tone, guitars of a lower-medium weight are often likely to rule the day: for example, a Tele or Strat in the 7–8 pounds (3.2–3.6kg) range. When it is also very well constructed, boasts excellent pickups and hardware, and is set up properly, a guitar of this weight will often blend good body and punch with an element of sweetness, richness, and depth, while also offering excellent sustain. To risk a generalization about guitars on either side of this optimum weight range, those that are far lighter can still sound great but might sometimes lean toward the 'snappy,' 'quacky' end of the spectrum, while those that are heavier can occasionally sound just a little dull and lifeless.

That being said, good guitars of all weights can also sound excellent and can be among the best instruments you have ever played or heard. Remember, we're dissecting the minutiae here, and there are no rigid conventions. Nonetheless, the above rule of thumb should help you achieve more consistent results than simply seeking the lightest or heaviest possible guitar. It's worth bearing in mind that some extremely light Teles can sustain like nobody's business, while others can be a little flat. To get slightly more 'real world' about it, consider the pervasive myth that early-50s Teles were all very light and sounded great. In fact, the bulk of the lightest Telecasters in existence were produced in the late mid 50s and late 60s. It's not uncommon to find early-50s blackguard Telecasters and Esquires that weigh upwards of 8.5 pounds (3.9kg), and some of these models have been among the finest-sounding Teles of any stripe that I have ever played or heard. In short, don't let the weight factor guide you more than the actual performance—and bear in mind that a tendency to either of the extremes is more likely to disappoint than yield exceptional results.

Bolt-neck guitars are made with several other body woods these days. Some, such as poplar, are worth avoiding if you're really on a tone quest. Others, like basswood, can offer very good results, usually heard in a well-balanced frequency range that's enhanced by prominent mids.

SONIC CHARACTERISTICS OF THE BOLT-ON NECK JOINT

As it happens, the process of screwing the neck to the body, which produces a solid but inevitably less 'seamless' neck joint than the glued-in necks of Gibson, Gretsch, Epiphone, and other more traditional makers, adds accidental tonal and performance characteristics to Fender guitars. Indeed, in conjunction with the design attributes detailed above, this construction has undoubtedly helped to define the characteristic 'Fender sound.'

Although an extremely well cut and fitted, screwed-together neck joint might be as tight (if not tighter) than a glued-in joint in terms of the force of pressure of neck wood on body wood, the body and neck will always remain very slightly decoupled from one another. This is due to an inevitable microscopic air gap between the two pieces that is there courtesy of the grain in the surface of the wood and dimples or irregularities within the finish on each piece. While the debate continues among qualified, respected luthiers as to whether such decoupling is favorable or not, and to what extent either way, there's little doubt that a bolt-neck guitar sounds different from one of glued-neck construction. While removing a Strat's neck screws and gluing the neck in place instead won't make a radical sonic difference (even if the neck joint wasn't designed to perform optimally as a glued-in piece), taking the same guitar and carving a deep-set neck tenon and body pocket on one side and gluing them together, while screwing neck and body together with a traditional Fender-style heel and pocket on the other, is likely to make them respond at least a little differently.

Some of the characteristics distinguishing bolt-neck tone are its percussive snap, a decoupling of the pick attack and the note's body and tail, the result of a minute delay between its initial pop and the sustain and decay of the note, versus the furrier and less distinct attack-body-tail of the response of, for example, a Gibson Les Paul or SG. I'm talking fine points here, extremes of nuance, but these are the infinitesimal details that add up to the final tonal signature of any breed of instrument.

Some guitar makers and players believe that too efficient a neck joint (one that is glued-in) contributes to a muddying of the frequency response, because the neck and body resonate at different frequencies, and the clash of these disparities sometimes cancels, mutes, or absorbs resonances that would otherwise enhance harmonic richness, sparkle, and clarity in less efficiently coupled neck-body joints. There is some logic in this thinking. Even when a neck and body are made from the same type of wood, the grain and orientation of those cuts of timber will usually differ. They will almost always have been carved from different sources, and will result in different masses and densities, too, however slight. Body resonance and neck resonance are also triggered by string vibration absorbed in different places and in different ways, through bridge saddles, nuts, or frets.

C   H   A   P   T   E   R   1

Consider the following analogy with recording studio microphone technique. By using two different mics placed in different positions, an engineer can potentially capture a bigger, richer recording of a guitar-and-amp sound. If those two recorded sources present adverse phase relationships when their signals are combined, however, certain frequencies will be cancelled out resulting in a thinner sound than either of the mics alone might produce. Can the transference of too much neck and body resonance create a similarly conflicting frequency relationship, one that adversely affects an instrument's overall tone? The analogy is far from perfect, of course, because we aren't talking about two versions of the same sound source captured at different positions in a room and blended together, but rather, the combined vibrations of two different pieces of wood. It's possible that there's some correlation here, but, as ever, the pros and cons of melding wood resonances in this way depend upon the tone you seek, and what is undesirable from one perspective might be favorable from another (that is, one player's 'dullness' is another's 'warmth;' one players 'shimmer' another's 'harshness,' and so on).

Even within the bolt-on field, the issue of neck-joint tightness and the virtue (or otherwise) of decoupling between neck and body continue to spawn plenty of arguments around the water cooler. I have a much-played 1957 Fender Esquire (long-ago 'Tele-ized' with the addition of a neck pickup) with a neck pocket that is so ill-fitting that if I remove the neck, I have to put considerable pressure on it to bias it toward the bass side while tightening the mounting screws—if I want to have any hope of getting the strings to line up in a playable fashion across the fingerboard from bridge saddles to nut (do it wrong, and my high E-string will be floating off the edge of the fingerboard). Get the thing secure, however, and it's a superb-sounding guitar. I also have a recently built Hahn 228 (a guitar constructed in the image of a blackguard Telecaster) with a neck pocket cut so precisely you can remove the mounting screws entirely and still carry the guitar around by the neck. Although I treasure the vintage Esquire, the Hahn sounds 'better'—bigger, fuller, livelier, and more harmonically responsive. This is a subjective assessment, nevertheless, and plenty of others might prefer the Esquire. What is objectively verifiable, however, is the fact that, although the Esquire has a more powerful bridge pickup than the Hahn (they are 7.76k ohms and 7.15k ohms respectively, made with similar magnet types and wire gauges), the Hahn is appreciably louder. In this, I believe, I am partly hearing that neck pocket, as well as a few other factors (a huge, quarter-sawn maple neck and a very efficient bridge, not least). The point of all this, however, is not to tell you why I purchased the Hahn—both guitars are outstanding, and belong on any list of tonally superior Teles—but to offer a living example of the way certain variables might interact to create nuanced differences in guitars that are otherwise built to the same, or at least extremely similar, templates.

To address the decoupling/neck-joint issue from a different angle, it is also worth considering a degree of additional decoupling that is sometimes regarded as necessary to guitars within the bolt-neck group. I'm talking 'neck shims' here. A neck shim is a thin piece of material that is cut from wood veneer, card, thin metal, or another substance and placed beneath part of the neck heel to adjust the angle of the neck, therefore facilitating a greater range of bridge height adjustment than the totally flat neck pitch allows. I know plenty of players (and I'm usually one of them) who will avoid shimming a neck at all costs, in the belief that putting that minute gap between the underside of the neck heel and the bottom of the pocket will kill off their tone. You can talk to an equal number of techs who have shimmed necks, however, as well as guitarists who have played such instruments, who will tell you that there is no noticeable difference in tone between the shimmed and un-shimmed neck, provided the guitar is set up correctly in each instance. A few will even tell you that bolt-neck guitars with shimmed necks sound better.

One of the latter is noted guitarist and tech Buzz Feiten, who believes that shimming its neck can dramatically improve a guitar's tone, as he revealed to Dan Erlewine in Erlewine's book *How To Make Your Electric Guitar Play Great* (Backbeat, 2001). In short, Feiten feels that the decoupling of two differently resonating wooden components does wonders for his guitar's tone. But of course, there are myriad examples of efficiently cut, tightly coupled, bolt-on neck-body joints in guitars that sound thoroughly outstanding; so where does that leave you?

To make this more than a merely rhetorical question, I would try all the great guitars you can get your hands on without, if possible, letting your knowledge of the efficiency of their neck pockets, their inclusion or exclusion of a shim, or any other such factors, influence your judgment before you hear what's coming out of the amplifier. At the end of any and all assessments I would still hold that, more often than not, the guitar that has been made well, with a tight, clean neck pocket and, therefore, a good, tight-fitting neck, and which can be adjusted satisfactorily to any reasonable playing action without use of a shim, is likely to be a better sounding guitar than one that fails in these departments. But, that said, if the Tele with the shimmed neck or the neck pocket showing a little airspace between the side of the neck heel and the bass-side bout sounds better to you than the one that you can carry around by the neck with the mounting screws removed, you know what to do, and don't let your preconceptions persuade you otherwise.

THE 25½-INCH SCALE LENGTH

Just as several component and design-based factors in Fender's seminal solidbody guitars worked toward brightness and clarity, their scale length also furthered those ends. The 25½-inch scale length used for the Telecaster and Stratocaster, as well as for the Jazzmaster that followed in the late 50s, and the vast majority of reproductions and emulations of these designs, emphasizes harmonic shimmer and brightness more than shorter scale lengths, factors that are further enhanced by these guitars' single-coil pickups and other features already discussed. You can get a 24¾-inch Gibson-style guitar to sound 'a little' like a 25½-inch Fender-style guitar, and vice versa, by changing pickups and components, but scale length is so fundamental to the inherent sound of either of these types of guitar that you can never entirely ape the sound of classics from either camp without building the instrument to the appropriate scale length in the first place.

Since the issue here is the scale length used by the archetypal bolt-neck guitar with single-coil pickups, I'll concentrate on the virtues of that model for the moment. Scale length is often thought of as the distance from the nut to the bridge saddle, but it is more accurately calculated as twice the measurement from the nut to the 12th fret, since most guitars have adjustable

saddles and the precise distance from nut to individual string saddle will therefore vary. In addition to feeling a little tighter and firmer under the fingertips—since they need to be placed under slightly greater tension than strings on a shorter-scale guitar to achieve necessary pitch at standard tuning—strings tuned to a 25½-inch scale length will genuinely sound different to those of the same gauges tuned to the same pitches on a guitar of a shorter scale. Put simply, this is because the harmonic nodes placed along the 25½-inch length of string are spaced a little more widely than those found on shorter lengths of string and have slightly more room to 'breathe,' if you will—so the harmonics shine out a little more prominently.

No doubt you already know something of the harmonics I mention, and probably use them in your own playing on occasion, resting a finger very gently on a plucked string directly above the fifth, seventh, or 12th fret (most commonly, although there are other harmonic positions) to summon their ringing, ethereal sound. These tones aren't present only when played in this manner; they and others are part of the harmonic makeup of any open string you resonate. When fretted strings are played, other harmonics are similarly accessed, although they occur at different points along the string.

For the same reason that a first-position open G-chord will ring more noticeably with harmonics than, for example, a barre chord G played at the tenth-to-12th frets (which will ring with far less of the shimmer and sparkle of its lower counterpart), longer scale lengths allow these harmonics to ring out more clearly because each will have additional space around it, allowing a more precise response.

Since 25½ inch is the longest scale length commonly used for standard electric guitars, these instruments inevitably offer more of this sparkle than instruments built to shorter lengths. They also, as a rule, produce firmer low notes, since both the clarity of their harmonic response and the greater string tension work together to produce a bold fundamental. Have you ever wondered why your Stratocaster with fairly weak, single-coil pickups always had a bolder, tighter, more piano-like low E-string than your 24¾-inch scale rock machine equipped with high-octane humbuckers? That Strat's scale length is a big part of it; its narrow, tight-sounding pickups also contribute, while the high-gain humbucker's width and power combine to further 'blur' the fundamental heard from the 24¾-inch scale guitar. To reiterate, you simply can't achieve the full 'Fender sound' on a Gibson-scale guitar, or vice versa.

SIGNIFICANT COMPONENTS

As touched upon briefly above, several other elements of the classic bolt-neck guitar's design and construction work toward the bright, clear tone that generally distinguishes these types of instrument. You can alter a bolt-neck guitar considerably, of course, by changing all or most of its significant components to those of a different breed of instrument, and that's exactly what several makers have done over the years since the traditional templates were first established. But thanks to the fact that great originators such as Fender and Gibson (alongside Gretsch, Epiphone, Rickenbacker, and others) tended to purposefully differentiate their designs, in the early days at least, rather than mixing and matching similar elements, their seminal bolt-neck and set-neck guitars remained entirely distinctive.

PICKUPS ON TRADITIONAL BOLT-NECK GUITARS

Fender Telecaster and Stratocaster pickups are dissimilar in nuanced but significant ways, although in the broad sense they are still more alike than different. While several things contribute to the legendary Fender brightness and twang (in short, a heightened high-end response), their pickups are often considered to be the heart of that signature. Beyond the characteristic sound produced by single-coil pickups in general, the particular shape and design of the pickups on Fender's initial electric guitar models worked together to produce a clear tone with accentuated highs.

Having established the tonal significance of scale length, namely that the longer the vibrating string the more space the higher harmonics have to 'sparkle,' we can now consider the component that picks up that vibration and translates it into an electrical signal. The narrower the magnetic field above that pickup—which is what interacts with the string vibration to create the sonic response—the tighter the focus of the signal it will produce. Both the shape of the coil and the positioning of the magnets in the classic Fender pickup designs serve to create a narrow magnetic field. That slender window is biased toward a clear, bright signal with tight note definition, and that's what we hear as part of the archetypal 'Fender sound,' whether from a Strat or a Tele.

The relatively low output of most such single-coil pickups also accentuates both their highs and lows, while vintage Fender pickups with coils wound toward the higher end of the spectrum, and therefore producing higher outputs, will produce a little more midrange content, although they will still be fairly bright and clear. In addition to the output level and magnetic field characteristics, the use of actual magnets as polepieces within these pickups, rather than a magnet or magnets mounted beneath the coil in contact with steel polepieces, further contributes to a bright, clear tone.

Stratocaster pickups are a bit narrower, and are usually wound with slightly fewer turns of wire, than Telecaster bridge pickups, and these variations differentiate their tone accordingly. Tele neck pickups are smaller and narrower still, and are also wound with thinner wire—specifications aimed at capturing a clear tone from the warm, full neck position. But by far the widest sonic disparity between Fender's two early classic models is down to the way the Tele's bridge pickup is mounted, not to mention the bridge design itself.

A traditional Tele bridge pickup is suspended by bolts (supported by springs or rubber tubing) from the bridge's thin metal base plate. This pickup also has a copper-coated tin base plate attached to the underside of its coil. The contact made between this base plate and the pickup's magnetic polepieces—and, via the mounting bolts, the metal bridge plate—affects the magnetic field somewhat, while also increasing the inductance of the pickup slightly. This adds some 'fatness' to the pickup, while the interaction between the bridge plate, saddles, and pickup influence the Tele's tone still further (more of which below).

Stratocaster pickups, which 'float,' suspended within the guitar's plastic pickguard, are less influenced by other factors of the guitar's design. As such, they act more purely as themselves, if you will: the pickup translates the sound of the guitar via its own fundamental design, without so much interaction from its mounting or other nearby components. Regarded in this way, the

Telecaster bridge pickup might seem like an imperfect arrangement, given that its performance relies heavily on the way that it is mounted. While that may be the case, the Tele pickup's arguably compromised engineering has become an inexorable part of the guitar's legendary tone, one that's extremely difficult to achieve when any of its several determining ingredients are subtracted from the recipe. Indeed, there are devoted Tele players aplenty who would hesitate at the prospect of *any* overarching 'improvement' to their instrument's time-honored design.

BRIDGES ON TRADITIONAL BOLT-NECK GUITARS

Although it appeared on the first commercially successful solidbody electric guitar, the original Fender Telecaster bridge remains unique to this style of guitar and was never deployed on other designs, as were so many later hardware components. With this type of bridge, the strings are anchored in ferrules inserted into the back of the guitar's body, from which they pass through drilled holes to emerge through a steel bridge plate before taking a rounded right-angle turn over the bridge saddles and on toward the neck. This simple configuration achieves excellent sustain, a firm attack, and a bright, ringing tone, yielding a sound that is virtually impossible to repeat with any other style of bridge, however similar the guitar might be otherwise.

The fact that a Telecaster's bridge pickup hangs from mounting bolts that are anchored in the bridge plate also influences this unique guitar's mojo. In addition to helping shape the magnetic field of the bridge pickups, the metal bridge plate—upon which the saddles rest, and through which they resonate—transfers some of the strings' vibrating energy and a little microphonics into the pickup, adding an element of edgy, metallic twang to the sound of the guitar. Several makers have sought to achieve the classic Telecaster sound without the metallic, slightly microphonic contribution of the bridge, which can, arguably, make for a tone that's too sharp and piercing in some situations. Tom Anderson, G&L, and even Fender itself (with the G.E. Smith Telecaster) have all made guitars in this general style, but with the bridge pickup mounted directly into the wood of the body or suspended from a plastic pickguard. A truly first-rate Telecaster, however, should blend the traditional bridge element into an overall sound that is rounded and warmed by the body resonance, with enough fatness from the pickup so that the final result is bright, with lots of sparkle, but filled out by plenty of bite and a little grind, without ever being harsh or shrill.

The Strat's 'synchronized' tremolo (or vibrato) bridge—and the countless copies and near-replicas which have followed it—introduces a variety of particular sonic elements to the guitar's overall tone, but it does so by interacting with string vibration and body resonance rather than directly with the bridge pickup. In addition to the individually adjustable, stamped-steel saddles and bridge plate visible on the front of the guitar (which themselves contribute some brightness and clarity to the Strat tone), an unseen 'inertia block' (or 'sustain block') bolted beneath the bridge plate, and into which the strings are anchored, plays a major part in shaping the archetypal Strat sound. The inertia block itself is an ingenious piece of design, and helps to make up for the resonant mass lost by the necessarily flexible coupling of vibrato to guitar body (tonehounds swear by the original, heavy, cold-rolled steel blocks deployed on 1954–71 Strats, and those on high quality reissues and reproductions, as compared to the less dense blocks that were later made from die-cast Mazak and other lighter, sonically inferior alloys). As such, it adds in some warmth, body, and low-end solidity that might otherwise be absent and is a crucial part of an overall tonal picture characterized, in a high quality Strat, by ringing chime and jangle with a slightly silky sizzle in the highs, an air of gentle compression, and a somewhat scooped midrange coupled to a firm bass response.

Aside from any tonal contribution by the bridge, the springs at its rear, which counteract the string tension and enable the unit to return to pitch following down-bends, add considerably to the playing feel of this style of guitar. Bend a Strat's G-string firmly, for example, and you will note how the bridge plate tips forward slightly. Pick an open high E-string but bend the G (without picking it) and listen to how the pitch of the high E dips. That action tells you that there's some give in the Strat's vibrato, and your fingers can detect this quality—a softness and springiness in the instrument's playing feel. This can make a Strat seem easier to bend than, say, a Telecaster, although not necessarily that much easier to achieve a given pitch with an up-bend, since that give in the bridge is dipping the strings' pitch at the same time that you are pushing up. Still, this is one of several things that contribute to the distinctive character of the guitar.

VARIATIONS ON BOLT-NECK DESIGNS

Many guitars set out to be nothing more than copies, or near-copies of Strats and Teles (sometimes with brilliant results), so the ingredients discussed above apply to them in the same way they would to the original instruments. Others stray further from these templates, although in an effort to modify the original formulas, the sound they make differs by degrees according to the extent to which the seminal elements of tone are altered in their design (which is not to say that any of these variations will sound worse, or better, merely different).

The most common modification to the Fender-style bolt-neck configuration was arrived at by players and manufacturers adding humbucking pickups to these kinds of guitars in order to replicate the success that Gibson was having with humbucker-loaded instruments in the late 60s and early 70s. Adding a humbucker to the neck position of a Telecaster became a popular option, for jazz and blues players in particular, and transformed a country and raw-rock'n'roll instrument into a surprisingly able performer in those other genres.

Fender introduced its own Wide Range Humbucker, designed by Seth Lover (inventor of the PAF, the world's first humbucking pickup), on the Thinline Telecaster model of 1971, and attached them to its Custom and Deluxe models soon after. The use of cunife (an alloy of copper, nickel, and iron) magnet polepieces, which are hard enough to be threaded, and therefore adjustable, makes these pickups sound bright, articulate, yet warm and fat-sounding, so the instruments that carry them retain at least a modicum of Fender character while leaning toward conventional humbucker tones, too. In the course of adopting a humbucker in the bridge position, with the pickup suspended from the steel bridge plate, these guitars lost seminal elements of the Tele bridge. Rather than sounding like a 'twanging Tele with a humbucker,' these instruments are a good two or three steps removed from a Telecaster circa 1952. Rather than aping a classic Tele tone, only with a little more thickness and grind dialed in, these dual humbucker-sporting Teles are entirely different guitars altogether.

When choosing a replacement pickup or contemplating the pickups in a new guitar you are considering buying, don't automatically succumb to the 'hotter is better' mythology. Granted, hot pickups have their place in many kinds of music: how else to explain the healthy market in high-gain replacement pickups? For styles where clued-in players want to achieve dynamics, nuances, musical subtlety, and finger tone rather than sheer power, however, the lower-gain pickup still rules the day. This simple fact was lost on a lot of players in the late 70s and 80s, when the replacement-pickup market first boomed and a 'hotter is better' mentality pervaded the guitar world. The trend was understandable given that this was also the era of anemic amps (the sun having set on the golden age of the tube amp a few years earlier), in which many players attempted to make a big rock sound with newer gear that just didn't possess the crunch factor of the vintage stuff. With the over-wound or ceramic-magnet pickups that proliferated at this time, those limp amps could be driven harder, achieving distortion with relative ease. It seemed like a perfect solution for some, yet innumerable players soon tired of the one-dimensional setup and grew nostalgic for the smooth highs, vocal tones, and touch sensitivity that they had once achieved using older equipment.

Many guitarists attributed these qualities, not incorrectly, to vintage instruments and to the way the old tube amps reacted with them. A major part of this interaction was down to the pickups. Although the humbucker had come to be viewed as the powerhouse of pickups, a close examination of an original Gibson PAF pickup of 1957–62 reveals a lack of DC resistance in the 10k–12k ohms range, as commonly found with later, high-gain humbuckers. The vintage PAF hovers down in

Perhaps surprisingly, Fender refrained from adding humbuckers to any stock Stratocaster model until well after others had started doing it as a post-factory modification. The 'superstrat' configuration, which at its most basic describes a Strat-style guitar with a humbucker in the bridge position, became popular with several rockers in the 70s, and made a stratospheric rise to prominence with Edward Van Halen's use of a Charvel S-style guitar with a rewound Gibson PAF humbucker. Modifying the basic template in this way obviously adds a thicker, creamier bridge-pickup tone, with more aggression and sustain. Since you can rarely have it both ways, it also inevitably results in the loss of some of the Fender-ish nature of the instrument: as midrange is emphasized and gain is increased, highs become thickened and lose clarity, while lows become rounder and usually a little less firm and 'piano like.' After the superstrat craze struck, the format was taken up by countless makers—Charvel, Jackson, Kramer, Ibanez, and others—and frequently included a high performance, double-locking Floyd Rose vibrato bridge, or similar. The addition of this highly-engineered vibrato took the core tone of these superstrats further from that of the original, vintage-style Fender Stratocaster—the new bridge tended to thin out the guitar's natural resonance slightly, so the tone became even more a product of the pickups (and a more extreme playing style, of course) than of an interaction between body, bridge, and pickups.

In developing his popular contemporary designs, Paul Reed Smith (PRS) evolved a template the 6.5k–7.5k ohms range, which is no hotter than plenty of single-coil pickups. The same relative 'coolness' applies to vintage Gibson P-90 pickups when compared to many modern replacements inspired by that classic single-coil design (it's also worth noting that a P-90 and a PAF humbucker in fact have very similar outputs, even though they sound quite different).

The idea that you can't rock with a low-output pickup is fallacious. Try telling that to Eric Clapton. who ripped it up in the 60s with PAFs on his original circa-1960 Les Paul Standard, and equally low-output 'patent number' humbuckers on an ES-335 and SG Standard; or to Pete Townshend, who in the late 60s powered The Who with two relatively low-gain P-90s on his SG Special; or to Jimi Hendrix, whose late-60s Stratocasters had weaker, single-coil pickups than those guitars generally carried a decade earlier; or to Stevie Ray Vaughan who followed him in the single-coil tendency.

All these players undeniably rock, and their low-output pickups help to get them there. And here's the rub: while high-gain pickups give you heavy overdrive tones and effectively nothing else, lower-gain pickups better translate the nuances of your attack, style, and dynamics, with plummy lows, sweeter highs, and less aggressive midrange. In short, they are more touch sensitive. They also overload the preamp stage of your amplifier or effects less than high-gain pickups, and thereby help to carry a full, round guitar sound along to other stages of the amp's circuitry, where some players feel the more delectable tones are generated, rather than clipping early and leaving you with nothing but heat and grunge. You *want* heat and grunge? Crank it up—you can still get there. That's what volume knobs, booster pedals, and overdrive effects are for. If you've yet to try low-gain pickups, do check them out: I'm betting you'll discover added nuances of tone.

that is often viewed as a hybrid of the Fender and Gibson styles. Although the company's top-of-the-line models are set-neck instruments, and their range now includes other differently configured variants, the core of the PRS line still blends characteristics from both Fender and Gibson camps, and its bolt-neck CE models are particularly fine examples of the hybridized approach.

The majority of PRS guitars are made to a 25-inch scale length, which influences both the tone and feel of the instruments, and was one of the factors that helped to make them a hit with players who wanted a little dash of Gibson with their Fender. The humbucking pickups that they most commonly carry facilitate many of the former maker's tricks, while the coil-splitting switching emulates some of the single-coil tones of the latter. Add to that a bolt-on maple neck and you're left with a snappy, articulate guitar that can pull off some twang and jangle when necessary but also remain sufficiently thick and warm for creamier rock soloing and crunchy rhythm parts. The PRS vibrato unit was also a clever reworking of the vintage Stratocaster model, deploying many of Fender's principles to achieve similar sounds while offering improved return-to-pitch stability.

Of course, PRS's blending of traditional humbucker-based characteristics with bolt-neck construction is nothing new, and many other makers have subsequently joined the game. As alluded to earlier in this section, we really are in a postmodern age of guitar design and

manufacture, and none of the old rules hold fast any more. The classic templates still provide the basis for the majority of guitars on the market, however, while the better instruments which blend elements from the otherwise distinct camps prove that putting lime in the coconut can satisfy certain tastes.

SET-NECK SOLIDBODIES

The glued-in neck (commonly called the 'set neck') has clearly been a staple of guitar-making for much longer than the 'bolt-on' neck: it was the method used for acoustic-guitar neck attachment long before the electric came along. When Gibson became the first major manufacturer to release production-model electrics in the mid 30s (Rickenbacker and a few others had actually produced electric guitars before Gibson, but only tentatively and in tiny quantities), the instruments naturally retained this cornerstone of their construction. The glued-in neck's standing in luthiery—and its use by established makers such as Gibson, Gretsch, and Epiphone (along with Martin and other acoustic guitar specialists)—meant that early bolt-neck efforts were often seen as cheap, second-rate, or sub-standard, and remained so in the eyes of skeptical players for many years after Fender's revolutionary guitars had been accepted by others. Aside from being seen as embodying design tradition and high quality workmanship, many set-neck guitars do possess resonant characteristics that result directly from this method of attachment. As pertinent as this is, the majority of these instruments tended to be distinctive in several other, unrelated ways, too; so it's not only the method by which their necks are attached to their bodies that differentiates them.

COMMON SET-NECK BODY WOODS

There are some variables in the woods used in groundbreaking, standard-setting set-neck guitars, although the archetypal examples fall in a fairly narrow range. Gibson's original trendsetter in this department, the Les Paul Model (later renamed the Les Paul Standard), popularized the combination of a carved solid maple top, glued to a solid mahogany body. This pairing has become one of the major established templates, and for good reason. A body made only from solid mahogany offers plenty of tonal depth and richness, usually heard as a blend of warmth and multi-dimensional texture. This tonewood template was good enough for the Gibson Les Paul Special and Junior, and the SG that followed, as well as several other outstanding guitars from other makers. Adding a maple top, however, brings increased clarity and high-end bite to what the mahogany already delivers, and helps to produce a more toothsome tonal picture overall.

Rickenbacker's prominent use of maple in solidbody models such as the 450 and 460 from the early 60s, along with the alder used in early examples of the 325 of the late 50s, gave another flavor to the set-neck recipe, but these guitars had a brightness and jangle that always made them sound and feel entirely alien to the set-neck category as we usually identify it. Equally anomalously, Gretsch's 'solidbody' Duo Jet was constructed of mahogany and maple like the Les Paul, but actually had several internal chambers providing airspace beneath its top, which was made from laminated maple pressed into an arch, rather than solid, carved maple. I will address this further in the section on semi-hollow instruments. The other significant solidbody wood of the early days of the breed, although it wouldn't prove itself immediately, was korina. Sometimes known as limba, this African wood is related to mahogany but is lighter both in weight and appearance, and offers distinct tonal refinements, too. Its use in the low-production, and now extremely rare, Gibson Flying V and Explorer models of 1958–59 established its presence in the set-neck guitar world and it has been revived for this use by several other makers in the intervening years, as well as by Gibson itself. Korina yields an admirable blend of resonance, warmth, sweetness, and sustain, which, all rolled together, give it a unique sound that's difficult to replicate precisely with other woods.

Naturally, anything goes today, and quality guitar makers have introduced ash, alder, walnut, oak, cherry, and just about any other viable hard or semi-soft wood you can think of—and combinations thereof, alongside more exotic alternatives—into their set-neck solidbody designs. While many of these have their virtues, they are used too infrequently to have established a template as such. To taste them, you really need to sample the individual guitars in which they appear.

SONIC CHARACTERISTICS OF THE GLUED-IN NECK JOINT

The act of fitting together two precisely cut pieces of wood in a dovetail or mortise-and-tenon joint, and gluing them together, has direct implications on the way string vibration travels through that joint. Guitars so constructed will usually sound different to those on which the neck and body are butted tightly together and held with screws, even if all the other ingredients of the respective instruments are identical. Some of the theory behind the sonic signature of the set-neck tone has already been discussed in the section on bolt-neck guitars—namely, the current thinking that tightly coupled set-neck joints might contribute to some 'sonic clash,' or canceling out of certain frequencies. Thanks to the more efficient transference of vibrations through the wood, some maintain, the neck resonance and body resonance may fight each other, leading to a darker sounding instrument.

In the previous section, we discussed this area in largely pro-bolt-neck terms, but let's now look at it from the perspective of set-neck guitars and consider how this efficiency of resonance transference might be seen as an asset. If the slight decoupling of the body and neck in the bolt-neck guitar can be heard as contributing to explosive attack and added harmonic sparkle, the modest muting of those characteristics in a well built, set-neck guitar leads to what some would call greater warmth, thickness, and body—the renowned 'creamy' Les Paul lead tone, for example. The traditional glued-in neck joint, with a mahogany neck appended to a mahogany (or mostly mahogany) body, as favored by formative makers Gibson, Gretsch, and Epiphone, and by countless subsequent manufacturers, does indeed enhance the smoothness of the picking response, when compared to most bolt-neck guitars. It can also make for excellent, although not necessarily 'superior,' sustain, since a good Telecaster can ring on into tomorrow. The key tonal characteristics to look for here—however much these terms might be overused—are smoothness, warmth, fatness, and creaminess; in short, a certain thickness and depth of voice which is present in the guitar itself, regardless of the pickups used on it.

Naturally, there's a wide disparity in the quality and general veracity of different glued-in neck joints, and even the hallowed Gibson neck joint has varied considerably over the years. Much is made of the long neck tenon used in early Les Pauls and revived in many of the better reissues, and this is definitely one of several keys to superior set-neck tone. It takes little effort to appreciate how elongating the tenon—the 'tongue' of wood at the heel end of the neck—into the body pocket is likely to aid sustain and resonance, and it's these characteristics that win praise in a guitar with an expertly made, glued-in neck. Such an instrument requires not only the longer, deeper joint, but also a well-cut tenon and pocket that are a good, tight fit in the first place (irrespective of glue), not to mention a correctly angled neck. The neck angles of Les Pauls (and other set-neck models) have varied widely over the years. The slight back angle of its necks is one of the significant characteristics of the Les Paul, but a neck that drops too far below the plane of the body top will necessitate too high a bridge setting and a weakened tone will result. Conversely, a neck angle that is too flat will drop the strings' break angle over the bridge saddles some way shy of the optimum, therefore impeding tone, and might also lead to difficulties with string-height adjustment in relation to pickup height. By and large, a joint angle (or neck pitch) of around four per cent is often considered ideal in a Les Paul. Other set-neck guitars which are made somewhat in the image of the Gibson classic, but which don't aim in any way to be precise copies, might be optimized with other neck pitches, depending on the design of bridges, pickup mounting, and so on.

Beyond the obvious factors of feel and playability—basic issues of personal preference—the sheer size of a guitar's neck also has an impact on the instrument's tone. Plenty of players hold firm to the simple adage that a big neck equals big tone. While there's some sense to this proposition, it might be just one of several elements that help to determine a guitar's voice, rather than the decisive factor, so it would be shortsighted to cling to this while ignoring other influences on an instrument's sound. It seems logical that sending a resonance down a larger chunk of timber is going to have different sonic results to sending the same resonance along a super-slim neck, but this is another one of those tone legends that's difficult to corroborate in any scientific way, even if the compiled weight of anecdotal evidence seems to have convinced plenty of players that the theory holds water. Some of the bigger-necked Les Pauls and Telecasters that I have owned have been among the most inspiring guitars I've played, although you can certainly find great-sounding instruments of all stripes with slimmer necks, too. For big, woody resonance and a lively response, with plenty of depth and richness when played through a clean, semi-clean, or mildly crunchy amp, however, this big-neck-to-big-tone equation proves pretty consistent (provided the guitar in question is well constructed and properly set up in the first place, of course).

In addition to the neck joint, and the pitch of the neck itself, the back-angled headstock on most such guitars also contributes to their sound. Gibson's creations from the 50s and 60s (and more accurate recreations of these) featured a headstock pitched at 17 degrees, and this rather steep angle gave the strings a desirable level of downward pressure in the nut slots, helping to optimize the transference of vibrational energy from string, to nut, to wood. Noting that many guitars with such steep headstock pitches were suffering neck-end fractures when accidentally knocked over, Gibson adopted a 14-degree back angle during the Norlin era (1969–86), but players came to see this 'improvement' as detrimental to the overall tone of the instrument. So, while the headstock raked back at 17 degrees might be a little more fragile, and can lead to some hitching of the strings in the nut slots causing occasional tuning issues, this feature is still considered an essential constituent of classic Gibson tone.

THE (SO-CALLED) 24¾-INCH SCALE LENGTH

The slightly shorter scale length of archetypal glued-neck guitars, as deployed on classic Gibson instruments—which, to be more precise, is closer to 24⅝ inches—also has a significant influence on the core tonality of these guitars. The more densely packed harmonics found on strings of this length, when compared to longer, 25½-inch strings, lead to a thicker, furrier voice; one, in fact, that could be described with many of the same adjectives used above to describe the resonant characteristics of the glued-in neck joint itself. A dip into the viniculturist's lexicon might freshen up these descriptions: 24⅝-inch guitars being "earthy and full-bodied, with a buttery finish," perhaps. What really matters is not the terms we use, but the fact that we understand what we're trying to describe, and know how that sonic image might suit—or run counter to—our goals as guitarists and tone crafters. If we think of the natural ring of the 24⅝-inch guitar as being 'round' and 'warm' we'll all probably be on the same page.

The slightly blurrier harmonic spectrum of these guitars means it's more difficult to get firm, full-bodied twang and top-notch sparkle out of them, although most good ones can fake it perfectly well, especially when they have decent, low-wind, vintage-style humbuckers or P-90s on board. But the point is, if tight fundamental and high-frequency harmonic sheen just aren't there in the first place, you can't pull them out of some other element further down the signal chain, or not in quite the way you can from a 25½-inch guitar, anyway. That said, it's difficult to get genuine 24⅝-inch warmth and creaminess from a 25½-inch guitar, and so, as with many of the considerations in this book, it's a 'horses for courses' scenario.

We've already broached the notion of the hybrid template, and with so many production models and custom offerings from different makers available today, the fact that a standard, classic design template doesn't quite achieve the multiple sonic characteristics that you seek shouldn't stop you looking for them elsewhere. For example, I have a guitar sitting here staring at me right now that was made by an outstanding luthier named Saul Koll, who is based in Portland, Oregon. It's a set-neck solidbody called a Superior and is very much a marriage of a Telecaster and a Les Paul Special, with other original twists. It has a glued-in neck (maple with ebony fingerboard), a wrapover bridge, a Jason Lollar 50s-spec P-90 neck pickup, and a bridge pickup by TV Jones that's really a melding of a Tele bridge pickup and a P-90. So far, this is probably telling you that it sounds fairly Gibsonesque. But stir in its 25½-inch scale length and solid alder body (with tasty early-50s Goldtop-style finish), and the end result is a guitar that really does sound like an amalgam of a Fender Telecaster and a Gibson Les Paul Junior or Special, with more hair and meat than the former, and more definition and sparkle than the latter. Without that bolt-neck joint and Tele bridge it will never sound exactly like a Telecaster, and without that mahogany neck and body, and 24⅝-inch scale length, it will never sound

exactly like a Les Paul Special. It does, however, blend other elements of the two rather beautifully into something that is all its own, and is, thus, perfect for many playing situations. Koll's hybrid of scale and components/construction isn't a new one: guitars like the Hamer Monaco, Duesenberg Starplayer Special, and the Nik Huber Dolphin, among several others, successfully blend the longer scale length with more Gibson or Gretsch-like components and features.

SIGNIFICANT COMPONENTS

The majority of elements at play in guitars built to the classic templates, as described in this section, tend to work toward similar sonic results. In, for example, the templates for vintage set-neck solidbodies—namely the Gibson Les Paul Standard, Special, Junior, and SG—several of the significant components enhance the fat, thick tones that are already presented by woods, design type, construction, and scale length.

Variations exist, certainly, and there are also cases where makers seek to achieve characteristics that are outside of the norm for the 24⅝-inch set-neck group, but the rule far outweighs the exceptions. Gibson was laboring throughout the late 40s, 50s, and early 60s to get more clarity and a better high-end response from its guitars, and many of the company's significant developments worked toward this end—not least the Tune-o-matic bridge, the Alnico V, Firebird, and mini-humbucker pickups—but the core tonality of the company's cornerstone instrument models have never been altered so significantly that they entered into entirely new sonic territory.

PICKUPS ON TRADITIONAL SET-NECK GUITARS

For a single-coil pickup, Gibson's P-90 always sounded pretty fat and thick. It had more high-end bite and grit than many of the humbuckers that would follow (although, it might be argued, not more than a truly great PAF), but nothing like the twang and treble sting of Fender's Broadcaster/Esquire/Telecaster pickup with which the Californian upstart's plank-bodied guitar made such a splash in the first place. Put another way, a Les Paul with P-90s certainly sounds very different from the same guitar with humbuckers, even when the outputs of the two different pickups are similar. Yet there's still something inherently 'Les Paul-ish' about either example. A 1956 Goldtop with single-coils will still sound far more like a 1957 Goldtop with PAFs than it will a Tele or Strat.

There's far more detailed discussion of this subject in my book *The Guitar Pickup Handbook: The Start Of Your Sound* (Backbeat, 2008), but suffice it to say that, as with any praiseworthy pickup, the P-90 owes its distinctive sound to several elements of its design and construction. Its wide and relatively flat coil shapes a magnetic field that is correspondingly wide, or at least wider than that above the tall and narrow coil of a Strat or Tele pickup, and the wider this magnetic window, the thicker (although not necessarily better or deeper) the tone. The use of adjustable steel polepieces charged by a pair of Alnico bar magnets mounted beneath the coil gives a grainy bite to the P-90's treble response (as opposed to the clearer, crisper treble of a similar pickup with Alnico poles), while also giving it a bump in the midrange. Original 50s and 60s P-90s weren't overly hot pickups, although some did come off the line with far more turns of wire than the average. On the whole, they hit the 7.25k–8.25k ohms mark, which is about the same range as original PAF humbuckers.

Gibson's quest for a viable humbucker in the mid-to-late 50s was more about squelching 60-cycle hum than reshaping the guitar's tone, but the PAF also brought distinct refinements to the guitars it landed on. While the summed signals from its pair of adjoining coils made it a little warmer and thicker sounding than a P-90 of similar specification, it was also smoother and, perhaps more surprisingly, boasted a nuanced yet distinctive treble snap that lent excellent definition to the front edge of every note. The combination of these characteristics, and general decrease in grittiness in the PAF when compared to the P-90, usually leaves the single-coil predecessor sounding more aggressive than the humbucker, a reversal of their respective signature sounds.

While the full-sized humbucker remained on the SG throughout the 60s (during which it gradually evolved in terms of construction materials but not in general design), Gibson dabbled in other pickup designs for other models, some of which have become classics in their own right. The Firebird humbucker, often mistaken for an Epiphone-derived Gibson mini-humbucker with a cover over its polepieces, was actually a new and original design, and a very different unit in just about every way other than its size. Following the brief to obtain a brighter, arguably more Fender-ish tone in the original 'reverse-bodied' Firebird models, this pickup carried side-by-side coils wound around Alnico bar magnets in a blade-style design. Mindful of the P-90 versus Fender-style single-coil debate discussed above, the Firebird pickup's designers placed the magnetic material *inside* the coil, rather than beneath it, feeding a separate steel blade or polepiece. This gave the humbucker a brighter, snappier tone, helping the all-mahogany, set-neck electric instrument fulfill its creator's objective to make a guitar whose brightness and crispness could rival that of Fender's Stratocaster.

The more prevalent mini-humbucker, with visible, adjustable polepieces in one coil, best known for its use on the Les Paul Deluxe of the 70s, was more of a squashed-down rendition of the full-sized humbucker, with steel poles and a bar magnet beneath the coils. Its narrower magnetic window and the decreased number of windings on each coil combined to give this pickup a brighter sound than that of most PAF-derived humbuckers; but, while plenty of Deluxes can sound great, the occasional 'hardness' and 'thinness' heard within the brightness on some examples of this unit might disqualify it from tonal nirvana for some players. For the ultimate verdict on the mini-humbucker we can look to the vast number of players who voted with their routers and hacked out enough maple and mahogany to fit full-sized replacement pickups in their 70s Deluxes.

Today, guitars made approximately in the image of Gibson's seminal templates are produced with a vast range of pickups, and thus they offer a little of just about anything to players who may be seeking some variety in their set-neck instrument. The majority of these do still represent some variation on the full-sized Gibson or mini-humbucker, or the P-90 that preceded it (either in a traditional soap-bar or dog-ear-sized housing, or in the shape of the recently popular humbucker-sized P-90).

C H A P T E R   1

BRIDGES ON SET-NECK SOLIDBODIES

By and large, the classic guitars in this category are known for carrying rock-solid bridges (and, if applicable, tailpieces), and this chunk of hardware is a crucial part of their tone. Variations in the small details, however, and, in particular, in the materials these components are made from, can make a big difference in the sonic success of these parts, and all Tune-o-matics, stopbars, and wraparounds are definitely *not* created equal.

It might seem like pure sentimentality, nostalgia, or simple force of habit that we tend to rate the original examples of so many components higher than most of the revamps that followed, but there's also some simple logic to this. A lot of research and experimentation was generally involved when these prototype parts were first conceived and developed, and so many of them arrived almost perfectly formed, or were quickly whipped into shape once teething troubles were ironed out (the Les Paul's original wrapped-under trapeze tailpiece comes to mind). In the ensuing years, however, the companies that made these parts, usually at the behest of corporate owners, made efforts to maximize production and profit while minimizing costs, so that cheaper materials and more expedient manufacturing processes were taken onboard. At other times, attempts to make certain components more reliable might have achieved that end but only at the expense of an instrument's tone (Gibson's aforementioned move to a 14-degree headstock pitch, for example). And in yet further cases, the shifting availability of raw materials and the lessening in quality of components by second-party suppliers sometimes forced unforeseeable changes in the basic performance of particular parts. In short, guitar makers were aiming squarely at creating high-quality products, even as they were inevitably yoked to the bottom line, and more often than not they achieved this. In the majority of cases, the generally superior metals and woods that they employed resulted in solid, richly-toned instruments.

The Tune-o-matic bridge and its derivatives are used on more set-neck solidbodies (and semi-hollow models, for that matter) than the wraparound unit that preceded it, but it is probably better examined in the light of Gibson's simple, stud-mounted bar bridge, where its several advancements can truly be appreciated. After a brief flirtation with its short-lived trapeze tailpiece design, from late 1953–55 Gibson's first solidbody electric guitar, the Les Paul, was fitted with a unit that would become known as the wraparound bridge (alias the wrapover, wraptail, or bar bridge). Originally made from lightweight aluminum and mounted on heavy steel bolts set into studs in the body, this bridge was also used extensively on Les Paul Junior, SG Junior, and Special guitars, as well as on some other models. It's an extremely simple design, and although it offers limited intonation adjustment (next to none, effectively), it provides an extremely solid anchor point that contributes to great sustain and a warm, full tone. Although it might seem counterintuitive, the light aluminum of its construction really helped this guitar to ring out with a sweet, open voice. The gentle curve of the top of the bar provides a break point for the strings that isn't as sharp as some subsequent designs, so the notes emanating from this bridge sound a little rounder and furrier, a character that many players really enjoy and one that can help to fatten up the overall tone of any guitar carrying such a bridge.

Gibson updated the wraparound bridge in the early 60s by adding a compensated saddle. Taking the form of a narrow ridge at the top of the bar that breaks to and fro to more accurately position the strings and create a sharper break point, this chunk of hardware is called a 'lightning bridge' thanks to the zigzag shape of its saddle. In some instances, it does indeed improve intonation somewhat, although this is another barely adjustable bridge. The narrow ridge adds a bit more definition to the meat of the note, too. On the whole, fans of vintage tone tend not to favor these over the more rudimentary 50s-spec wraparound units, unless they are part of the original equipment on an early-60s SG Junior or similar.

Gibson's next advancement in bridge design arrived in 1954 in the form of the Tune-o-matic/ABR-1, which has usually been partnered, on non-vibrato solidbody electrics, with a stopbar tailpiece. The stopbar (or stud) is really just the same hunk of aluminum (later steel) as the wraparound bridge, with the strings loaded straight through the anchor holes from back to front, rather than loaded through the front and wrapped back over the top of the bar. Used as a tailpiece, this unit makes another extremely solid anchor point, and the Tune-o-matic likewise provides a solid and precise bridge and saddle unit. Its main virtue is often thought to be its adjustability, allowing precise intonation of individual strings via independently adjustable saddles, although it also brought a sonic shift to the table, too. By providing a sharper break point (or 'take off' point) for the strings, the peaked saddles of this bridge lend a little more clarity and precision to the notes than is available from an original wraparound bridge. The results are usually heard in the form of a little more high-end shimmer and improved note definition within chords. When set up properly, and mounted on a good guitar, this bridge/tailpiece pairing offers outstanding sustain, too.

Original Tune-o-matics were made from zinc and plated in nickel, with nickel-plated brass saddles, and units of this construction are still preferred by purists. The zinc and brass combination is solid but not overly heavy as a unit, and helps you to hear the ring of the strings more than the density of the bridge itself. Some players also ascribe a certain magic to the combination of this medium-weight bridge and a stopbar tailpiece of an even lesser weight.

The original ABR-1 version of the Tune-o-matic tends to be the connoisseur's preference, and not the Nashville version that followed. The former is mounted on relatively narrow steel bolts that are set directly into the wood of the guitar, while the thicker, heavier mounting bolts of the Nashville bridge are set into steel studs in the body top. The ABR-1's more direct journey from string to wood seems to be a part of its sonic personality. The Nashville is made from the zinc alloy Mazak, as are several other later renditions of the Tune-o-matic. Its longer saddle-adjustment travel and more secure adjustment bolts were intended as an improvement on the original ABR-1 design, and it can sound fine on a good guitar, although tonehounds tend to go for ABR-1s made to original specs, or renditions of the design by companies such as TonePros and Pigtail, among others.

There are many other set-neck bridge designs out there, of course, but relatively few offer any significant variation on these templates. Among the more noteworthy alternatives is the bridge often used by Hamer which includes six independent saddles on a bridge plate not unlike that of a hardtail Strat, with through-body stringing. Solid and reliable, configurations such as these do sound a little different from the classic Tune-o-matic and stopbar pairing, with a slightly higher meat-to-bite ratio and excellent sustain.

C H A P T E R   1

A few modifications of the wraparound design deserve honorable mentions, too. Among these are PRS's aluminum effort, with slots to keep the strings in place and compensated ridges for improved intonation, Wilkinson/Gotoh's simple but clever design fitted with either one or two adjustable saddle segments for the G/B and A/D string pairs, respectively, and Pigtail's compact yet fully adjustable unit.

Several other variations on the Tune-o-matic and wraparound themes exist, but perhaps the most significant modification occurs when a vibrato tailpiece is partnered with one of these popular bridges. A common scenario in this regard involves the installation of a Bigsby tailpiece, either at the factory or as an after-market modification, although there are several additional variants. Indeed, there are several different types of Bigsby vibratos, although they fall into two general categories: those with roller bars to increase the string tension over the bridge, and those without. As a general rule, most Bigsby units will take a tiny bit of meat out of a guitar's core tone and add a bit of jangly 'zing' to the attack. Those units *sans* roller bar usually affect a more noticeable change, since they often result in a slight decrease of the strings' break angle over the bridge saddles, and therefore a minor decrease in the heft of the overall tone.

On some guitars, however, this is one of a handful of ingredients that might contribute to a magical, or at least distinctive, tone. Many Gretsch models, for instance, get their characteristic

TONE TIP — Pickup Height

The majority of readers probably know that adjusting their guitar's pickup height will affect its output; fewer, perhaps, will realize the ways in which such adjustments can influence their instrument's tone. The instruction you most often encounter, when aiming to achieve the hottest sound possible from the pickups that are already in your guitar, is to lift the pickups themselves as high as you can get them, short of letting them hit the strings, or raising them to a point where the magnetic field starts to exert pull on the strings and interfere with their ability to vibrate freely (the effect of this can be heard as a slightly dissonant, atonal sound, like an out-of-tune harmonic that follows the root note). There's a lot more to pickup height adjustment than merely maximizing volume, however, and a little consideration of the other variables will add a new tweaking tool to your tone arsenal.

Consider the issue from the flipside: lower your pickups down into the body a little more than is standard—that is, position them *further away* from the strings—and you can be sure of giving the strings plenty of unencumbered air in which to vibrate. One result of this is, inevitably, a little less output, but that's something you ought to be able to live with; after all, that's what the amp's volume control is there for. Rather than worrying about what can be lost with this adjustment, consider what you can achieve: a tone that's woodier and more resonant, with greater dynamics, touch sensitivity, and a livelier feel to the playing response. Pick lightly and it's clean-yet-warm; dig in harder and you get increased drive and output but without a big sacrifice in note definition and clarity. It is important to make such adjustments gradually, of course—tweak, test, and re-tweak—and naturally you don't want to lower your pickups to extremes that will lead to severe loss of output or tone.

percussive jangle—a major part of the characteristic 'great Gretsch tone'—from the decreased downward pressure on the saddle(s) of a floating bridge that results from using a Bigsby unit. There are also plenty of emulations (what the hell, *copies*) of Bigsby vibratos out there. Some cheapen the design; others, like the Duesenberg Tremola, arguably improve upon it.

On vintage set-neck solidbodies, the other most likely vibrato candidate is the Maestro Vibrola which appeared on several models in the SG line-up in the 60s, as well as on a few other Gibson and Epiphone guitars. Probably as notable for its absence as for its presence on vintage instruments today, since players seemed to be removing them in droves for many years, they really aren't bad units, all in all. Simple and sturdy, they accomplish their vibrato action fairly efficiently and don't seem to be any more significantly detrimental to a guitar's tone than the larger Bigsby units. They do, however, often seem to suffer slight return-to-pitch problems, a malady probably equally attributable to the bridges with which they were paired (often 60s-era compensation-ridge wraparounds) as to the Vibrolas themselves.

Right behind the Maestro is the Burns vibrato found on many mid-era Gretsch solidbodies, in addition to the Burns guitars they were first appended to. Loathed by some players but enjoyed by others, these units are simple, solid, and fairly efficient (if limited in their pitch-bending travel) and don't tend to hamper the tone of any guitar they are attached to—at least

Note that adjustable polepieces are not generally intended to influence overall output level or tone; they are mainly provided as a modifying facility for achieving good string-to-string balance and are usually best adjusted to follow the curve of your guitar's fretboard. Dog-ear style Gibson P-90 pickups occasionally prove the exception to this rule. Since these pickups have no means of overall height adjustment, you might occasionally need to raise the polepieces to achieve a little more output, or lower them further into the coil to soften the sound. Often, however, you can purchase or construct mounting-ring shims to lift the entire pickup unit a little closer to the strings when more extreme adjustments are required.

Any adjustment in pickup height in two-pickup guitars needs to give some consideration to balancing the output between the bridge and neck units. In most cases, the neck pickup is positioned a little lower than the bridge pickup, because the broader vibrational arch of the plucked string over the neck pickup, which is closer to the center of the strings' length, already makes for a greater output and beefier sound. These days, many guitars are made with calibrated pickup sets to account for this (and many pickup makers offer their units in such sets), but in the past, most pickups were similarly wound, and output levels between neck and bridge often varied considerably.

None of these suggestions are definitive directives. Different approaches suit different playing styles and tonal preferences. It's best to experiment with different heights and see what works for you.

If you really do want more drive and intensity to give you that hot, compressed crunch for lead sounds, you might want your pickups a little closer to the strings, within reason. If you want more balance, air, warmth, and definition, then moving them a little further away (lowering them into the guitar) may well do it for you.

no more than so than the questionable bridges they are sometimes partnered with. From quirky to clever, the range of other contemporary set-neck vibratos is extensive, although few have taken a hold on the market. The exception, and the remaining unit worthy of discussion here, is the PRS vibrato tailpiece. As mentioned briefly in the Bolt-neck section above, Paul Reed Smith developed this bridge as an update of the Fender Strat vibrato (PRS originally undertook their design for Carlos Santana who wanted a vibrato "like Fender's … that would stay in tune"). It differs from the Fender design in several ways, but its solid block, streamlined design, and efficient motion all work together to provide a very usable vibrato action, with little detriment to tone compared to a similar guitar equipped with a fixed bridge. This unit represents the most popular alternative vibrato seen on set-neck guitars, given that PRS Artist, Singlecut, and similar models carry it (although it also appears on many thousands of PRS's bolt-neck CE models).

SEMI-ACOUSTIC AND HOLLOWBODY ELECTRICS

Once, this category would have been populated mainly with Gibson ES-335s and their ilk, Gretsch Duo Jets and the like, several Rickenbacker models and, possibly, 'thinline' hollowbodies such as the Gibson ES-330 and Epiphone Casino, which are not 'semi' at all, merely thin. In the past couple of decades, however, there has been an enormous boom in semi-acoustic models, their popularity the result both of their characteristic tonal properties and their physical lightness. These guitars divide into two main categories: the semi-acoustic guitar that was designed as a thinline hollowbody with a solid block or blocks added internally, and the chambered instrument that was initially designed as a solidbody, with wood routed from the back before the cap is glued in place.

Strictly speaking, hollowbody electrics (which are also often electric arch-top guitars) are fully acoustic—whether thinline or full-depth—with none of their internal space taken up by body blocks or the like. In this sense, they are, technically, fully acoustic guitars, although many are made with more rigid top support, in the form of braces or tone bars, than would usually be found in a genuine acoustic guitar that is primarily meant to be played unamplified.

Since any wood that is made to resonate by vibrating strings will play a major part in determining a guitar's core tone, different types of semi-hollow and hollowbody electric guitars, constructed with different configurations of timber, can certainly be expected to exhibit distinctive sonic properties. It is worth noting that the inherent qualities of the acoustic ('unplugged') tones of these instruments readily translate into distinctive sounds conjured through certain pickups or in conjunction with certain bridge and tailpiece combinations which tend to have other specific characteristics when used on solidbodies. Or, put more simply, all the components you thought you were familiar with on a solidbody will sound a little different on a hollowbody, because, inherently, the guitars themselves sound a little different.

TONAL CHARACTERISTICS OF SEMI-HOLLOW ELECTRICS

Originally, the advantages of semi-hollow electric guitars, in terms of sound and performance, were essentially seen as those of fully hollow electrics. By and large, early examples of these types—which mainly means the Gibson ES-335 and its brethren, the uncontested seminal template for this category—were designed for habitual arch-top players who secretly craved a dash of the new solidbody models' performance, rather than for solidbody players who wanted to pretend to play arch-top acoustic-electrics. Although from our 21st century perspective they might seem like an evolutionary missing link between the hollow arch-top and the solidbody, the semi-acoustic didn't properly hit the market until almost a full decade after the arrival of the mass-produced solidbody guitar. Nevertheless, it did so as a solidifying of the acoustic arch-top, if you will, rather than as a lightening of the solidbody.

Having noted the benefits of the solidbody electric instrument, Gibson and its more traditional adherents sought some of these new characteristics but housed in a hollowbody-*style* electric guitar. The solidbody was particularly successful in combating the feedback from which genuine hollow electric instruments often suffered when played at higher volumes, and it also offered greater fidelity by way of improved string definition and enhanced high-end content, along with better sustain. The 'compromise' may seem a simple one today—place a chunk of solid wood in the middle of the hollow guitar body—but it was a revolution at the time. To cut to the chase, the design of the Gibson ES-335, constructed of pressed-arch maple ply, front, back, and sides, with a solid block of maple running down the center from tail to neck, achieved all of its objectives, while retaining a degree of hollowbody character in the hollow wings visible beneath its dual f-holes. Tonally, that meant a juicy blend of air and roundness, and a certain organic depth to the midrange response, but with plenty of punch, cut, and clarity, along with admirable sustain.

Given identical components, an ES-335 won't sound an awful lot different to a traditional Les Paul Standard, but it will never sound quite the same, either. To the brutish thump and grind of the Les Paul's attack, the ES-335 will offer more bounce and compression, with a slightly warmer, woodier follow-through. If you want the beef and mustard of a Les Paul or an SG along with their characteristic sustain and cutting power, but would like to feel a little more wool than cotton in your weft, a little more of the creamy goodness of the great outdoors, an ES-335 might well be your instrument

Gibson's original semi-hollow models, and the better of its reissues, really do rule the day, although plenty of other companies now make excellent and occasionally somewhat original semi-acoustics, too. Having played plenty of genuine ES-335s, both vintage and contemporary models, I have to say that there really is a certain magic to examples made to the late-50s and very-early-60s specs, with PAF pickups, nickel-plated hardware, and so on. What's more, a handful of 1958–62 ES-335s run impressively against type, and are capable of whipping out all the thick, creamy, bluesy neck-pickup warmth and wail you could ever want while also chiming and jangling sweetly in the bridge position, with really breathtaking bite and clarity overall. For all that vintage magic, contemporary instruments shouldn't be overlooked: the best of them continue to offer the exemplary qualities of the original semi-acoustic template.

'Short block' Gibson ES-335s from the 70s, which were made with a maple block that extended from the neck to just behind the bridge, are often excellent guitars, but they do sound a little different from the archetypal, full-block ES-335. The use of a trapeze tailpiece on these

later models (there being no wood in which to anchor the studs of a wraparound tailpiece) and the additional acoustic body space both help to reduce the meat in their attack slightly while making them somewhat prone to feedback. As with any design, these factors are likely to vary from instrument to instrument. The fact that the modification was made to reduce weight rather than tweak the guitar's sound (in an era when Norlin-owned Gibson concentrated harder on production numbers than on tonal results) should tell you something, but good examples of these models can still give a lot of satisfaction.

Vintage Epiphone Sheraton and Guild Starfire IV instruments are of roughly comparable quality with the early Gibson instruments. Both have bodies made with laminated maple and center blocks, glued-in necks with scale lengths of approximately 24¾ inches, and a pair of humbuckers, although the pickups on each are a little brighter and 'thinner' sounding than the PAF (or similar) humbuckers used on Gibson semis. The mini-humbuckers on the Epiphone definitely add some jangle and chime to the format but can still wail through a cranked amp. The almost full-sized humbuckers on the Guild also serve to enhance the guitar's shimmer and give a rough stab to its sound, something like a cross between a PAF and a Gretsch Filter'Tron. They can occasionally be somewhat microphonic, too, but a little of that adds some edge and liveliness to the tone of a good Starfire, so long as it doesn't segue into extreme squeal at high volumes.

Plenty of copies and rough emulations can get you into the ES-335 ballpark. Guitars from the Yamaha SA family usually offer good quality construction and excellent value, as do many Ibanez, Greco, Tokai, and Samick semis from the late 70s onward. If one of these has 'good bones' to begin with, it can usually be tweaked to suit a player's tastes with a quick change of pickups. Heritage's H535 is made to specifications very close to the ES-335, by a company launched by several former Gibson employees working in the company's old Kalamazoo factory. Take from that what you will. Other impressive variations on the theme include Hamer's Newport and Monaco III, and Collings's I-35, although each of these strays somewhat from the laminated-with-block construction and takes us toward territory that deserves an independent assessment.

Gaining in popularity with pros and enthusiastic amateurs alike in the last few years, Duesenberg's Starplayer TV is another semi that takes elements of ES-335 construction and runs with them in some entirely new directions. The single-cutaway design includes a solid wood center block and laminated maple back and sides, but with a solid spruce top, all crafted into a body that's considerably smaller than that of Gibson's archetypal semi (closer to that of a Les Paul, in fact). The spruce adds a little sweetness and richness to the voice, while the guitar's 25½-inch scale length, another departure for its 'type,' increases the sparkle and clarity factors somewhat. Blending vintage spec bridge humbucker, a P-90-style neck pickup, and Duesenberg's own simple but effective reworking of a Bigsby-style vibrato, the end result is something close to a hybrid of Gibson, Gretsch, and Fender: a new voice that a lot of major players are clearly enjoying—Mike Campbell, Brad Rice, and several Nashville studio cats among them.

TONAL CHARACTERISTICS OF CHAMBERED OR 'SEMI-SOLID' GUITARS

To differentiate between a semi-acoustic and a chambered guitar, think of the latter as an instrument made with what starts as a solid block of wood, but has some of this routed away to create airspace within the body. The last two decades have seen a vogue for such semi-solid instruments, in tandem with the trend toward lighter guitars in general. The design of these guitars varies quite widely, from instruments with just a little wood removed to those that are more air than wood by the time the router is done chewing, and they include several examples from both the bolt-neck and set-neck camps. An example of a bolt-neck with just a little wood removed would be the Fender Telecaster Thinline; for a set-neck routed to more acoustic proportions, think PRS Hollowbody. Between these models, the range is vast and accounts for just about any conceivable variation of the format.

Contemporary chambered guitars tend to differ further from semi-acoustics in that they are often made with solid (if hollowed-out) woods, while classic semis are made with laminated tops, backs, and sides with solid center blocks. One of the originators of the format, the Gretsch Duo Jet, was constructed with a laminated, pressed-arch maple cap on a routed mahogany body, and confused the picture somewhat by billing itself as a solidbody. We're all willing to forgive it, however, because it is truly one of the all-time great guitars as far as distinctive tone and character are concerned. A classic example of a semi-solid guitar, the Duo Jet was unveiled in 1953 as direct competition for both the Fender Telecaster and, in particular, the Gibson Les Paul. As already mentioned, it was inherently different from either 'rival' instrument, although it was superficially similar to Gibson's candidate for the solidbody crown. Few players of the day probably thought enough about the distinctions between 'solid' and 'chambered' guitars, and the pockets of air in the Duo Jet's mahogany body aren't enough to give it any obvious 'acoustic' properties, although they do certainly help to shape the overall character of the instrument. Of course, a Duo Jet is different from a Tele or a Les Paul in several additional ways, and arguably its voice exhibits less of the character of its wood resonance than it does the sum of other ingredients employed in its construction. Among the significant factors that influence the Duo Jet's tone—in addition to the chambered mahogany body with a fairly rigid, arched, maple-ply top—are its floating bridge (a solid-steel rocker bar, threaded roller saddle, or intricate Melita bridge piece on an unfixed ebony base), its glued-in mahogany neck, a Bigsby or trapeze tailpiece, a pair of DynaSonic or Filter'Tron pickups, and its scale length of approximately 24⅗ inches. All of the above translate into the distinctive Gretsch sound, often described as bright, snappy, chiming, and jangling, but with plenty of furry roundness and enough warmth to give it some body. Those adjectives apply to the sound of the Duo Jet, regardless of which of the two distinctive breeds of Gretsch pickups are fitted. The single-coils and humbuckers do distinguish themselves in definable ways, however, and are worthy of further analysis.

The Gretsch DynaSonic (originally made by DeArmond as the Model 200, recently reproduced by a few other manufacturers) is a single-coil pickup with a rather unusual design. It uses Alnico V rod magnets as individual polepieces within the coil, as do Fender pickups, but the DynaSonic's are long and rather wide-diameter rod segments, and these play a significant part in the sound that the pickups produce. These poles are attached by a 'monkey-on-a-stick' arrangement to individual steel brackets which are threaded onto narrow bolts to allow for independent adjustment of each pole (the appearance of both screws and poles in the top of the

pickup gives some players the impression that they are humbuckers), and the interaction of this extra steel further affects their response. In addition, these pickups are wound with very thin 44-gauge wire (compared to the 42 gauge used for most Fender single coils and Gibson PAF-style humbuckers and P-90s), and have a relatively beefy inductance of around 3.35 henrys. The result is a pickup with silky high-end content for plenty of twang and chime, but also a thick, balanced midrange and a firm low end.

Gretsch's own Filter'Tron humbucker was designed in the mid 50s by Ray Butts, at the request of stellar picker Chet Atkins, at around the same time that Gibson's humbucker was in development, but it was unveiled a little later, at the summer 1957 National Association of Music Merchants (NAMM) show. While we often think of the move from single-coil pickups to humbuckers in terms of a tonal shift from bright and clean to warm and fat, the arrival of the Filter'Tron on several up-market Gretsch models heralded no such transition. Made with two side-by-side coils, wound with a relatively meager 3,000 turns of 43-gauge, poly-coated wire, with six adjustable steel poles in each coil and an Alnico V bar magnet mounted below and between them, the Filter'Tron was a clear, crisp humbucker with chime and definition in spades, which was just what Chet was after. Its relatively wide magnetic window still gives it some meat and depth, but it's not one to drive the front end of a big, clean amp into distortion the way some beefier humbuckers will do.

Gretsch fans of different camps debate the relative virtues of 'Trons versus 'Sonics *ad infinitum*, but both are undeniable classics, adept at doing their own sweet thing across a range of genres, from rockabilly to country, British invasion, punk, and beyond. Indeed, these are a pair of pickups that break the 'humbuckers rock and single coils roll' mold.

Perhaps the other most notable chambered vintage guitar was produced by Rickenbacker. Its 360 model and other similar variants boasted scimitar (or 'cat's eye') sound-holes, which advertised the fact that these guitars had some airspace under their hoods. They were made very differently from Gibson's ES-335, with which it was roughly contemporary. That said, as discussed by Tony Bacon and Paul Day in *The Rickenbacker Book* (Balafon, 1994), with reference to the first-hand memories of former Rickenbacker salesman Joe Talbot, the 360 really wasn't perceived as a rival to Gibson's semi so much as it was a competitor with Fender's solidbodies, which had the bright, cutting sound that so many players desired at that time. By joining two slabs of solid maple to a maple and rosewood 'through neck' (not a set neck as such, but closer to that territory), routing it out from the back, and closing off the work with a fillet of wood, Rickenbacker designer Roger Rossmeisl produced a guitar with a super-crisp response and good resonance, but with considerably less weight than a solid-maple slab.

Despite a more Gibsonesque scale length of approximately 24¾ inches, the 360 really was chasing Fender's popularity with the pop-rock crowd, and its tonal appeal was all about brightness and shimmer. The pickups Rickenbacker devised were crucial to the success of the guitar in this regard, and to the birth of 'jangle' in general, and are still a cornerstone component if you're looking for that tone. Rickenbacker's seminal 'toaster top' pickup arrived in 1957, made by a company that was one of the first on the electric-guitar scene but which really hadn't made great inroads into the market since the unveiling of its horseshoe pickup in 1931 and the simple lap-steel and Spanish guitars on which it appeared. Although its cover leads some to assume it's a humbucker, the toaster top is actually a single-coil pickup with one row of six individual Alnico polepieces running under the cover's silver center bar within a single coil of wire, rather than two rows and two coils under each of the black inlays either side of it. Most were wound with very fine 44-gauge wire (although there are reports of some using thicker 42 and 43 gauge) to a DC resistance of around 7k–8.5k ohms—some higher, some (especially very early models) lower. The result was a pickup that was brighter and less punchy than such numbers might imply, given that higher wire gauges produce higher impedance levels, but without the same levels of overall output that pickups wound with 42-gauge wire to similar readings will provide. Nevertheless, good vintage toaster tops do offer some thickness and grit amid the glimmer and twang, as so many early records by The Who and The Beatles attest. To get reissue toaster tops sounding closer to the originals, many players have literally unwound some of the wire from the coil, taking them from the 10–12k ohms mark right down to 7.5k or so, to bring more chime and clarity to their tone.

In 1969, Rickenbacker got into the high-gain movement with a pickup that it unequivocally dubbed the Hi-Gain Pickup, although it has become better known as the 'button top' for the row of six black, button-like polepieces that protrude through its chrome cover. These poles, made from steel, ran through a very similar coil to that of the toaster top to contact a pair of ceramic bar magnets mounted below. Since it carried the same turns of wire as the toaster top, but was charged by more powerful ceramic pickups, this was indeed a hot single coil, and the steel-poles-in-coil formula gave it some added grit and snarl besides. As such, it tends not to be the preference of fans of old-school West Coast or Brit-pop Rickenbacker tone, although Paul Weller of The Jam and Peter Buck of R.E.M. have both made major noises with these pickups, and they definitely have their place in the pickup pantheon.

Performance-wise, Rickenbacker—whether loaded with toaster tops or button tops—etched out a reputation for guitars that were more adept at rhythm work (jangling arpeggio styles in particular) and simple lead riffs than wailing rock solos. Good models, when set up properly, can be smoothly playable, but determining elements such as the general sound of the instruments and the feel of their necks have led to more conspicuous adoption by players who favor rhythm with an occasional melodic lead aside—Pete Townshend, John Lennon, George Harrison, Roger McGuinn, Peter Buck, Tom Petty, and Mike Campbell among them.

For many makers today, chambering an otherwise solid body has been a matter of weight reduction rather than sonic fine-tuning. Gibson chambers many of its USA-made Les Pauls these days (although usually not its Custom Shop models) in an effort to turn the heavier mahogany stocks available into guitars that are palatable to a playing public no longer willing to drag around an 11 pound (4.98kg) instrument, like so many did in the late 70s and early 80s. The company does give some consideration to the tone of these instruments, however, and has experimented with the placement of the 11 weight-reducing chambers beneath the maple top so as to enhance the resonance and overall sonic character. The result is an instrument that might, to many ears, sound little or no different from a completely solid Les Paul made with lighter mahogany, producing a slightly rounder, more vowel-like midrange.

C H A P T E R   1

Several smaller, high-end makers also deploy routed chambers but with arguably even greater attention to the tonal implications of the procedure. The work of German luthier Nik Huber is a case in point. In addition to using alternative woods, Huber's Redwood model, for example, comes in at an extremely comfortable 6 pounds (2.72kg) or so on average, but still has the depth, attack, and sustain of the single-cutaway, set-neck solidbody that it appears to be. In the bolt-neck camp, makers like Tom Anderson have also subtracted some of the wood on many models to create light yet extremely responsive, solid-sounding guitars.

Both of these models conceal their airspace, in the physical sense, by using solid tops without f-holes, although they make the chambering evident in their promotional literature (something which Gretsch carefully overlooked back in the 50s). Fender had placed concealed chambers in some 'standard' Telecasters before showing off the routing in the prominent f-holes of its Telecaster Thinline model, released in mid 1968. Produced largely as a means of reducing the weight of the ash stock supplied to Fender at the time, the routed Thinline did nevertheless present a slightly rounder tone than the solidbody Telecaster, with a little more midrange honk.

HOLLOWBODY ELECTRICS

To clarify, we're talking here about guitars designed primarily as electric instruments but constructed with fully hollow bodies, rather than flat-top acoustic-electrics and the like. I won't explore the world of carved, solid-topped, arch-top electrics in great detail here, as these represent a specialized subject in their own right, although they are worth touching upon.

The carved, solid spruce-top guitar is the instrument that launched the hollowbody electric breed. Although Fender successfully jumped the starter's gun with the solidbody electric in 1950, Gibson had been the premier name in 'electric Spanish guitar' manufacture since the launch of the first of its kind, the ES-150, released by Kalamazoo in 1936. A rather basic instrument in many ways, and loaded with a hulking, primitive, but still desirable 'Charlie Christian' blade pickup, the ES-150 was nonetheless revolutionary. It was the grandfather of the many arch-tops with floating or top-mounted pickup that followed over the next decade and a half, and inspired competition from Epiphone, Gretsch, Guild, and others.

These were the guitars used by the cutting-edge guitarists who helped shape mid-20th century popular music; players such as Danny Cedrone, Scotty Moore, Junior Barnard, T-Bone Walker, and Chuck Berry morphed country, western swing, and blues into the new music that would set the airwaves on fire. Their instruments' fat, often woolly and feedback-prone sound was also what inspired the electric and thinline semi-acoustic instruments that followed throughout the 50s. Which is not to say such hollowbody electrics can't sound outstanding. Obviously they can: a good, carved-top arch-top, fitted with the right pickup, can thoroughly astound you with its depth, richness, and harmonic nuance. But, with very few exceptions, their domain is jazz, and in this book we're mainly addressing the broad realm of rock and its various derivatives. Steve Howe's prog-rock high jinks on a Gibson ES-175 notwithstanding, rock'n'roll on a hollowbody electric usually means either a Gretsch 6120, or similar, or a thinline hollowbody such as a Gibson ES-330 or Epiphone Casino, or something made along those lines.

After making some inroads into the jazz world with a few of its big-bodied arch-tops in the late 40s and early 50s—as a sort of third-tier maker (at best) behind Gibson and Epiphone—Gretsch found its niche in a big way with laminated-bodied arch-top electrics that appealed to the 50s and 60s rock'n'roll crowd. As Gibson had with its 1949 ES-175, Gretsch reasoned that an amplified guitar wouldn't need the resonant nuances of a hand-carved arch-top made from solid wood, and that a more robustly braced top and body made from pressed laminated woods would be a viable alternative when rammed through a couple of 6L6 output tubes and a Jensen speaker, as well as being more feedback resistant (not to mention more affordable to produce). In addition to any general design points, signing Chet Atkins to promote the model was a major coup, and since so many of the cats copping his elegantly country-fried licks would soon be transmuting them into rock'n'roll, the 6120 soon crossed over to the new pop arena.

From its release in 1955 until 1958, the 6120 carried DynaSonic pickups and was manufactured with a simple, parallel top and back brace that left the 2⅜-inch-deep body fairly lively, especially when played at high volume. Filter'Tron humbuckers were added to the model in 1958 and the bracing was bumped up to include a block or 'sound post' in the center of the body that partially locked the top and back together. This was an effort to tighten up the front and back a little and get them vibrating in unison, thus reducing undesirable feedback howl. The changes meant that there were two distinct responses and tonalities from these twin breeds of single-cutaway 6120s. The design would change further in 1961 when a double-cutaway model was launched.

As already discussed in the context of the semi-solid Duo Jet, DynaSonic and Filter'Tron pickups produce quite different sounds but don't necessarily follow the light/bright, heavy/warm dichotomy into which so many single-coil versus humbucker battles are pigeonholed. That said, given single-coils and a more lightly braced body, the 6120 of 1955–58 sounded sweet and clear, with plenty of bite, yet still presented a lot of the sensitive, touchy-feely response and round warmth of a fully hollow arch-top.

The 1958–61 6120, on the other hand, was tighter and a little sharper, with slightly better sustain, while still offering plenty of roundness courtesy of its humbuckers. As we've also discussed in relation to the Duo Jet, the bridge and tailpiece configurations of these Gretsch guitars contributed to a certain percussive zing and jangle in their tone, elements that have become their archetypal tonal signature.

With the double-cutaway 6120 Chet Atkins Hollow Body model, Gretsch thinned the body down to a depth of two inches and also closed off the f-holes in a bid to further squelch feedback, at Chet's request. The guitar also picked up 'a zero fret' (an additional fret placed right in front of the nut, in the 'zero' position), a design point that some players find a little quirky. The instrument still offers a classically Gretsch package but is quite a different proposition from either version of the 6120 models of the mid-to-late 50s—guitars which are still much-favored by the rockabilly crowd and which, to my ears, best exhibit the clanging, twanging snarl that has come to define the Gretsch tone.

Often mistakenly referred to as a semi-hollow guitar thanks to its outward resemblance to an ES-335, the Gibson ES-330 (like the extremely similar Casino made by stable-mate

manufacturer Epiphone) is actually a thinline hollowbody guitar. Its P-90 pickups also distinguish it from the humbucker-loaded ES-335, but even before you plug it in, the ES-330 is a patently different beast. Its body mirrors the dimensions of its older sibling (the ES-335 arrived in 1958, a year before the ES-330) but it lacks any form of solid center block, and also has a neck-body joint at around the 16th–17th frets, rather than at the 20th as on the ES-335.

The shifted neck joint in itself would alter the ES-330's tone, since it puts the guitar's bridge nearer to the center of the large lower bout—in the position of the bridge on a traditional arch-top, in fact, aligning it with the center points of the f-holes—and gives the guitar a deeper, thicker voice as a result. In terms of design, it is essentially more of a thinline guitar aimed at jazz players than it is a pseudo-jazz instrument for the rockers (a fact ably demonstrated by Grant Green's brilliant early recordings, made with an ES-330). Compared to 'proper' jazz guitars, however, the ES-330 is unusual in having its Tune-o-matic bridge set directly into the wood of the guitar's top and the parallel top braces beneath it, rather than carrying a floating bridge, as did Gretsch's semi-solid Duo Jet.

Being truly hollow, if thin, the ES-330 can suffer from unwanted howl more than the ES-335 and its ilk. In addition to its potentially jazzy warmth, however, it can exude a richly cutting tone through a semi-cranked tube amp, thanks in no small part to those P-90s—excellent in raw rock'n'roll and roots-rock contexts. Thanks to The Beatles' guitarists, all three of whom played a Casino at one time or another, Epiphone's variation on the form is often considered more popular, but the humble ES-330 definitely has its fans, too. One step below in perceived status, Gibson's ES-125TCD offers many of the same tricks as the ES-330 but in a single-cutaway body with unbound neck and floating bridge. Adjust your expectations accordingly, although these are undoubtedly fun guitars and have been gaining in popularity in recent years.

Several companies offer contemporary takes on the Gretsch hollowbody electric theme, although, as good (and good value) as many are, there's little to distinguishes most of them, or not enough at least to make them worth lengthy discussion here. Plenty of custom builders will of course give you their rendition of 'the ultimate 6120', at a price, and instruments of this kind—Saul Koll's Duo Glide Almighty comes to mind—can do a phenomenal job of out-Gretsching a Gretsch on some occasions.

Emulations of the Gibson thinline and full-depth mojo are perhaps more common. One such is the Reverend Pete Anderson Signature model, built to a 24¾-inch scale length with a set neck and a 2⅜-inch-deep body made from a laminated spruce top and laminated maple back and sides. A 'hollowbody' to all intents and purposes, it replicates some of the post-1958 Gretsch 6120's characteristics by incorporating a proprietary 'uni-brace.' Although just half-an-inch (12.7mm) wide, this brace connects the top and back through a portion of the body, along the bass side, running from the neck block to a block set beneath the fixed Tune-o-matic bridge. Intended to reduce unwanted feedback while also tightening tone and sustain somewhat, this construction puts the Pete Anderson somewhere between the semi-acoustic ES-335 and the fully hollow ES-330, while the guitar's in-house P-90 pickups find it tending more toward the bluesy tones usually associated with this pair than the bold twang that originally made Anderson famous as Dwight Yoakam's lead guitarist.

PERIPHERALS AND EXTRAS

Plenty of other bits and pieces are used to put electric guitars together, and while some of these are custom-made by individual manufacturers for specific instruments, the majority of them are somewhat generic, at least in the sense that they can be swapped and retrofitted between many different types of guitar. Such components include nuts, frets, tuners, pots, and switches—all of which occasionally need replacing on otherwise healthy guitars (the end of their natural lifespan by no means sounding a death-knell for the instrument). All can also be upgraded without major surgery to suit the individual player's requirements in sound or feel, although many such jobs are still best left to a professional. We really ought to include the finish of the guitar in this category, since it is the final ingredient in the overall package, and as such it does deserve some consideration from a tonal perspective.

NUTS

Many players give little thought to that thin, slotted strip of organic or synthetic material that lies across the end of the fingerboard and guides the strings on their way to the tuners, or consider it only as it affects tuning and playability. The stuff from which your guitar's nut is made also plays a major part in shaping your tone, however. In partnership with the bridge saddles, the nut is one of the two 'anchor points' that determine the speaking length of your string (a job it shares with the fretboard when you play a fretted string) and it greatly affects both the way in which the strings ring, and the amount of vibrational energy that is transferred into the neck and body of the guitar.

The nuts on better vintage acoustic guitars, and many electrics, were often made from bone, and this organic material is still preferred by many makers and players today. Bone has good density, can be shaped fairly easily, is relatively hard-wearing, and generally enhances resonance and sustain. A bone blank can, however, contain irregularities that aren't always obvious to the luthier who cuts the nut from it; so it isn't always as consistent a material as it might appear. Occasionally, tiny pockets within the bone can lessen its density and impede resonance, while the fragility of some stocks can lead to chipping and early failure. Usually, it's pretty reliable stuff, and sounds great, but it's worth being aware of its imperfections. These inconsistencies have led some makers and players to use synthetic alternatives made from Corian or Micarta. Corian is a material that is commonly used in kitchen counter tops; it's a hard yet workable substance that provides good sustain and pleasant, balanced all-round tone. Micarta, a compound of phenolic resins, is a little softer and easier to work than bone, but still dense enough to provide a tonal upgrade on cheaper plastic nuts.

Several makes of self-lubricating nuts are popular with players who make heavy string bending or vibrato use a major part of their style. Graphite-based nuts provided an early form of self-lubrication, offering excellent return-to-pitch capabilities along with durability and good tone. PRS's proprietary nuts were among the initial graphite nuts, while Graph Tech's black, Teflon-lubricated TUSQ XL nut is a popular modern component (their white TUSQ nuts offer a more traditional-looking alternative). Super-slippery Delrin nuts have also become popular lately. Each of these is a worthy alternative for players who either ask a lot from their vibratos

or simply want nut slots to remain slick and snag-free. While the cheap PVC plastic nuts and, even worse, *hollow* plastic nuts found on some 'budget' guitars are widely considered to represent the nadir of guitar hardware, many players are surprised to learn that one of the most prized vintage electric guitars of all time, the Gibson Les Paul of 1958–60, carried a nut made from nylon. Nylon 6.4, to give it its full title, was a super-hard, semi-self-lubricating material that provided excellent nuts for many Gibson instruments in the 50s and 60s, until it was discontinued due to its toxicity. Nylon 6.6 is the closest alternative available today. Some players have gone as far as cutting replacements from Nylabone dog bones, nylon cutting boards, and other household products in order to obtain a similar look and feel, although those are made from slightly different types of nylon.

As with so many of the components of tone, it is perhaps most important to be aware of the range of different nuts available, rather than cling to the idea of some 'ultimate nut.' As long as your guitar carries a nut made from one of several materials that offer some sonic veracity, the exact selection you make will depend on what kind of tone you are trying to achieve with your instrument. Whether it's the brightness and clarity of Corian, the warmth and smoothness of graphite, or the depth and high-end edge of nylon 6.6, the choice is yours. As with many guitar components, it's virtually impossible to accurately compare and contrast different nuts on the same instrument. You need to weigh up the opinions and descriptions of others, sample as much of what already exists on available guitars, and, finally, take a leap of faith.

FRETS

Like so many components of the electric guitar, and those related to the neck in particular, frets have a major impact on both tone and playing feel. When we talk about the 'feel' of a neck, a major part of that is really the tactile quality of the frets. The board part of any fingerboard is of relatively little consequence feel-wise, compared to the way the frets themselves feel under the fingertips of your left hand (assuming you are a right-hander). From wide and low, to narrow and high—and many variables in between—each fret yields a different 'touch,' and, in turn, inspires and encourages a different way of playing. What's best depends on what you want to achieve. Wider frets are often preferred by heavy benders, while narrow frets are often the choice of guitarists looking for a sharp, precise feel. There can be plenty of compromise in between: play as many types as you can get your hands on and see what works for you.

While most guitarists who give any thought at all to their frets usually do so in terms of the basic issues of tactile response and condition (especially if the frets are rough or pitted), players should also consider whether or not the ends are sharp when they slide up the neck, or if they are too low to get any grip. Frets are also a tonal component, thanks to their contribution to the overall make-up of any guitar. As such, frets of different types, made from different materials, of different shapes, and with different states of wear, will directly affect the sound a guitar produces, over and above its playing feel.

When a guitar string is depressed against the fingerboard, the fret takes over from the nut as the anchor point which determines the speaking length of that string, and, therefore, transmits the vibrational energy into the neck and, in turn, body of the guitar. Contemporary fret wire is commonly made from one of two materials. The more traditional is a steel alloy that contains approximately 18 per cent nickel-silver (also called 'German silver'), actually a silver-free alloy of nickel and copper. The less traditional alternative is stainless steel. The former is in far wider use, although the latter seems to be growing in popularity.

Traditional nickel-silver frets are actually made from an alloy that is relatively soft and can't be relied upon to last the entire lifetime of a guitar. They have evolved as a compromise between tone and durability, and as they are far and away the industry standard they really do hold a tonal monopoly. As such, it's a little pointless trying to describe 'the nickel-silver fret sound' in light of all of the other variables at play on any given guitar. That said, frets obviously need to be sound and well seated to do their best vibration-transference work, and they need to retain an adequate depth of pit-free crown surface to be playable. Beyond matters of age, stability, and condition, the size of fret wire (its width and height, or, taken together, its 'profile') will contribute a slight tonal variable. The three broad categories of fret profile are narrow, medium, and wide (or jumbo), and each has a slight influence on sound as well as feel.

Many players are convinced that fatter wire equates to fatter tone, and there could be some logic here, considering that the more metal in any fixed component usually means a greater vibrational coupling between string and guitar. Too much metal, however—as with heavier bridges and tailpieces, on occasion—and you might find the component sucking up the vibration, rather than passing it on and letting it ring. Players such as Stevie Ray Vaughan, Kenny Wayne Shepherd, Rory Gallagher, and innumerable others have opted for guitars with wider frets that were originally manufactured with narrow 'vintage'-gauge fret wire. In many cases, of course, this is a subjective 'feel' phenomenon as much as it is a sonic one, and wider frets are certainly easier to bend without choking out. Wider frets also present marginally less distinct noting than narrow frets, so the move from narrow to jumbo perhaps makes most sense from the blues player's perspective.

Narrow frets present a more precise termination point for the string's speaking length, and can yield more shimmering harmonics and a tighter, better defined note as a result. Determining which frets are right for you will require a triangulation of sorts: you have to balance the way the fret allows the string to vibrate and determine pitch with the extent it transfers additional energy into the neck wood, while also considering the way it bends and feels to the fingers. In the end, the feel element probably matters most to the majority of players.

In addition to a fret's width, its height will also affect playability. Even wide frets are difficult to bend when they become worn down significantly from their original height, and low frets make satisfactory finger vibrato more difficult to achieve. I have come across some otherwise gorgeous vintage guitars that were just begging to be played, but which were in an impracticable condition thanks to the ultra-low frets that their owners were loathe to change, probably for reasons of authenticity (Gibson's original 'Black Beauty' Les Paul Custom of the 50s, and the SG-shaped Les Paul Custom of the early 60s, were known as 'fretless wonders' because they were made with super-low frets right from the start. It made them fast, but tricky to grip or to bend strings on). Of course, you can get your frets too high as well. Frets that are too tall will lead some players to slip out of pitch, because any extra finger pressure actually bends the string

downward behind the back of the fret and raises the note slightly. High frets can sometimes feel like speed bumps when you're working your way up the neck.

Stainless steel frets, rare until recently, are in wider circulation now and can be considered a second standard of sorts. The same considerations of profile and feel apply here, of course, but stainless steel fret wire certainly does wear a lot better than nickel-silver, and it can be expected to last a lot longer under comparable playing conditions. Stainless steel frets also feel a little harder and slicker under the fingertip, which is to some players' taste, but not others. Some makers and players claim stainless steel frets give a guitar a harder, harsher sound than nickel-silver, but many other respected luthiers will refute this. Once again, it's the quality of 'feel' that will most likely sway players toward or away from stainless steel more than any other single factor, not to mention their willingness to part with the extra cash required to install these much harder frets.

Gauge preferences and any personal conclusions regarding the gauge/tone ratio aside, condition remains a prime consideration with the frets on any guitar. It's probably best to consider them a consumable: you might get ten or even twenty years of life out of your frets, but when they are worn down too much for a good milling you just have to have them replaced.

TUNERS

Mainly a functional component which you can pretty much ignore when they're working smoothly and efficiently, tuners do also play some part in shaping the tone of any guitar, as does anything to which a vibrating string is anchored. Exactly what part they play, and how they play it, are issues I will leave for others to document. Tuners are a subject I have examined extensively over the years but about which I continue to find compelling, contradictory arguments.

It seems like every major rock and blues-rock player of the late 60s and 70s was convinced that heavier tuners, and the increase headstock mass they necessitated, helped to improve sustain on their guitars. Jimmy Page, for one, has always sworn by the die-cast Grovers he swapped for the lightweight Klusons on his Les Pauls, and for a time it seemed more difficult to find a Les Paul or SG with original tuners than without. Those were certainly happy days for makers like Grover and Schaller. Along similar lines, Groove Tubes founder Aspen Pittman has filed patents for two products intended specifically to increase a guitar's headstock mass—a brass strip known as the Fathead, designed to be mounted at the back of the headstock under the tuners, and a brass clamp of sorts called the Fatfinger, which is more portable and clamps to any headstock. Pittman swears by the increase in sustain that these can bring to any guitar.

It's also worth considering any number of high-end acoustic guitar makers who use extremely light, open-backed Waverly tuners on their exquisite creations. Or, for that matter, arch-top guitar luthier Robert Benedetto, who told me several years ago, and expounded to similar effect in his book, *Making An Archtop Guitar* (Centerstream, 1996), that heavier tuners deaden resonance at the headstock end and that light tuners, ideally with light ebony buttons, are the way to go for ultimate tone. Benedetto knows his stuff, although Jimmy Page is hardly a tone lightweight.

And so it goes. On occasion, in the guitar world, different voices of seemingly equal authority will swear by theories from opposite sides of the fence. Ultimately, as is so often the case, it isn't a matter of better or worse, simply 'different.'

POTS AND SWITCHES

Anything your signal passes through can have an effect on your tone, and it passes through at least one pot or switch at all times, sometimes several. Terms such as 'tone sucking' and 'true bypass' are buzz-phrases of the recent effects pedal boom, and are usually used to describe the supposedly detrimental affect of running your signal through certain pedals. The truth is, the only way to get zero tone-sucking would be to hard-wire your guitar's pickup straight to the cathode of the amp's first preamp tube with very short lengths of wire. Most everything your signal passes through along the way, even when you connect the guitar directly to the amp with a relatively short cable, can rob you of at least a little of your tone, and most likely will.

There's nothing that can be done about this—not even the most committed tonehound would seriously entertain the idea of standing rammed up against the back of a Vox AC30 with a Telecaster's bridge pickup soldered straight to pin two of a Mullard ECC83 tube. I mention the inevitable tone sucking of virtually all electronic components by way of admitting that, yes, quality counts, and good components *should* deplete a little less of the good stuff than lesser ones do. Put briefly, this tone sucking takes the form of a slight decrease in highs and a loss of a little of your guitar's potential 'sheen.' We think of running straight to amp with a high-quality cable of a reasonable length as being the road to total tonal purity, but many of us will also have experienced the magic of the original Fender Broadcaster switching network which sends the guitar's single bridge pickup via the tone control in the middle position, but bypasses the tone control in the back position. The latter setting is perceptibly brighter and hotter. Similarly, the standard Stratocaster wiring scheme, which sends the bridge pickup straight to the output (via the master volume pot) was designed to keep it as bright as possible in an age where treble was king. In each of these cases we see how the tone pot robs the signal of a bit of high end, and the volume pot does the same. Well-made pots will often do it a little less, or at least will be more consistent in their slight theft of highs, but perhaps more to the point, the value of the pot in the circuit will also greatly influence its effect on your sound, especially with regard to high-end content.

Provided you (or your guitar maker) are using quality potentiometers in the first place, the main thing that is likely to concern you, from a tone perspective, is the value of your volume and tone pots. Values of between 250k ohms and 1 megohm are used for each position, and there's a considerable difference in the way these extremes interact with your guitar signal. The lower the volume pot value, the more highs it cuts, even, to some extent, when it is fully 'on.' Fender used 250k-ohms audio taper pots exclusively from 1950 to 1969, and that has become the traditional value for single-coil pickups, which can usually handle (and will sometimes benefit from) the slight attenuation in highs. In fact, from 1969 the company began using 1 megohm pots on the Telecaster, and some of these guitars can sound slightly spiky as a result.

To eke more highs out of its humbuckers, and its fatter-sounding P-90 single coil, Gibson has traditionally used 500k-ohms pots. Guitars that mix humbuckers and single coils are likely to carry 500k-ohms pots, too, rather than risk a too-dark humbucking tone with 250k-ohms

pots. Armed with these simple facts, you can easily see how you might taper your own pickups' response by giving some thought to potentiometer values, or how you might track down and correct some unwanted darkness or brightness that is actually induced by this unsuspecting component, rather than being any flaw inherent in the pickups or in your guitar in general.

The values of the tone pots affect their response, too, although the more noticeable factors with these are usually their taper and the value of the tone capacitor that is attached to them. While audio-taper pots are more often used for volume controls, makers have used different tapers for tone pots, and different players seem to express equal preference for audio and linear alike. The values of the tone pots affect their response, too, although more notable factors in the performance of these components are their taper—the rapidity with which they roll off highs—and the value of the tone capacitor that is attached to them (explained below). With these pots, you might note that nothing much happens until the last third of the knob's rotation, although that's the way a lot of people like it. A linear pot, on the other hand, does what its name suggests, and decreases output or treble fairly steadily from fully clockwise to fully counterclockwise. If anything, you are more likely to see this pot used in the tone control position, where Gibson employs it on its contemporary models (as do many other makers) in place of the audio pot of old. Some players also like a linear pot for the volume control, although more tend to prefer the gradual roll-off of an audio pot in that position. What's 'right' or 'wrong' depends upon what works for you, or what *doesn't* work for you: if all the action happens too quickly or too slowly for you, see what you've got in there now and try the other flavor of taper in its place.

Often, these days, players seem to be more interested in tinkering with tone caps than with tone pots themselves. A traditional, passive guitar tone control consists of one of the potentiometers we have already discussed, with a capacitor (or 'cap') wired from its 'output' terminal to ground. Together, these form a simple low-pass filter that, as the control is turned down, continues to let low frequencies pass through while shunting increasing amounts of highs out of the signal (these are also called 'treble bleed' networks). As such, it might be less confusing to think of them as 'high cut filters' rather than 'low-pass filters.' This little filter's shelf, the position on the frequency range above which highs begin to be cut, is determined by the value of the capacitor used. The larger the value of the capacitor the lower on the frequency range this cut-off point will be set, and the darker the overall tone will be as you turn down the control. Standard tone-cap values are between capacitance values of .1µF ('µF'—also sometimes written as 'mF' or 'MFD'—which stands for microfarads—the 'µ' symbol representing 'micro'), the largest commonly used, and .01µF, and values between these, such as .022µF and .047µF are quite popular. Fender's bright pickups were commonly attenuated with a .1µF cap on vintage Strats, for example, to give a more noticeable darkening as the tone controls were wound down, although .05µF (or .047µF) is more common today. Gibson used .022µF caps on the Les Paul to avoid making it too dull when the filter was applied, and this remains the most popular value for humbuckers.

In addition to the value of the tone cap used, its make and composition have latterly become hot subjects for tweaking. Capacitors are made of several different types of material, and each is considered by some to have its own sonic properties. More often a consideration of amplifier circuits than of guitars and perhaps only likely to make minimal impact, capacitors have become a major point of exploration for guitar modifiers looking for another variable to fine tune. The types range from cheap ceramic discs to vintage paper-and-foil units, and Mylar, polyester, Teflon, and polystyrene capacitors, as well as hallowed (and expensive) paper-in-oil types. In each case, the ascribed name indicates the dielectric (or insulator), which is the material that determines the flow of electrons from plate to plate within the capacitor and governs its capacitance. Caps made from different types of dielectric are still built with a wide range of values, which are determined (to put it simply) by the thickness of the material between the plates. As with so many of the finer points of electric guitar tone, certain materials have taken on magical status, as have caps produced by certain makers. At the top of the tone cap heap come several types made by Sprague, including the vintage 'Bumblebee' and 'Black Beauty' caps found in old Les Pauls, and the NOS ('new old stock') Vitamin Qs that are all the rage today.

Both the type and value of your tone caps would seem to be contributory tonal factors only when the pot is turned down low, but even with the tone pot on 'ten,' the cap is loading the pickup and causing a slight alteration in tone from that pickup's straight-to-amp sound. As such, a change in cap value will also change that load, and might be heard by some ears (although not by others), even when the tone control isn't turned down at all. Of course, the tone cap comes into play more fully when you start rolling down your tone control, which some players never do. I've often heard it said that a change in value (say, from .1µF to .047µF or .022µF) can be heard by most, even with the tone control on full, but that the different qualities of various types of capacitors (ceramic, polyester, paper-in-oil, etc) can only really be heard when the pot is set to 'zero.' This is something we can all test for ourselves, so there's no point dragging out an already long-standing argument here. If you belong to the 'woman-tone' club, however, and needs to have the tone pot wound back part way to feel like you're truly interacting with your guitar, you should hear a difference certainly between tone cap values, and possibly between tone cap makes and types, too.

To revisit the point we came in on, however reputable your parts, traditional guitar wiring circuits and control networks are likely to suck a little of that precious tone before it even exits the Switchcraft jack; it's an inevitable result of the way the hardware works on any electric guitar. That said, some guitars benefit from a little of the perceived 'warming up' achieved by the loss of some highs through an inefficient wiring and potentiometer network, and eliminating this treble-loss by 'fixing' it might suddenly render your prized instrument spiky and harsh.

FINISHES

Finish is usually a major point of consideration for vintage spec sticklers, but is often ignored when it comes to tone-influencing components. We should certainly discuss finish within the context of tone, but I throw this out as a subject for consideration rather than declaring any hard evidence on the matter. The popular theory has it that nitrocellulose lacquer is the most beneficial of common finish types, from a sonic perspective, other, perhaps, than bare wood with a light oiling for protection. That's not to suggest that there is anything inherently tone-

enhancing in nitrocellulose itself, but rather that its relative porosity, the way that it hardens with age, and the fact that it is usually applied rather thinly (while also thinning further with age) allow a guitar to resonate and 'breathe' more fully. There is no doubt that many of the finest-sounding electric guitars in existence, both vintage and contemporary, have been made with nitrocellulose finishes. There are, however, many other fine-sounding guitars in existence which wear polyurethane finishes. Paul Reed Smith, Nik Huber, John Suhr, and Roger Giffin, among several other high-end makers, are all happy to use polyurethane to coat their guitars, and these are makers known for their attention to detail and no-compromise approach to tone.

So what should we conclude? "It isn't so much the type of finish used, but the skill with which it is applied, the thinness of the final finish, and, more than anything, the quality of the guitar itself," says Scott Lentz, a highly respected guitar maker and finisher. "I use polyurethane on all my guitars," he adds, "and only use nitro if I'm doing something by request of a customer that has to be to exact vintage specs. The truth is, though, in a blind test, *no one* can hear the difference between a poly and nitro finish, not when the finish, and the guitars, are done right."

This is another of those areas where a quick and accurate A/B test, blind or otherwise, is just impractical. You could, theoretically, prepare two different guitars that you feel are 'identical' in every way other than their finishes—one nitrocellulose, one polyurethane—and compare them under the sonic microscope and they will perhaps differ, marginally. However, variations in body and neck wood stocks, pickups, and other components are more likely to create noticeable disparities than are dissimilar finishes. Sure, many of us like to have our guitars the way they were in the golden years of the 50s and early 60s, and perhaps there's nothing wrong with that, but as far as pure tonal considerations go, there is simply little to choose between nitro and poly.

If your 'poly' is polyester rather than polyurethane, however, you are probably right to feel the paint is impeding your tone. Occasionally a source of confusion when the words are shortened, polyester is a thicker, hard, hermetically sealing finish, often used on more affordable guitars, and one that can indeed dampen the tonewood's resonance somewhat. Around 1968, Fender replaced the nitrocellulose finish on its guitars with polyester (it's also known as a 'thick-skin' finish). Applied in order to increase the general durability and longevity of the guitars, the modification is seen by some as early evidence of the decline in Fender's quality under CBS, who'd bought out the company in 1965.

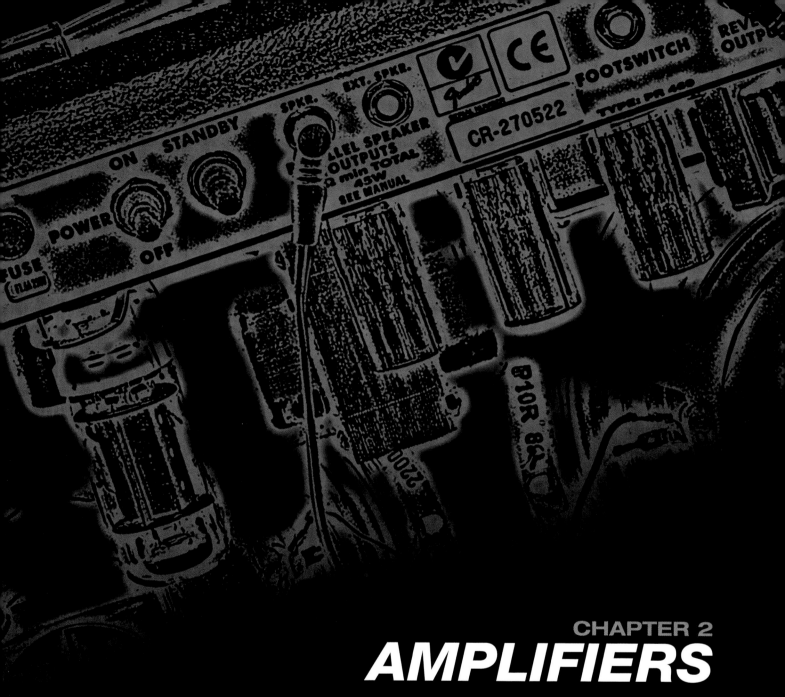

CHAPTER 2
AMPLIFIERS

Over the past 15 years or so, guitarists have given more consideration to their amplifiers than ever before. Yet, there is still a tendency for even great players to obsess about every little detail of their precious guitars while giving comparatively little thought to the amp they plug it into, beyond the scant descriptions in the manufacturer's promotional literature.

Most enlightened connoisseurs understand that, in setting any gear budget (and whether considering new or used equipment), you really ought to allocate as much cash to the amplifier as you do the guitar, otherwise you are unlikely to get the best out of the instrument you've sunk the majority of your money into. In fact, you would do well to spend around 60 per cent of the allocation on the amp and 40 per cent on a guitar (with a little consideration for a pickup upgrade if necessary). In any case, while your hands and your attitude are a big part of what makes that guitar sing, the thing you call 'your tone' only exists once it all comes out the back end of the amplifier.

As much as every link in your signal chain—guitar, pedals, amp, and all the cables that connect them—contributes to your final sound, your amp itself is one hot, glowing box of individual components that each contributes to a greater tonal whole. Your tone isn't just shaped in one instantaneous *shlumpf* inside the box, but is the amalgam of what each step, from input to output (via the speaker), does to it along its journey. Not only will the way that each of those steps is designed alter your tone, but minor differences in components along the way can add up to a big difference at the output stage, too.

As the late Ken Fischer of Trainwreck Circuits once put it: "I can take a schematic from any amp and just change some parts, and make it sound like a completely different amp." And to hammer this point home, Fischer offered a pertinent example from the effects world. "Get a Clyde McCoy wah-wah, an early Vox wah, like Hendrix or Clapton would use, and a new Jim Dunlop CryBaby wah-wah. Every component value and schematic is completely identical. So why does the old Clyde McCoy wah have a much more vocal sound than the new CryBaby? It's got to be in the details, in the components." Apply that thinking to amp design, and you can multiply the variables exponentially.

No single amp is really good for every kind of music. There are a few that excel at one end of the spectrum and can fake the other end pretty impressively, perhaps with the aid of the right distortion pedal, but getting it all, authoritatively, is asking a bit much. A more realistic goal, however, should be to find an amp that is the most expressive and best-sounding instrument for the kind of music you play most; and if your church gig requires you to cover Cream, Dwight Yoakam, Jimi Hendrix, and Slayer back to back on the same Sunday morning set list, buy a digital amp and be done with it. For the rest of us, just a few different sounds—those obtainable from a couple of channels and the twist of half a dozen knobs at most—should be plenty. The rest you can do with a few pedals, if you even need them.

Perhaps this sounds good to you in theory, but you feel you really need a vast palette of tones at your fingertips? I encounter many players who seek extreme versatility in their amplifiers, hoping to get something to sound just like Luther Perkins one minute, Stevie Ray

Vaughan the next, and Dimebag Darrell after that—and all that from traditional tube amps, too, not modelers with 60 digital presets. The inescapable fact is that even the best amps out there won't offer this kind of flexibility. However, crank up almost any really virtuous tube amp to a bit past half way, then play your guitar with the volume firstly at around 50, then 80, then 100 per cent, and you'll probably discover three outstanding and very usable tones. What's more, play these with your own style and attitude and you'll probably sound better, ultimately, than you will by trying to imitate Messrs Perkins, Vaughan, or Dimebag.

For all that, emulating the tones of others isn't a bad place to start. If your own tone quest is just beginning, you will undoubtedly learn a lot by trying to cop the tones of other great players. I would argue, however, that achieving your own tone and playing like yourself will ultimately be more rewarding than any imitations you pull off, however convincing.

So, let's begin this chapter by looking not merely at the marvelous variety of tube amplifiers out there, and the infinite variety of stages in the signal chain within those amps, but also considering the elements within those vinyl or tweed-covered boxes that contribute most significantly to tonal virtue.

AMPLIFIER CATEGORIES

We will work our way inside the box with a brief look at the different genres of amps available. I might have my favorite amp, and you might have yours, but if we are both right-thinking people neither of us will write off the other's choice. Whether a Dumble, Trainwreck, Fender, Matchless, Peavey, or Traynor is your idea of tonal heaven, it might not be the next guitarist's. As discussed above, different types of amps serve different requirements; that's just the way it is. But within that range of different types we can make some sort of distinction between the merely 'good' and the 'great,' and hopefully discern a few ways to move your own particular amp toward the latter category. Having agreed on some ground rules about the terminology we'll use, it will be easier to progress with the more in-depth discussions about what goes on under the hood.

Vintage and Vintage-Style

Our old friend eBay might define vintage gear in its listings as 'pre-1980,' but that's too broad a span for our purposes. There were plenty of pre-80s amps made to more modern specifications, and many that have been made far more recently (and are being made right this minute) that fit what is more accurately described as a 'vintage style' category. So, let's set the boundaries of 'vintage' around non-master-volume amps that are also, for the most part, made with hand-wired circuit boards, which is to say made *without* printed circuit boards (PCBs).

Before the true vintage amp era ended, in the early 70s, with the rise in popularity of Mesa/Boogie's high-gain Mark I combo and the gradual addition of master-volume controls to amps by major makers like Fender and Marshall, the majority of tube guitar amps had a fairly simple structure, however many extra features such as reverb, tremolo, and multiple channels they might have carried. These usually included a single preamp stage per channel, sometimes in addition to an extra gain make-up stage to enable the use of a more involved EQ circuit

TONE TIP Use Your Guitar's Volume Control

No, I haven't put this in the wrong chapter. I am making this point here because it really has as much to do with how you use your amp as how you play your guitar. During what I reverentially refer to as the First Golden Age of Tone, the late 50s, 60s, and early 70s, this was second nature to great electric guitarists, but it seems to have fallen from the knowledge bank in the 'high-gain era' of the late 70s and 80s, when multi-channels, footswitches, superchargers, and hotrods ruled the day. Long before the ascendancy of channel switching and massive pedal boards, legendary rock players had perfected a straightforward means of achieving clean crunch and vivid lead tones directly from their guitars. To achieve this, they set their tube amps for the best lead sound they could muster, then turned the guitar's volume knob down a little for some crunch and a little more for a clean tone. That was it: the volume control was used like it was meant to be, as a remote appendage of the amp's controls. Work with this yourself and you can get a lot

out of this control right here in the 21st century.

Now, this technique might seem to work best with vintage-style tube amps, including newer amps made to those classic templates, but it can also do wonders for either the clean or lead output of a channel-switcher. With certain vintage amps, however—a Fender 5E3 Deluxe or Vox AC15 for example—this technique might be the only way to achieve any headroom and still make use of the lovely, full-blown tube distortion that you bought the thing for in the first place. After a certain point, these amps don't get any louder (I'm thinking, in most cases, of volume settings between about three o'clock and five o'clock on the dial), they just break up and compress more. Crank them up, however, and wind down your guitar's volume control, and you get surprisingly rich, dynamic clean tones that are often far more appealing and playable than the tones achieved by turning the amp down to a comparable volume and the guitar turned up all the way. In between, you get thick crunch and lead tones, and these are very

without any loss of signal, straight into any of a handful of popular output topologies. That really was about it, and any 'extras' on the control panel were peripheral to this circuit path.

One significant factor of the vintage-style amp is that you'll usually find a fairly direct relationship between the volume setting and the amount of breakup in the tone. This can vary widely from model to model, of course. For example, a tweed Fender Deluxe breaks up extremely early while a Twin does so very late, if at all. There is a 'what you see is what you get' relationship between the volume control and the output level, and no other factor is intervening in that relationship. If you want it to break up, you turn it up. If it still doesn't break up, other than physically modifying the amp, there's nothing you can do to change that, other than to add some external influence such as a pedal or a guitar with hotter pickups.

Another significant characteristic of the vintage-style amp is that, given the simplicity of its signal path, there is essentially nothing to get in the way of your tone. Whether it's an affordable Harmony H430 or a highly collectable Vox AC15, if the components are up to spec, the amp is in good condition, and the tubes are fairly fresh, you should get plenty of expressive tonal veracity out of the thing. Players' gradual discovery of this fact, alongside the realization that a

C H A P T E R 2

difficult to replicate with overdrive or distortion pedals.

All of this might seem just a little too easy to be true, but it works for very scientific reasons that have to do with the electrical interaction between a guitar and a tube amplifier. Every note you pluck is transmitted to the amp in the form of an electrical current of a certain voltage. Turn your volume controls down, and a lower signal voltage is sent to the tube. Pick the string very lightly and the signal voltage decreases, and because there's a direct correlation between the level of the signal voltage which that first preamp tube registers and the degree to which the amp distorts, you've got a very real and direct means of controlling your distortion levels at the guitar's volume control, and even with your own pick attack. Try it out. Play around with your amp levels, learn where you need to roll your guitar's volume control(s) to in order to achieve the desired changes, and you'll soon discover you have far more control over your tone. There's nothing wrong with overdrive pedals and footswitch lead channels, but this is a nifty tool to have in your box.

Many guitars darken up a little when you turn them down because the loss of highs is emphasized more than the overall volume cut. Some players work with this, using it to mellow out their tone, brightening it up at full-volume for solos that really cut through. Other players find the 'turn it down' technique problematic and cure this by adding a simple 'treble bleed' network to the volume control, usually consisting of a small .001uF capacitor placed between the input terminal on each pickup's volume potentiometer (the terminal to which the pickup's own hot lead, or the hot lead from the switch, is connected) and the middle terminal on the pot.

Some guitar techs also like to add a small 150k–300k-ohms resistor in the same position so that some lows pass through, along with the highs, guarding against the tone thinning out too much.

If you play around with interactions between guitar and amp in some of these ways, the chances are you will discover a magical—and magically simple—means of governing your instrument's tonal dynamics and those clean, crunch, and lead tones.

good vintage amp isn't always an expensive collector's amp, has driven up prices of less iconic models in recent years. As a result, it's harder to get your hands on a Traynor Guitar Mate, Ampeg Reverberocket, Selmer Treble'N'Bass, or just about anything made by Valco; but this lesson has been a boon to guitar tone in several other major ways.

One benefit of this renewed appreciation of vintage amps is that it has encouraged several modern manufacturers to create new, great-sounding, and extremely reliable vintage-style amps. This trend has made the vintage-amp tone available to any player with a little money to spend, even if they can't find, or afford, a working B or C-list vintage amp, let alone anything from the A list. I'm really describing today's 'boutique' amp world, which thrives on reinventing vintage designs, often with a few useful new twists thrown in. A great many such amps are near-clones of vintage originals from Fender, Vox, Marshall, and even Gibson and Valco, but others are more original, combining semi-original renditions of vintage circuits in new and useful ways.

As a general group, these are amps for players who want to generate their overdrive tone by cranking up the amp itself, and by using the guitar's volume to clean it up again if and when they need something tamer. These models are also popular with players who use booster or

overdrive pedals to achieve their lead tones. The main drawback with such amps is that, as discussed at the start of this category, you are pretty much stuck with that near-linear relationship between volume and distortion, and if you need that amp-distortion for your tone to work and it doesn't happen until the amp hits a volume that's too loud for a particular playing situation, you're in a tight spot. There are attenuators and isolation boxes and other 'add-on' fixes, but as for the amp itself, you get what you get and you don't get upset.

Master-Volume Amps

Master-volume (MV) amps, which I have already mentioned in helping to define the parameters of the vintage-style amp, introduced a new era in gain crafting. Canadian manufacturer Traynor often claims to have been the first to introduce an MV control on its amps, specifically the YSR-2 Signature Reverb model of 1969. Randall Smith was putting an MV on his custom-made pre-Boogie creations before that time, although these amps were of a different type entirely. Fender introduced the MV to its range in 1972, on the Twin Reverb and a couple of other large models, and Marshall brought in the feature in 1975. The theory behind the circuit is a good one: turn up your channel volume (preamp gain) to get the tone you're looking for and use the MV to control the overall output level. In practice, however, the first generation of MV amps didn't always work entirely satisfactorily.

One reason for this is was that many of the first production amps that received MV circuits, particularly the Fender Twin, were designed to play loud and clean throughout their range anyway, producing little break up without some external goosing of the front end. Setting the channel volume on one of these to max and reining in the MV could produce a little fizz, but rarely any truly satisfying overdrive. Allied to this is the fact that the overdrive produced by most early MV models was nothing like the fat, juicy effect that players had previously achieved by cranking up vintage, non-master-volume amps, so these newfangled models could seem inferior on this front, too. Finally, many amps of the early-to-mid 70s that featured MV controls were already beginning to suffer tonally when compared to their predecessors, thanks to the general downgrading of circuits and components and to the sonically detrimental effects of modifications made for the sake of safety and reliability. For all of these reasons, many of the master-volume models became emblematic of a general decline in the sound of certain once-seminal amp designs.

But these caveats are reserved for the early days of MV, and you can expect teething troubles with any new technology. In the subsequent years, several creative makers have developed extremely useful MV controls on great-sounding amps, plenty of which are such stellar tone machines that we often think of them more as 'vintage-style' amps, or vintage-leaning boutique amps, and forget that they do in fact carry master-volume controls. Examples of such amps are the flagship Matchless models, the DC30 and the smaller Lightning, Bad Cat's Black Cat and Cub, TopHat's Club Royale and King Royale, Divided by 13's CJ11, and Goodsell's Super 17 MkIII. None of these are what we commonly think of as 'master volume amps,' yet they employ such a control to good effect, and without significant detriment to their overall tone (although many players will argue that they still sound their best with the MV maxed and, therefore, out of circuit).

C H A P T E R 2

High-Gain Amps

A large proportion of players who are looking beyond vintage-style tone (whether in an old or new amp) are in fact pushing *way* beyond that template, using what we call 'high-gain' amps. The term 'high-gain' is really used to describe the preamp structures of such amps, although they almost invariably carry master-volume controls to help them do their thing. Although a handful of creative, lone-wolf amp makers were tinkering with such notions in the late 60s, Randall Smith was the first to successfully launch a line of high-gain amps, with the designs that would evolve into the Mesa/Boogie Mark series.

Smith not only concocted one very hot preamp stage, but strung together several, spilling one over into another in a method that came to be known as 'cascading gain.' Where a tweed Fender Bassman, for example, had one gain stage plus a cathode-follower stage to drive the tone stack, the Boogie Mark 1's lead input had three gain stages plus a gain make-up stage for the EQ, with two volume controls and a master to govern the gain overspill before it all hit the phase inverter (PI) and the output tubes. Although the details of others' designs have varied, this is essentially the route taken by many makers of high-gain amps in the years since Boogies made their mark and includes such names as Soldano, Bogner, Rivera, Peavey, Carvin, Engle, and others.

In most high-gain amps, the output stage is really no different to that of bigger vintage amps or more traditional MV amps; it is there to amplify the high-gain signal that is fed into it, and is usually made to be a fairly firm and robust platform for that purpose. As such, the distortion produced by a high-gain amp is almost always preamp-tube distortion, except perhaps when you wind up the volume (gain or drive) controls *and* the MV high enough to get the output tubes cooking, in which case you'll probably still get mostly preamp-tube distortion with an element of output-tube distortion blended in.

Fans of fat, dynamic, transparent, vintage-style tube distortion extol the merits of generating your crunch at the output stage, which can only be done by keeping the front end of the amp relatively clean yet bold, but driving the signal hard into the PI and the output tubes to induce some clipping there. In fact, *pure* output-tube distortion is extremely rare, and that hallowed vintage tone is still usually a combination of some preamp clipping, often a pretty good whack of PI clipping, and a little output-tube clipping, too. In most amp designs, the output tubes really aren't going to start breaking up until the amp is roaring loud, and that's something that few of us have many opportunities to indulge in with anything other than an amp of 15 watts or less. That said, it can sound great if you do get to that volume, and often it packs the kind of dynamics and harmonic saturation that make an amp a real pleasure to play through.

None of which is intended to imply that high-gain amp distortion can't be extremely satisfying and inspiring. Some schools of thought disparage preamp-tube distortion as 'fizzy' and 'buzzy,' and when executed crudely it certainly can be, but as produced by some of the better amp designs it can also be extremely juicy, rich, and touch-sensitive. This is also just about the only way to achieve singing, 1,000-pound-violin sustain at less than foundation-rattling volume levels, as an early proponent of cascading gain, Carlos Santana, has been ably demonstrating for four decades.

In the better breeds of high-gain tube amp, the harmonic sparkle and depth of tone can be

impressive, irrespective of the genre of music you play. Randall Smith talks of the "morphing" of harmonics, an ineffable quality that gives added dimension to a good high-gain amp like a Boogie Mark IIB. "Not only do the harmonics need to be the right ones, but you want them to morph," says Smith. "That's something we look for at Boogie. You don't want them to just be steady, you want them to intertwine and interleave and move around—it's almost like a subtle chorus effect."

CONSTRUCTION METHODS

Players today are more aware than ever before of how the tricks inside the box were put together, and many have strong opinions about the amp construction methods they prefer. There are several types of hand-made circuits which tend to get the best rap, but there's a hierarchy even among these. Some might place genuine point-to-point wiring at the top of the heap (if only because of the implied labor-intensiveness of this method), with hand-soldered components mounted on printed circuit boards lower down, and varying types of machine-loaded and solder-dipped printed circuit boards (PCBs) down further still. Before examining each type a little more closely, however, it's worth noting that amps made to any of these formulas can and do sound great, and it's important to consider, and credit, the circuit design and the veracity of the construction, not merely the construction method, when making a judgment. Ultimately, it is most important to plug in and play and try to let your ears and heart guide you, rather than to be swayed by any suppositions or prejudices about what's going on under the hood.

Point-To-Point Construction

In the past, the question of whether or not a guitar amplifier was a 'point-to-point' (PTP) design wasn't even an issue. Back in the 50s and 60s, all major tube amp manufacturers loaded their circuit boards by hand, and soldered all the connections and the wires between board, sockets, and switches by hand, too. Although Fender kept making tube amps this way through the mid 80s, Vox Sound Ltd started making the AC30 and other models using PCBs in 1970 (having taken the reins from original Vox manufacturer JMI), while Marshall started using PCBs in its amps around 1974. Slowly but surely, as players began to hanker for the older designs, guitarists noticed that one obvious difference between the old models and the new was the way the circuit boards were constructed, particularly the way the guts of the amps were wired up. The PTP versus PCB debate duly caught fire.

Before dissecting the subject more thoroughly, let's lay some groundwork by way of a few definitions. A printed circuit board is a glass-epoxy or phenolic-resin board, with a thin plate of copper on one side (sometimes both sides), onto which circuit components are soldered. Electrical connections between components on such a board are created by etching away certain portions of the copper plating to leave copper 'traces' (this is the so-called 'printing' process). These traces look like narrow tracks, and their pattern determines the signal, power, and grounding paths around the circuit. Manufacturers moved over to PCBs for amplifier construction for a number of reasons. If you plan to make a lot of the same design of amp, etching PCBs to a precise and carefully laid-out pattern will often provide more consistent and reliable results than wiring up each circuit individually, with slight variations in wire positions and lengths according to which worker on the line assembled the unit. Often, PCBs will also have components loaded onto them by machine, and have their solder connections made all at once in a process called 'dipping.' In short, PCBs are used because, in some cases, amp manufacturers consider them the best option for consistency and reliability, but also often simply because they are a more cost-effective means of manufacturing an amplifier.

A point-to-point circuit, on the other hand, is one in which all connections between components and the trace-less (non-etched) circuit board are hand-wired. To be strictly accurate, however, a genuine PTP circuit is one that uses no circuit board at all but makes all of its circuit connections directly between components, using the leads of those components themselves and very little wire: a resistor connects the input jack to the preamp tube socket, a capacitor connects the output from that preamp tube to the volume control, and so on. In truth, this kind of circuit is extremely rare. It is most commonly seen today in amps made by Matchless, Bad Cat, and Star, and in some vintage amps from Gibson, Valco, very early Fender models, and a few others (most of the *very* earliest guitar amps used PTP construction, in fact, because they were generally simple enough not to require the imposed logic of a circuit board). In the genuine PTP amp, the signal path is usually as short as possible, which can help minimize interference and noise in the circuit, and the circuit flows logically from input to output. Often in such cases, tube sockets are placed close to the position at which they are used in the circuit, rather than all in a line toward the back (for example). The circuit itself, therefore, tends to look very much like the schematic diagram from which it is built. Fans of PTP manufacturing say the logical signal flow and short wire runs make for a bolder, richer tone, too.

Alongside the virtues there are also a few potential downsides to PTP circuits. If executed poorly, they can be prone to a lot of noise and electrical interference, since an inexperienced builder might not adhere rigorously to critical considerations such as keeping signal wires and power supply wires from running close or parallel to each other, and so forth (rest assured, however, that the makers of the aforementioned modern PTP amps are *experienced* builders and have carefully considered such matters). Also, even in high-quality, well-built PTP amps, components can sometimes be more difficult to access and disconnect than those in other hand-wired circuits using non-PCBs, thanks to the rat-nest intertwining of components and connections. In addition, physical stresses—such as the heat from tube sockets, or the movement that occurs in a tube socket terminal when a tube is wiggled loose for replacement—might impact directly on components in the PTP circuit, rather than on the flexible wires making connections in other types of hand-wired circuits. Of course, the labor-intensiveness of PTP circuits also contributes to the extreme expense of some amplifiers.

Other Hand-Wired Circuits (Eyelet Board, Turret Board, etc)

Often, when guitarists are discussing so-called PTP amps, the circuits in these models really aren't true point-to-point construction at all but are made using a variety of other techniques. Among these types are eyelet boards, as most commonly found in vintage Fenders and Ampegs; tag or turret boards, as used in vintage Marshall, Vox, Hiwatt, and Traynor amps, among

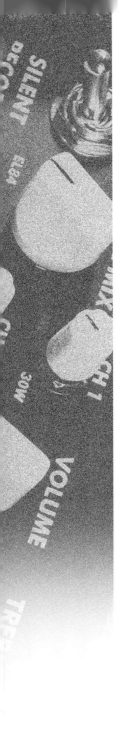

others; or terminal strips as seen on vintage makes such as Valco and Gibson, and in modern amps like TopHat and Goodsell. The boards used in each of these amps are made from insulated, non-conductive fiber into which metal eyelets, posts, or terminals are mounted. Signal-shaping components in the circuit—namely resistors and capacitors—are soldered between these terminals, while the wire connections going from points in the circuit to other components within the amp are also soldered to them: jacks, switches, potentiometers, tubes (via tube sockets), and transformers. These direct-wire connections are what lead many people to mistakenly refer to such amps as 'point-to-point,' a slight misnomer that's easily forgiven.

When built well and laid out logically, with an efficient signal flow, these boards yield extremely well-toned amps, even if they might involve a few more inches of wire through the course of the circuit (a minimal, possibly inconsequential consideration). Good examples of this kind of construction have the advantage of being easy to repair, since almost any component can be changed by desoldering two easily accessible joints and lifting out the part, as well as being extremely rugged and hard-wearing, since the circuit board offers the components some insulation against heat and vibration. In fact, none of these methods, executed properly, has any significant downside, other than that they are rather laborious, thanks to all the hand-soldered joints and hand-wired connections required to manufacture them, and are therefore generally found in amps with hefty price tags. As a result, makers that use this type of circuitry today generally fall into what we call the 'boutique' realm, which includes brands such as Victoria, Dr Z, Cornford, Mojave, Clark, 65amps, Bruno, Reeves/Hiwatt, and many others. Upscale models from major makers, such as Marshall's Hand-Wired series, many of Fender's Custom Shop amps, and Vox's new AC15H models, employ these techniques.

Printed-Circuit-Board Construction

A rugged and well laid-out PCB can certainly present an efficient and low-noise signal flow, as can a well-designed, hand-wired circuit, and the use of a PCB doesn't necessarily indicate a lower quality product. Randall Smith used PCBs in his Mesa/Boogie combos when he founded the company in the early 70s, and he still does. "Right from the beginning, I wanted consistent, repeatable results from my amps," Smith told me recently, "and quality printed circuit boards provide the best means of achieving that." Certainly the early Boogies can be considered among the forefathers of boutique amplifiers, and a lot of hand wiring still went into constructing these high-gain lead monsters. Other makers of quality boutique amps such as Soldano, Rivera, Koch, and Vero also use PCBs, as do the 'standard' lines from Fender, Marshall, Vox, and all contemporary amps from Traynor, Laney, Ampeg, Peavey, Crate, Krank, Randall, and numerous others. That said, you will generally notice a difference between the PCBs in the higher priced tube amps that carry them and those in the most affordable. A thick PCB with wide tracks, a fluid layout, and easily accessible parts can still make for a great-sounding and easily-serviced amplifier. Not all PCBs are created in this way, however, and some are much harder to service than others, or certainly harder than almost any good hand-wired amp.

In many cases, the quality demarcation is found not in the circuit board but in other places and for other reasons: for example, if tube sockets and/or pots, switches, and jacks are mounted directly to the circuit board or to the chassis, with flying leads between sockets and board, rather than with direct solder connections to the board for such components. More economical production often sees sockets, switches, and pots soldered directly to either the main PCB or, preferably, to one or more secondary PCB. When this is done, however, these boards can be prone to cracking with excessive vibration or movement (the kind that occurs when you wiggle a tube to remove it from the socket, flip a switch repeatedly, or just regularly throw the amp in and out of the tour van). Boards can also be damaged over time from too much direct heat passed on from tubes. Build an amp, however, with a thick, rugged, well-designed PCB, carrying high-quality components, mount the switches, jacks, potentiometers and tube sockets to the chassis itself—which provides excellent heat dispersion and resistance to physical stress—and you've got a product that should run with many of the big boys of the hand-wired world.

In addition, the types of components used in the circuit—resistors and capacitors in particular—often vary widely according to price and construction technique. PCBs that are machine loaded with these parts and which have all their terminals soldered at once in the aforementioned 'dipping' process usually don't carry the higher-end components, which are often physically larger and less efficient to work with (in addition to being more expensive). Instead, these tend to use smaller, more generic components from the wider consumer electronics industry which the loading and dipping machines are designed to work with. These also tend to be the amps that are harder and more time-consuming to service; sometimes, in fact, as is so often the case with the PC or DVD player you send back to the factory for repair, a technician might simply pull out the entire circuit board and replace it rather than try to diagnose and locally repair the precise problem itself.

None of this is to say that you need to sell your granny and run out right now to buy a PTP or hand-wired guitar amplifier. Hand-crafted US or European-made goods in any corner of the consumer market cost a lot more than mass-manufactured or assembly line goods, and I don't mean to imply that the extra expense is justified for every player out there. Makers of quality tube amplifiers that use PCBs still employ a lot of hand assembly in the manufacturing process, and, clearly, plenty of great pros record and tour with amps such as Fender Bassman Reissues, Vox AC30TBXs or Custom Classics, Marshall JCM800s or TSL100s, Mesa/Boogie Mark 1s and Triple Rectifiers, Soldano SLOs, Peavey 6505s, and many other righteous models that carry printed circuit boards. Having said that, both pros and hobbyists regularly derive virtuous tones from any of a number of the hand-wired tube amps that are available—whether new or vintage models. The important point here is that it's worth knowing the major differences in circuit design when you undertake your own search for tone, so you can more intelligently assess the elements in the models you are drawn toward, and hopefully understand a little more about what makes them tick, and why.

CIRCUIT STAGES

As mentioned at the beginning of this chapter, any tube amp—simple or complex—is the sum of a number of stages, each of which shapes the guitar tone as the signal passes from one to the next. The way that individual stages in the circuitry amplify and filter that signal, and the

quality and value of the components in that part of the circuit, all play a part in your final tone. If you're looking for ultra-tight bottom and sharp, shimmering twang, you're just not going to get it from an amp in which two out of three stages are predisposed to give you compression and dirt. Likewise, you won't achieve spongy, brown, garage-rock tones from an amp that was born to give you a firm response and plenty of headroom. Knowing a little about what goes on inside the box, therefore, can help you understand how to achieve the sounds you're looking for or why you just *can't* wring them out of the amp you have been sweating over. To that end, let's track a range of tube amp topologies stage by stage, spending a little time on what makes each link in the chain tick and noting how different circuits and components can affect your sound.

Preamp Stage

A guitar amp's 'preamp' is often said to include everything between the input and the phase inverter (PI, as explained below), including any gain or tone-shaping stages along the way. For our purposes, however, it makes more sense to break out the preamp proper as the gain stage, or stages prior to the tone controls, which is how things fall in the majority of tube amps.

Once your signal ducks through that quarter-inch input, the first thing it encounters, in most cases, is a single 68k 'grid-stopper' resistor put in place to stop oscillation in the tube; then it's a short, straight trip to the input of the first tube stage in the preamp, where it already begins to be amplified. As the name implies, the preamp—any preamp, effectively—is merely a small amplifier designed to bring an audio signal up to a level that the power amp can deal with and thus boost to a more substantial level ready to be converted to audible airwaves pumped by a speaker. The guitar amplifier's preamp contains a gain stage that boosts the signal (usually one half of a dual-triode tube, most commonly a 12AX7), a coupling capacitor that helps to determine the desirable frequencies to be passed along to the next stage, and a volume control (technically known as a 'variable resistor') to let the player determine how much of the signal to let through. Other capacitors and resistors do the jobs of conditioning the power supply and biasing the tube (that is, setting its operating level).

The preamps of legendary amplifiers such as the Fender Bassman 5F6-A of the late 50s, the Vox AC30 of the early-to-mid 60s, and the Marshall 'plexi' of the late 60s, contain precisely these ingredients and no more. In these preamps the signal passes through a 68k resistor, one tube gain stage, a .02uF capacitor, and a 1M volume control. In most cases, in standard-gain amps at least, after this point it's bye-bye preamp, nice knowing you. But as ever, the beauty is in the details—or in some cases, the lack thereof. Each of the same elements of a different make and/or composition will introduce subtle sonic changes: a metal film resistor versus a carbon comp (the older 'carbon composition' resistor types), a polyester versus a polystyrene or paper-in-oil capacitor, a GE 12AX7 tube versus a Mullard ECC83, a 12AX7 versus a 12AY7, and so forth.

Since the dawn of the 'boutique amp' era, two decades ago, there has been a lot of talk, hype even, about the qualities of these individual components in the signal chain, and coupling capacitors have themselves gone through a renaissance of sorts. Beginning in the mid-to-late 90s, there was a trend among many amp makers to acquire the fanciest, most high-fidelity signal caps available. Paper-in-oil caps were all the rage for a time, until some makers found that some types weren't happy with the high voltages produced inside many guitar amps. Several kinds of audiophile caps also had their 15 minutes of fame, although few of even the larger boutique builders use components such as these on a regular basis. Some makers think you can go too far in this quest. As Mike Zaite of Dr Z puts it, "Where I draw the line is … I don't want to build an amplifier that's like a stereo—a high-fidelity type of amp. I still want to build an instrument, something with a little character to it. And I find that when these guys start using gold chassis and pure, oxygen-free wire, and all these really expensive resistors and capacitors, the more they spend, the worse they sound, to my ear. You're not making a guitar amp to reproduce prerecorded music: you're making an instrument to *make* music. I find that some of the little warts and quirks, some of the lesser components, when married together correctly, give a better output."

Whatever the veracity of Zaite's opinion, the debate still rages about what tonal nuances are produced by miscellaneous component types used within a circuit. You *might* hear changes in quality relating to types of coupling caps in some circuits, and both hobbyists and boutique makers often spend considerable time sampling these components and selecting the ones that they feel help to optimize the tone they are looking for. What you should certainly hear is any change in coupling cap values. Also known as 'tone caps' or 'blocking caps,' coupling caps perform two jobs simultaneously: they block DC current from entering the circuit in front of them, while also helping to determine the frequency response of your signal. The name 'coupling cap' derives from the fact that they often join two circuit stages together, and they are also used further down the line to couple tone stack to PI, and PI to output tubes.

In the preamp stage I have just described, the coupling cap connects the output (or plate) of the preamp tube to the input of the volume control, and helps to voice the circuit while doing so. Each of the classic amps mentioned uses a .02μF (or .022μF) capacitor here. This is a popular value, and is a good choice for a full, balanced tone at this stage. Other common values include the .1μF coupling cap in this position in a 5E3 Fender Tweed Deluxe from the late 50s, and the .05μF (or .047μF) in some other designs. The rule for voicing in this stage is that a lower value capacitor will decrease the signal's low-frequency content, while a higher value cap will increase the bass response. The final outcome will, of course, be further shaped by other stages down the line—so what you seem to hear as brightness or bassiness won't always seem to correspond directly to what's going on in this position.

In addition to the frequency-shaping achieved by the coupling caps, any capacitor attached to the cathode of the preamp tube will also help to voice the stage. Since the mid 50s or so, the majority of amplifiers have used cathode-biased preamp designs, which means that the cathode of the preamp tube is connected to ground (earth) within the amp via a resistor of a value that determines the tube's bias (its operating level). In many amps, this is 'bypassed' by a capacitor, which is to say the cap is also connected from the tube's cathode pin to ground (which is sometimes achieved simply by soldering one end of the cap to the resistor's tube-side connection point and the other to the ground-side connection point). Although your signal does not pass through this cap, its use here gives a 'boost' to the preamp, while also voicing it further: the lower the value, the fatter the boost; the higher the value, the brighter the boost. A 25μF cap is common for a 'fat-boost' bypass cap, in which case an electrolytic capacitor is used for reasons

of size, while .68μF is a frequently-used 'bright-boost'—as found in the 'brilliant' channels of many Marshall models, for example. A popular feature these days is a three-way boost switch to offer fat/off/bright options by selecting either or none of these caps, an option used on many TopHat amps and others.

Blackface Fender amps of 1963–67 and the silverface models that followed, and some amps designed along similar lines, do things a little differently, and don't use coupling caps, or even configure their preamp/tone-stack stages, in quite the same way I have described here. In these models, the first gain stage runs straight into the tone network, then into the volume control, and on into a second gain stage (the second half of a 12AX7 or 7025 preamp tube) that makes up signal level lost in all that tone-shaping circuitry. Rather than using a coupling cap to join preamp-tube plate to volume control, these stages are 'coupled' by the entire tone network, including the various tone caps that are part of it. Changing the values of these caps will alter the way the tone controls perform, and can, to some extent, change the amount of gain that they pass along to the stage that follows.

High-gain amps that use the 'cascading gain' technique mentioned above have further gain stages in their preamps, usually placed before the tone stage, although occasionally after. These gain stages are often as simple as the single gain stage that we have already discussed, as used by the more traditional amps, and they largely repeat the process, with another potentiometer added to rein in drive levels as required. Some makers add a few extra tricks along the way in order to ramp up the gain somewhat differently at different stages. The Mesa/Boogie Mark 1 adds another gain stage before the tone stack and another after, in addition to the gain make-up stage immediately following the EQ network. Marshall's JCM800 preamp adds another half of an ECC83 for one more gain stage in front of the tone stack, and Soldano's SLO was designed with three gain stages in lead mode and two in clean/crunch mode. And for every added gain stage there is another opportunity to condition and voice the signal as it makes its journey— more coupling caps, more cathode-bypass caps on the preamp tubes, and so forth.

By the same token, if not placed very carefully, the more complex multi-stage preamp might also mean more clutter, and more places for the tone to slip through the cracks as unflattering voicings or harmonics are introduced, or as something in one or more stages goes a little south, even while the gain continues to remain high and sizzling. Where these levels of gain are required, the better amps do a beautiful job of providing it. When it isn't needed, however, many players find they prefer the open voice and direct response of simpler preamp topologies.

EQ Stage (Tone Stack)

In breaking out the first gain stage as 'the preamp,' it implies that you're done with pre-amplification duties there. In truth, the EQ stage that follows often plays an equally important role in shaping the gain structure in addition to its primary equalization duties.

The topologies of tone-shaping stages—referred to as 'tone stacks' by amp techs because of their piled-up appearance on many schematic diagrams—vary far more than those of first gain stages in tube amp preamps. Many early amps, smaller ones especially, had no tone controls at all (the tweed Fender Champ, for one). The signal went straight out of the volume control and on to the output stage via a second coupling capacitor, and this lack of any tone control certainly affected the inherent tonalities of these amps, as well as their gain structures. Others, such as several smaller Vox and Marshall amps, the tweed Fender Deluxe and its siblings, and many smaller contemporary boutique amps, have just a single tone control, while everything from the Fender Bassman mentioned above to larger Marshalls, and most modern channel-switchers, have a three-part tone stack with bass, middle, and treble controls.

The number of controls, the way they are configured, and the value of the capacitors they employ for frequency shelving will clearly affect the signal passing through them in different ways. More controls don't add more tone, they merely provide more fine-tuning over what's there. If anything, more controls can sometimes deplete tone slightly—or deplete level, in any case—and require further gain stages to make up the loss. In any event, while passive tone stacks (the most common type) add a mid control to what was previously a two tone-control amp, they don't actually lend the unit any more midrange frequency, they merely provide more precise governance over how much of that midrange stays in the signal. The two-control amp governs its midrange content by the voicing of the EQ network and the relative settings of the bass, treble, and volume controls: turn down the lone bass and treble controls, turn up the volume a little, and you should hear more midrange in your tone.

Beyond that, even the placement of the tone controls significantly influences how they perform, and can also affect the gain structure of the amplifier. Amps with just a single control labeled 'Tone' usually carry extremely simple treble-bleed networks that tap off the highs as you turn them down. Since these types of controls—as seen, in different variations, on the Fender 5E3 Tweed Deluxe (and several earlier tweed amps), Vox AC15 and AC4, Matchless Spitfire, and many other amps old and new—aren't directly in the signal path they do little to damp down the gain, and don't require another tube stage to bring the gain back up from the tone stack, as do other configurations.

One of the legendary 'step-ups' from these one-knob wonders is the two (or three)-pot tone stack shared by the larger tweed Fenders of the late 50s, the classic Marshall JTM45 and JTM50 Plexi, and even the Vox AC30 Top Boost unit. On Fender's larger, narrow-panel tweed amps of 1955, the single tone pot was upped to a pair to give separate control over treble and bass. A presence control was also included, although this functioned in the negative-feedback loop between the speaker output and the cathode of the PI, and not in the tone stack itself.

The actual tone controls on these amps were configured in what's called a 'cathode-follower' stage, between the cathode of a second gain stage made up of two triodes (an entire 12AX7/ECC83-type tube) and the input to the PI. This positioning has become legendary among many guitarists for yielding great dynamics and player sensitivity—the phenomenon often referred to as 'touch'—and for helping to make the amps that carry such circuits especially sensitive instruments in themselves. In addition to shaping the tone of the guitar signal, this versatile, interactive circuit also helps to shape the feel of the gain structure, which varies somewhat depending upon your control settings. This tone stack reached its zenith on Fender's 'F' series Bassman and Twin circuits of 1958, in which a middle control was added for the first time, presenting a three-knob tone section plus presence control.

C H A P T E R   2

As much as the hallowed Vox Top Boost tone circuit is raved about, it was really just another rendition of the cathode-follower tone stack seen on the narrow-panel Fender Super, Pro, and low-powered Twin several years earlier, and also on the Gibson GA-70 and GA-77 of the mid-to-late 50s. Applied to a quartet of EL84 output tubes in cathode bias, with no negative feedback, everything sounds a little different on the Vox than it did on the US-made amps, giving the impression of a 'brilliance' channel rather than the fat, chewy tone stack of the tweed amps, although the EQ network is doing the same thing on all of them. Reproduced on countless boutique recreations of tweed Fender amps, this cathode-follower tone stack also pops up on many popular amps inspired more by the Vox formula, such as TopHat's Club Royale and Super 16, Matchless' DC30 and Lightning, much of the Bad Cat range, and others.

Other than the handful of more original EQ stages on the market—Dr Z's rendition of the Baxendall tone stack on the Z-28, which greatly increases gain as you turn up the bass and treble controls, comes to mind—the other most common tone stack is that best known from Fender's black and silverface circuits. First seen on many brownface amps of the early 60s, this tone stack places the bass and treble (and sometimes middle) controls after the first gain stage, but *before* the volume control and a second gain stage, generally known as a 'gain make-up stage.' This configuration leads to a little more fidelity and clarity in many circuits, at the expense of some of the juicy touch sensitivity of the tweed amps' cathode-follower tone stack. All of which, of course, along with other changes in the amps, served Leo Fender's ongoing quest for brightness, definition, and headroom. The presence of the extra gain stage behind these tone stacks hints that they also have a say in gain structure, not just in EQ, and experienced players of great blackface amps will tell you that the setting of these controls, and in particular of the treble control that feeds the signal on to the volume and the second triode stage, can be a big part of what makes one of these beauties sing.

Output Stage

A tube amp's output stage begins with the phase inverter (PI, or 'driver'), a network of related circuitry and another preamp-type tube, which does the job of splitting the signal into two reverse-phase signals to feed the output tubes. The stage ends at the other side of a transformer that converts the output tubes' yield into a signal that will power a speaker. Each of these sub-stages in the output section—PI, output tubes, output transformer—has a major impact on the voice of the amplifier, and the components that connect them play their part, too.

Different PI topologies have different sounds in themselves. The signal passes through this tube and the circuitry before and after it, so the tube and component types and their quality and configuration will obviously have some effect, however subtle. In addition, some types of PI circuits impart a little of their own distortion to the sound when pushed hard, while different PIs 'drive' the output tubes in different ways: some inspiring good headroom, some leading to an earlier onset of distortion, so they play a major part in how the output tubes themselves will sound. Players rave about vintage Fender tweed amps of the 50s, but relatively few are aware that Leo and co went through at least three different evolutions of phase inverter design in that decade alone, all with very different sonic and distortion properties, before arriving at the version that has become the most-emulated PI topology of all time for large, high-output guitar amplifiers. Even in the late 50s, Fender was using two different types of PIs in models that might seem to be of similar size, the tweed Pro and Bassman, for example. The former still carried the cathodyne or 'split-phase' inverter best known for its use in the 5E3 Deluxe, where it is part of the brown, fuzzy magic of that little distortion machine. The latter had advanced to the long-tailed-pair PI, known for its increased fidelity and headroom, and only used on that 4x10 'bass' amp, the high-powered Twin, and, oddly, the 6V6-powered Tremolux.

Today, the vast majority of amps use the noble long-tailed pair, which presents a bolder, truer signal to the output tubes than the cathodyne inverter, and contributes some of its own distortion to the picture when pushed more than lightly. Amps still using this dirtier PI include, of course, reissues and replications of the tweed Deluxe, along with emulations of the Pro, Super, low-powered Twin and Bandmaster, as well as many renditions of brown and blackface Fender Princeton amps. For players seeking a little more thickness and dirt at lower volume levels, the cathodyne inverter can be a real boon. Those looking for optimum clean bite and twang at low-to-medium volume levels, however, or more clarity and definition amid the overdrive of amps pushed harder, are likely to find it in models with long-tailed-pair PIs (which covers almost everything else out there).

The even more archaic paraphase inverter is still venerated in some circles, too. A noteworthy ingredient of the earlier TV-front and wide-panel tweed Fender amps, as well as many Gibson models, this PI was also present in many Valco-made amps right up to the early 60s (although a few, notably the Gretsch 6156 Playboy, upgraded to a cathodyne inverter), and continues to appear on recreations of these such as the Victoria Amp Company's ElectroKing and a handful of renditions of the Supro Model 24. Known for its throaty, mid-forward tone, the paraphase inverter also adds a good dose of its own distortion to the sound, which is usually heard as a warm, thick, creamy blues tone and felt in the plentiful compression of the amps that carry it. From the PI, the signal passes to the output tubes via a further pair of coupling caps, sometimes in series with resistors (or a quartet of resistors, in two parallel strands, in the case of an amp with four output tubes).

For guitarists who have owned the same amp for many years and had to re-tube it every 12 or 24 months or so following periods of rigorous gigging, it'll come as no surprise to hear that the output tubes are one of the most influential single links in the entire sound chain. Weak, badly mismatched, or wrongly biased output tubes can seriously impede an amp's sound—even satisfactorily operational but poor quality tubes can choke its tone significantly. Beyond mere functionality, however, different types of tubes, and even different makes of the same type, have varying sonic signatures which sharp-eared players can detect and use to their advantage. Factors like the DC voltage level that the tubes run on and the ways in which they are biased also affect tone and performance greatly—and not necessarily in a 'more is better' fashion. If variety is the spice of life, output tubes offer a sizzling jalapeño to the tone connoisseur.

Different types of output tubes will, of course, have their own signatures, and these characteristics will be discussed in a tube reference section a little further on in this chapter. But even when the exact same output tubes are employed, differences in the way the circuitry

surrounding them deals with these tubes can lead to very different sounding amps. To illustrate this, let's take the example of two Fender amps with approximately the same name, hailing from just a few years apart in the company's manufacturing chronology. The 5E3 tweed Deluxe, discontinued in 1960, is a common reference point for small blues and rock'n'roll amps; it is often rated at 15 watts, but realistically puts out about 12 watts of sweet, spongy, early-breakup tone (which can verge on the loose and farty with a high-output guitar and advanced volume settings). On the other hand, the blackface Deluxe Reverb, introduced in 1963, puts out a solid 22 watts of relatively firm, crisp power, which makes for a good deal more perceived volume, however you slice it. Both use a pair of 6V6 output tubes. Granted, there are different things going on in the preamp and tone-shaping stages, too, but the majority of the sonic differences, and certainly the difference in output levels, take place at the output stage. In the tweed Deluxe, a combination of lower voltage levels, cathode biasing, lack of a negative feedback loop, and slightly smaller output transformer (OT) accounts for its softer feel, dirtier tone, and lesser volume compared to the Deluxe Reverb, which has fixed bias, high plate voltages for 6V6s, and a negative feedback loop to tighten up the response and the low end a little. Similar formulas apply to other amps, often without such broad differentiations but with relatively similar sonic results.

As a further example of the results of variables in output stages, consider another pair of Fender amps, both late-50s tweed models: the 5F4 Super-Amp and the 5F6-A Bassman. Both use a pair of 6L6s (or 5881s) in fixed bias, class AB, and both have negative feedback loops. The Super realistically puts out about 28 watts, however, to the Bassman's heftier 40 watts. Why? The Super only has around 420 DC volts (VDC), give or take a few volts, on the plates, as compared to the Bassman's 445 VDC or so, it has a cathodyne PI verses the Bassman's long-tailed pair, and it has a smaller OT. These three factors add up to a significant difference in tone, feel, and volume. The Super also had only two ten-inch speakers compared to the Bassman's four (originally intended to power Fender's newfangled electric bass guitar), so the latter amp's full whack would have blown those fragile little Jensen speakers in short order.

Examples don't need to be entirely Fender-centric, although the way the company's amps evolved does make for some pointed lessons in these variables. We might, however, also consider that Marshall's EL84-based '18-watter' and '20-watter' of the late 60s and early 70s produce a different feel and tone partly due to higher output-stage voltages in the latter, or that the 50-plus watts of a Marshall 1987 model running two EL34s, and the 30 watts of a Victoria Regal II running on the same tube pair—alongside the *very* different sounds of the two amps—are due to several different considerations regarding operating class, tube bias, and voltage levels, all within the output stage.

Much of the above discussion regarding the different sonic results of different output stage topologies revolves around issues of output-tube bias, a topic that often slips into the 'class A versus class AB' debate these days. The term 'class A' gets slung around by amp makers more than hot hash off the griddle at a Memphis greasy spoon, but by its very nature the label can be misleading. When it comes to tube amp classifications, class A isn't intended to define 'the best' of a range of amps; rather, it's a term used to define a particular operating class with very specific *technical*—rather than qualitative—parameters behind it. Add to that the fact that it's a lot easier for an amp-maker's marketing department to claim that an amp is class A than it is for any player, or even product tester, to prove that it is not, and you've got a potential maelstrom of misinformation to contend with.

Many of the phenomenal, iconic models already discussed—the tweed Fender Bassman, blackface Twin Reverb, Deluxe, and Super Reverbs, Marshall JTM45 and Plexi, Mesa/Boogie MkI, Soldano SLO, and so on—are not regarded as class A amps; they are class AB. On the flip-side, the Fender Champ (whether tweed, black, or silverface), Vox AC4, Gibson GA-8, Kalamazoo Model 1, Wards Airline GDR-9012A, Silvertone 1481, and plenty of other similar 'practice,' 'student,' or 'budget' amps are categorically class A amps, even if they were not promoted as such in the trade ads of their day.

Definitions of operating class in tube guitar amplifiers are really pretty simple. We'll look briefly at these definitions as they apply to 'push-pull' (PP) amps, which constitute the majority of models other than the little single-ended amps listed above (and a few newer tricksters).

In a push-pull amp, with two output tubes or four tubes working in two pairs, one tube or pair of tubes works to amplify the peaks of the signal (the waveform, looking like a rolling pattern of hills and valleys) while the other tube or pair of tubes amplifies the valleys. In other words, one tube 'pushes the hills' while the other 'pulls the valleys,' then they swap. Since alternating current (AC)—that which carries your guitar signal from stage to stage within the amp—has constantly alternating hills and valleys, each tube of the PP setup receives a steady stream of each. In the majority of guitar amps, each side of the PP setup actually shuts down briefly during some part of the cycle, when the other side is at its peak of current flow. That looks crazy on paper, but, of course, it all happens so fast that there's no audible gap in the performance. Thanks to the fact that the 360 degree waveforms that are being amplified by each side of the PP setup are in reverse-phase to each other, there's no volume loss as one side dips and the other rises. The majority of the world's guitar amps function in this way, including classics like all the big Marshalls, Fender Bassmans and Twins, Dumbles, Mesa/Boogies, and so on. Indeed, as we have already discovered, amps that perform as I have just described are class-AB amplifiers. By definition, one side of the PP tube pair of a class-AB amplifier rests for at least some portion of the cycle (when measured at maximum volume before clipping). In simple terms, that's really all there is to the definition of class AB, or all that you need worry about at least. It's also worth noting, however, that sharing the load makes output tubes configured in class AB a little more efficient power-wise, and in performing this way they tend to help amps sound a little tighter, firmer, and punchier.

An output section operating in class A, on the other hand, has the tube or tubes working the entire cycle of the waveform (when measured at maximum volume before distortion). This is true even of push-pull amplifiers, where both tubes are sending the signal along to the OT together at all times, not alternately resting as with class AB. As such, class-A output stages are somewhat less efficient than those on class-AB amps, which can be driven to higher output levels. Players and amp makers often talk of sweeter distortion in class-A amps, but true class-A operation actually has less distortion content at a given output level, although a smoother onset of distortion when it comes, and one that is sometimes described as being more

harmonically complex, too. But the fact that these definitions of operating class are measured at maximum output *before* distortion should tell you something. A lot of voodoo is talked about class A, particularly by amp company marketing departments eager to sell you a particular new model. The sound of a true class-A setup, operating according to its technical definition, is something quite different to that which the advertising slogan 'a real class-A tube amp' means to imply. Relatively few amps fit the definition for class A beyond debate, which is not something to worry about at this juncture. The characteristic sound of different classic tube guitar amps is determined by far more than just their class definition.

Designers seeking true class-A performance in PP amps achieve it by manipulating two factors: the DC voltage delivered to the output tubes, and their bias setting. They force the tubes into this state of constant operation by carefully setting their bias point, which is a very complex matter (roughly speaking, we can equate a tube's bias with a racecar engine's idle). In short, class-A amps are usually biased very 'hot' (that is, their output tubes run on the hot side of what is acceptable), which—when such amps are built correctly, and this bias is used for the right reasons—can make them very tonally rich.

Such biasing is most often achieved in class-A amps, as well as in some amps that are *purportedly* class A, by a method known as 'cathode biasing.' The sound of the so-called class-A output stage will be most familiar to guitarists, as heard in the Vox AC30 and AC15, or other amps that follow those templates. Now here's the rub: cathode-biased amps, whether they are class A or AB in the purest technical sense, have a discernible sound, which itself has come to be associated with some of the supposed characteristics of an amp that is labeled 'class A.' This sound is harmonically lush, shimmering, with sometimes just a hair of grain and looseness, and fairly smooth when cranked up into distortion. Often it is not particularly tight, punchy, or bold, or at least is less so than a more efficient fixed-bias output stage, in relative terms. Former Matchless designer Mark Sampson, who now builds his own amps under the Star brand, is very much pro-class A. "For guitar amps, I think class-A amps are the best. They give the best harmonic content. In terms of numbers and power, it's lower, but who cares—it's just as loud. I can make a needle move on a meter and it says 50 or 60 watts, and I can make the same needle move at 300 watts, but when I put a dB meter in front of it and the 30-watt amp is louder, who cares? Because nobody is looking at the needle: they're listening to it, in real life."

Sampson's views notwithstanding, in the strictest sense neither class is better or worse than the other, it all depends on what you're seeking to achieve with your tone. However sweet the notion of class-A tone might seem, players looking for specific sonic qualities, whether they be round jazz tones, tight country twang, or thumping metal, are most likely *not* going to glean fully satisfactory results from a class-A amp.

In addition, and to compound matters, most amps billed as being class A also lack something we have touched on before, the negative feedback loop. Applying a little bit of an amp's output signal in reverse phase back to the front of the output stage (the input of the phase inverter), via a network known as a negative feedback loop, can help improve the overall tightness and definition of its sound. Ergo, excluding a negative feedback loop further contributes to some of the tonal qualities that are already being emphasized in the cathode-biased amp. You can bet your bottom dollar that almost any amp you encounter that's billed as class A will lack such a loop, and whether or not anyone is ever going to heft it up on the work bench, attach the meter and scope, and determine whether it is truly operating in a class-A configuration, such an amp will still produce what is commonly considered the 'class-A sound.' Guess what you'd find inside a Vox AC30? That's right: cathode biasing, and no negative feedback loop. And the same goes for amps like the Matchless DC30, Bad Cat Black Cat 30, TopHat King Royale, Mojave Sidewinder, Dr Z Stang Ray, and others that follow the AC30 template (in addition to all the smaller amps that emulate the AC15). Other amps that are cathode biased, with no negative feedback loop, include the 50s Fender Deluxe, Gibson GA-20, GA-30, and GA-40 Les Paul Amp, early-60s Selmer Selectortone, the late-60s Traynor YBA-2 Bass Mate, WEM Dominator, plenty of Valco-made amps like the Supro Model 24, and countless others.

A few paragraphs ago I listed a number of smaller practice amps that qualify, by definition, as genuine class-A amps. These are known as 'single-ended' amps, which is to say they have just one output tube. When one tube is working all on its lonesome in an output stage, it is categorically operating in class A because, of course, it cannot shut down at any portion of the waveform. As employed in guitar amps, single-ended tube output stages only ever stray into the medium-sized amp at best, and the lower end of the category at that, in the form of dual single-ended amps (also called parallel single-ended). Dual-single-ended amps, of which the Gibson GA-8 is the only one in that aforementioned list, use a pair of output tubes working in parallel to increase their potential output power. Rather than working in turns, like the PP pair, however, these are really pretending they are a single tube for operational purposes, both pushing the same signal all the time. Modern production examples of these are fairly rare, and include THD's BiValve and Victoria's Regal II, both of which are about the largest single-ended amps I can think of (both are dual-single-ended).

Even with two output tubes, such amps are still very inefficient compared to PP amps using the same tube complement. A design such as the GA-8 probably only puts out between 8 and 10 watts compared to the 15-watt rating of an amp like the PP Gibson GA-20 or Fender Deluxe, while the Victoria Regal II's maximum output is around 30 watts from a pair of EL34s, which could produce 50 watts or more in an efficient class-AB push-pull design. Still, the topology provides one way of getting a little more power out of a true class-A design than the measly four watts of a Fender Champ.

In other words, an amp's class definition can provide some clues about its likely tonal palette, but the potential for misinformation means you should play as many amps as possible, whatever their class labeling, before making any big leaps. Home in on the heart of your tone according to which amplifier feels and sounds right to you and works best for your style of music, and let categories and class descriptions be damned.

Before moving on from discussions of amp class, however, I want to clarify the issue of output-tube biasing a little further. The two main forms of biasing used in tube guitar amplifiers today are 'cathode biasing' and 'fixed biasing.' 'Bias' is a term used to describe the way in which a tube's operating level is set, usually with a resistor or a simple network that determines how

efficiently the tube translates the operating voltages applied to it into guitar signal amplification. The terms for these two techniques can be misleading: fixed-bias amps, those made post-1963 at least, very often carry bias adjustment pots, and in most cases it's necessary to adjust their bias levels ('re-bias' them) when you replace the output tubes. This is the case with all the larger Fender and Marshall amps, and others made to those templates, although early fixed-bias tweed and brownface Fender amps, some Mesa/Boogies, and others, have a preset-bias network that is not adjustable.

In contrast, cathode-biased amps most often have their bias permanently set, with a resistor tied between the cathodes of the output tubes and ground. When changing output tubes in these, just pop in a fresh set and away you go. Class-AB amps are usually fixed bias, while almost all class-A tube guitar amps you will encounter are cathode biased (although not all cathode-biased amps are class A, in the truest sense, as we have discovered).

Once the output tubes have done their thing, the signal runs straight from the output pin of the power tubes to the input of the output transformer (OT), which is known as the OT's 'primary.' The OT that you can see hanging from the underside of many an amp chassis (they are usually the smaller of two or the middle-sized of three) plays a part that would initially seem purely functional, in that it transforms a high-impedance current from the tubes to a low-impedance current that will drive a speaker. But as the entire product of your sound chain up to this point passes through it—with only one link in that chain to follow—you can bet it has a significant impact on your sound.

Factors such as the OT's efficiency, or lack thereof, its physical size, the ratio at which it converts the current, and many other factors, will affect how it will sound, and the way in which it converts your signal into one capable of pumping a speaker—and, therefore, becoming sound waves again—is enormously significant. Roughly speaking, bigger transformers (in a relative range determined by the output tubes in the amp) offer more headroom and better bass response; or, simply put, they provide a more accurate reproduction of the signal that the tubes send them. On the other hand, some vintage types exhibit juicier distortion, while more efficient modern designs offer impressive clarity and definition. OTs can be designed to roll-off low frequencies that might overload speakers, or to exhibit other frequency related characteristics. As with virtually every component we have analyzed so far, the choice is less about bad, good, better, or best, but rather one that acknowledges how various OTs contribute (sometimes greatly) to different tonal results. That said, guitarists have been known to obsess excessively over OTs, their specs and performance, and while careful OT design and construction (or selection) is almost always a significant part of any thoughtful amp designer's job, you won't always affect radical tonal transformations in an amp simply by swapping OTs. It's a big part of what goes into the overall sonic picture, but still merely a part, right alongside most of what goes on in the circuit prior to this stage.

Other factors, what we might call 'side chains,' are often involved in the performance of an amp's output stage, and, indeed, across all its circuitry, but none are as significant as the aforementioned negative feedback loop. In simple terms, this loop taps a portion of the output at the OT's secondary (that is, the output side of the output transformer) and feeds it back in negative to, most commonly, the input point of the output stage—at the phase inverter. The result is some suppression of resonant peaks and extremes in the frequency response, and what we hear is a tighter, firmer operation with more headroom, and a harsher onset of distortion when it finally arrives. Removing the loop (or never installing one in the first place) lends an amp a rawer, more aggressive voice, usually with a pronounced midrange response and a smoother onset of distortion, but with less headroom and a looser feel overall. Either option has its function, depending on your sonic goals.

Power Stage

A tube amp's power stage is not in the signal chain itself, but it provides the fuel that keeps the engine burning, and the amount of fuel it provides, and the speed at which it can cough it up at times of high demand, greatly influence the feel and, to some extent, sound of the amp. This stage consists of the power (or mains) transformer, the rectifier, and the filtering stages that clean and condition the current on which the tubes feed.

The power transformer (PT) is a purely functional device, but as with everything inside the chassis—and especially any component meant to handle high voltages—quality obviously counts. The PT takes the power from your domestic wall socket and steps it up to the higher voltage required by the amplification duties of the tubes, while splitting off lesser voltages to run the tubes' AC-powered heaters (filaments) and that of the tube rectifier, if there is one. This latter component is where we begin to encounter variables that the player will really notice.

The humble, oft-misunderstood rectifier comes in two main flavors: tube and solid state. In this postmodern and occasionally misguided world of tonal 'semi-awareness,' where any guitar gear possessing a glowing glass bottle is generally assumed to be better than gear without, it's important to understand that solid-state rectifiers are not implicitly inferior to tube rectifiers, merely different. Among tube rectifiers, there are also many different types that offer different performance characteristics according to the needs of different amplifier designs. Different types of solid-state rectifiers exist, too, although very similar types tend to be used in any given era of amp design, according to the best components available to do the job.

In basic terms, a rectifier is the component within a tube amplifier that converts the two lines (positive and negative) of AC from the amp's power transformer (PT) into a single line of DC that lets the preamp and output tubes perform their amplification business. In doing so, a rectifier also increases the resultant DC voltage level slightly—in fact, the voltage levels are increased twice on their way to the big output tubes. The AC comes into the amp from your wall socket at around 120VAC in the US or 240VAC in the UK, is ramped up by the PT to around 330VAC (in a Fender Deluxe Reverb, for example) and converted by the rectifier to around 400VDC to feed a pair of 6V6GT tubes. So, a rectifier converts AC to DC, simple as that. It is not in the signal chain, meaning the portion of the amp's circuit that carries your guitar signal does not pass through it at any time—which is not to say that the rectifier has no impact on the sound that your amp produces.

Both preamp and output tubes sound and perform differently when fed different voltage levels; so a rectifier that converts your PT's 330VAC to 400VDC will result in your amp

sounding a little different to how it does with a rectifier that converts it to 350VDC, or even 384VDC. In addition to the pure robustness of a rectifier's conversion duties, two other factors compound its influence on your sound. The first is the speed at which it accomplishes the AC to DC conversion, something which will be distinctly felt at either extreme—as a tight, fast, responsive, and articulate performance in the amp with a swift rectifier, or as a slightly soft, spongy, 'compressed' performance in one with a slower rectifier. The second factor is the speed at which the rectifier recovers from heavy demands upon its conversion duties (sometimes called 'sag'), when, for example, you are hitting the guitar hard for aggressive passages with the amp turned up loud. These aspects combine to greatly affect the impression of attack, compression, dynamics, and touch-sensitivity that any tube amp gives you, and it's these factors—more than any tonal considerations—which make players respond to the performance of their rectifiers, whether they know it or not.

Tube rectifiers are four-pin tubes that, more often than not, fit into octal (eight-pin) sockets. Given their similar sizes and mounting configurations, they can often be mistaken, at a glance, for output tubes. Only four pins are connected internally, two of which take in a 5VAC filament voltage supply from the PT to heat the tube so it can function, and two that take in the high-voltage AC current for conversion. The DC current comes out through one of the pins that are *taking in* the filament supply. That sounds impossible, I know, but one pole of the AC (which is bipolar, hence 'alternating current') can enter while the lonesome DC exits. There are also nine-pin tube rectifiers, such as the recently fashionable EZ81, as used in the early Vox AC15 and Marshall 18-watt amps of the mid 60s, although only four of its pins connect internally. These look a little like an EL84 output tube, and fit the same type of socket. Some small, early guitar amps also use diminutive seven-pin-socket rectifiers such as a 6X4 or 6X5 (again, with only four pins 'live'), but these are rarely found today.

Solid-state rectifiers take the form of diodes, usually used in sets of two, four, or six, most commonly configured in what is referred to as a 'bridge.' They form a chevron, of sorts, the two 'ins' corresponding to the top ends of the 'V' and the 'out' being the central node where they join to send the DC on its journey. The two strands of AC go in, and one strand of DC goes out. Solid-state rectifiers require no filament voltage, because they don't need to be heated up like tubes in order to function.

Until the late 50s, almost all guitar amps used tube rectifiers. Even high-powered amps that required a lot more current, such as Fender's tweed Twin, still used tube rectifiers, but the demands put upon them by four 5881 (or 6L6GC) output tubes running at high voltages were almost more than they could handle (some even boasted a pair of tube rectifiers working simultaneously to get the job done). Toward the end of the 50s, the arrival of reliable and affordable silicon diodes provided manufacturers of high-powered amps with an excellent solid-state alternative to tubes. Using these diodes meant amp designers could deliver even higher voltages to the output stage, thus squeezing even more power from the tubes, and could provide this power with less-intrusive sag, giving the big amps a more immediate and consistent response. Using solid-state rectification also demanded less from an amp's PT, since no separate rectifier filament (or 'heater') supply was required.

When, in 1960, Fender switched to using silicon diodes for rectifier duties in many of its Professional Series amplifiers (including the blonde Twin, Showman, Vibrosonic, and other models), its advertising literature bragged that "… modern silicon rectifiers are used rather than glass tubes. This feature reduces chassis heating and reduces servicing problems." Those weren't their only virtues. It so happened that silicon diodes also cost a fraction of the price of tubes, and without the need for a five-volt filament supply, the transformers used in amps that employed diodes for rectification could be made without this extra winding, and therefore cost considerably less to manufacture. By eliminating the mounting socket that a tube rectifier required, Fender made a threefold saving.

For all that, solid-state rectification really is beneficial to certain amp designs, regardless of economics; many manufactures used them for the 'right' reasons, from the tonehound's perspective, and still do. As I said above, the old 'tube good/solid-state bad' dichotomy that is often spouted by amp aficionados doesn't really apply here. In addition to those great early Fender amps, and some of the larger blackface models that followed them, legendary amps employing solid-state rectification include Marshall's plexi and metal-panel JMP50 and JMP100 rock monsters, Hiwatt's thunderous larger creations, Mesa/Boogie Mark Series amps of the early 70s and beyond, not to mention modern classics such as the Soldano SLO and Peavey 5150.

Of course, where there's a penny to be pinched, some manufacturers will indulge, meaning that many of the more affordable smaller tube amps marketed in the past couple of decades, which might have benefited in tone and feel from tube rectification, were instead made with solid-state units. The slight delay that a tube rectifier produces when hit hard, which gives an amp a compression-like playing feel that is also referred to as 'sag,' can be a big part of the magic in some tube amps. It softens the front edge of the player's pick attack while producing an enticing, explosive 'swell' of notes just behind that attack, and can often make an amp feel more dynamic and touch-sensitive, resulting in a more tactile playing experience. Players and philosophical amp designers alike will also tell you that they sometimes hear more 'breath,' 'air,' and 'dimension' in tube-rectified amps, a sort of bloom and spaciousness in the notes that gives them extra depth and texture.

For examples of rectifier squash, listen to almost any vintage electric blues recording where the soloist is cranked up and hitting it hard, or turn straight to Neil Young's amplified work in which his battered Les Paul is mercilessly slamming his narrow-panel tweed Fender Deluxe. In addition to the beloved Deluxe, other amps from the golden age of tone that employed tube rectifiers include Fender's tweed, brown, and blackface Champ, Princeton, Deluxe (and Deluxe Reverb), and Super (and Super Reverb); Vox's AC15 and AC30; Gibson's GA-30 and GA-40 Les Paul; Marshall's JTM45; and many Valco-made amps. Reissues of these models from Fender, Vox, and Marshall follow their originals in terms of rectification (although the early Bassman reissue came with a plug-in solid-state rectifier), and almost all 'boutique' amp makers of note—including 65amps, Carr, TopHat, Victoria, Matchless, and plenty of others—lean heavily toward tube rectification. Some other small amp designs, however, exhibit plenty of pF squash from the output tubes, and adding rectifier sag to that would make them too soft for a satisfactory performance. Cornford's highly regarded Harlequin, for example, has solid-state

C H A P T E R   2

rectification behind its juicy, single-ended, six-watt output, as does Bad Cat's five-watt Mini II.

Different types of rectifier tubes offer different levels of AC-to-DC conversion. The most common small-amp rectifier tube is the 5Y3GT, as found in the old Fender Champ, tweed Deluxe, and many vintage Gibson amps. This tube works fine in small combos that put out anything up to about 15 watts, but even when hit hard in a cranked version of one of these it can start to sag noticeably: cool, in the right place; potentially frustrating when you're looking for punch, speed, and clarity. At the other end of the scale, the GZ34 (or the 5AR4 in the USA, which is not identical, but operationally equivalent) has long been considered the king of the rectifier tubes. This powerful, sturdy unit not only makes more DC out of whatever AC you show it, but does so very elegantly, with great efficiency and relatively little sag, while still inducing many of the most-loved characteristics of tube rectification into its amp's performance.

Between the 5Y3GT and GZ34 are a number of mid-powered rectifier tubes like the 5R4, 5U4GB, 5U4, and 5V4, which yield AC/DC conversion with ascending efficiency, and are generally seen in mid-sized amps. Rectifier tubes can sometimes be swapped up or down one level, when, for example, you find it preferable to run your tubes at slightly higher or lower voltages. Such a change should only be made with reference to the advice of your amp's manufacturer and a qualified tech. And be aware that swapping *down* a level is usually safe, while swapping *up* a level often is not, unless you or your tech first ascertains that other elements within the amp's design are prepared to handle higher voltages. Also, it's important to know how much heater current the new tube draws, and to ensure that this is within the capabilities of your power transformer. One occasion that could call for such a swap might be that of a vintage amp that was manufactured in the days when domestic AC supplies in the United States were around 110 volts, but which now has to contend with your wall socket putting out anything from around 118 to upward of 125 volts.

As with preamp and output tubes, different makes of the same type of rectifier tube, and even different examples that came off the line from the same factory on the same day, can perform their duties a little differently. By this I mean that if you obtained three NOS Mullard GZ34s or three Sovtek 5Y3GTs from the same year of manufacture, popped them into an appropriate amp one after another, and measured the DC voltages that each put out, you would find slight variances.

Tube amp freaks know only too well that any all-over amp modification also involves obtaining a range of good rectifier tubes and testing them all in their amp to see which one makes it tick most sweetly. If you go to these lengths yourself and find a particular rectifier that your amplifier seems to groove on, it might even be worth 'blueprinting' that stage of your amp. Take it to a qualified amp tech and have them measure the level of DC voltage coming out of the rectifier (referred to in the trade as 'B+') and note it down for posterity. Next time you need to change rectifiers, try a few until you find one that gets you as close as possible to the one that had your amp sounding its best. Be aware, however, that even today's more reliable domestic power supply will vary from town to town, or even from one side of town to the other, or according to time of day, demands of the season, and other factors. Plugging the same amp, with the same rectifier, into a socket giving off 118VAC in Cleveland and then another socket providing 124VAC in Cincinnati will result in different voltage levels within the amp. Finally, if you do change your rectifier for one that produces a different DC voltage level within the amp, be aware that many fixed-bias amps will need to have their output tubes re-biased, which is another job for a professional.

Beyond the rectifier, the DC voltages are also subject to the filtering of electrolytic capacitors and sometimes a choke (a small transformer with a single input and output). Electrolytic capacitors, often called 'filter caps,' are the big can-like capacitors found in the power supply— often located, unseen, under that 'cap can' on the back of 60s and 70s Fender amp chassis, or in upright cans on the tops of vintage Marshall and Vox chassis. They also appear as smaller pieces further up in the circuit for other filtering or bypass duties. As AC power filters, no signal passes through them, but they do affect an amp's sound according to how well or poorly they perform their job of 'cleaning up' the power supply. Unlike signal capacitors, electrolytics are polarized and will be connected with their positive side toward the voltage supply and negative side to ground.

Put simply, electrolytic capacitors are used to remove AC ripple that is left in the DC power supply after it has undergone the rectifier's AC-to-DC conversion. Left untreated, this ripple can cause a number of problems generally associated with unwanted noise. These can take the form of a pulsating current, a dirty hum, a flabby and distorted low-frequency response, or even ghost notes, which sound something like a dissonant harmonic following along behind the true note. None of these are desirable, and it is the filter capacitor's job to eliminate them.

Any guitar amp will have a number of filter caps in the power supply chain, with other smaller versions in other sections of the circuit. I don't know of any popular (or playable) designs that carry fewer than three filter caps in the power supply, usually linked at their positive ends by resistors that drop the DC levels down to those required by each of the subsequent stages being filtered and supplied. In addition to merely helping to remove potential noise artifacts from the power supply, the size and placement of the selected filter caps help to determine the 'sharpness' of an amp's sound, and the firmness of its bass response in particular. In this way, even though no signal passes through these cans, their quality and accuracy can influence your tone for better or worse. A good designer will consider a number of factors when selecting cap values, however, and it isn't simply a matter of 'bigger is better.' Tube rectifiers are only happy with so much filtering in the first position, for one thing. A solid-state rectifier and large-value filter caps work hand in hand to help powerful amplifiers offer a tight overall response and firm, bold lows (which are, of course, defining criteria for any bass amp). On the other hand, over-filtering can sometimes choke and tighten up an amp that might sound more dynamic and open with lower-value caps in the power supply. Once again, the choice of electrolytics comes down to individual sonic goals and player tastes.

The pure quality of this component is also significant, as it is with practically every element in the circuit. Audiophiles can get extremely hung up on the virtue of electrolytic caps in their tube hi-fi amps, and the respected types can easily cost more than $100 a unit; with several such pieces required in most amps this can become a pricey preoccupation. Quality counts in filter caps for guitar amps, too. Better-respected electrolytics come from makers like Sprague Atom,

C H A P T E R 2

Illinois, LCR, JJ, and a handful of others, and while these don't approach audiophile prices, they do represent one of the larger expenditures within the amp chassis, after the transformers and tubes have been accounted for, and commonly go for around $5 per piece (compared to the 50 cents cost of smaller, generic, bulk-buy electrolytics) depending upon size and quality.

Some power supplies include a choke in the DC rail in place of one of the large dropping resistors between filter caps, but it performs a job that is far more 'filter' than 'resistance.' Rather than dropping the voltage down like the resistor, the choke is further smoothing the residual AC ripple from the DC voltage. It is a common component of amps seeking a tight, bold delivery (or of almost all amps of 30–40 watts or more), or of some small amps in which AC noise is of particular concern. Some players and designers feel that a choke can, well, 'choke' the sound of certain small amps a little, and that these sound hotter and more open with the component omitted. Of course, other such small amps are built without chokes simply because it's cheaper to do so. Either way, it is yet another variable that is best judged subjectively, although larger amps will almost always need a choke to sound their best.

TUBES

Any discussion of tube type or tone, and the quality of new versus old, is likely to open up a very big can of worms. For all else that's going on in an amp's circuit, a switch of tube brand or type has the potential to make the most dramatic tonal alteration achievable from a single item swap (other than, perhaps, a speaker change).

All amplification tubes carry at least four elements within their vacuum-sealed glass bottles: cathode, grid, plate (also known as an 'anode'), and filament (or 'heater'). The most basic types are called 'triodes,' named for the first three critical elements (the filament is a constant, so it's ignored in the naming process). Pentodes, which account for most output tubes and a few preamp tubes, carry two further grids, a screen grid and a suppressor grid, which essentially help to overcome capacitance between the control grid and the plate. In simple terms, a tube's job is to make a small voltage into a big one, and the four basic elements of the triode, or five elements of the pentode, work together to make this happen.

You might not have thought about it in these terms before, but each time you pluck a string you are creating a small surge of voltage within the coil of the pickup, which is sent to the input of your amplifier. This signal voltage is applied to the grid, which we can think of as the input of the preamp tube. As the voltage on the grid of the tube increases with the plucking of the note, it causes electrons to boil off the cathode and onto the plate at a correspondingly increased rate. This is how the sound gets bigger. Amazing, isn't it? So much of the magic of a tube guitar amp's sound is created in that plucked string/small voltage/electron flow/increased voltage relationship, and while the laws of physics govern precisely how this happens, it remains an essentially straightforward reaction and interaction. And as you can imagine, it is open to plenty of variables, too, with different brands and types of tubes offering discernibly different sounds. One of the most mutable features of the tubes is the manner in which it distorts, whether to a slight degree, during normal duty, or more significantly when pushed to near its limit.

As already discussed in a number of contexts, distortion plays an enormous part in creating

TONE TIP   Try Your #2 Input

One of the things many players love most about humbucker-loaded guitars, and even some with fatter, single-coil pickups like P-90s, is that they yield a hot, fat, full-throated sound that can drive an amp harder than thinner, Fender-type single-coil pickups. Plug your Les Paul, SG Special, ES-335, PRS CE22, or Hamer Monaco Pro straight into a vintage-style tube amp, crank it up, and wail. It's the way that blues, classic rock, and even heavy metal were born.

Sometimes, however, you want a cleaner, tighter, more focused sound from guitars like these, for rhythm playing, jangling arpeggios, or for styles of music a little further removed from the grinding rock context. These guitars can provide clarity and definition when called upon to do so, fear not, but achieving this tonal shift is a less frustrating endeavor if you take a couple of tips to heart. Note that this—like the guitar volume control tip earlier in this chapter—is a technique that most serious players were aware of back in the 50s, 60s, and early 70s, but which somehow drained from the knowledge pool in the high-gain era of the late 70s and early 80s when, more often than not, players wanted *more* gain, not less.

The solution to cleaning up that fat-sounding guitar is a simple one: show the amp's first gain stage a slightly lower signal from the guitar in the first place. How? Simple: plug yourself into your amp's #2 channel for a change, provided it has one. Guitar pickups create a low voltage signal that is translated by an amplifier into the high-watt output that drives a speaker. The higher the voltage from the guitar itself, the more likely it is to distort the first stage of the amplifier (most likely a 12AX7 preamp tube, or similar), and the hotter the pickup, the higher the voltage. Most players have long ignored input #2 because they assume they want the highest gain level at the front end at all times, but plugging into the lower-gain input drops the dirt down a notch before it can distort the first gain stage of the amplifier, which is to say the first preamp tube, and lets you retain greater clarity and definition and more perceived brightness throughout the following stages of the amp. Distort that first gain stage and there's no way of getting the clarity back; but give that first tube an easier signal to handle and you achieve greater headroom throughout the amp, and can still pump yourself up to required output levels with the volume control, or even drive the output stage into a fatter, fuller form of distortion if you desire.

With the help of any good A/B/Y pedal, you can even use the difference in gain levels between the average #1 and #2 input to create an instant, preset boost that in many cases is just enough to take you from clean rhythm to clean or slightly crunchy lead tones. Plug into the A/B/Y selector pedal, and connect its 'A' out to input #2 and 'B' to input #1. 'A' yields your clean tone while the 'Y' selection (both) gives you a boost of about 6dB for leads (when connected in this way, many amps sound about the same when merely switched between 'A' and 'B' because of the way the inputs are now ganged together; but selecting 'Y' gives you the hotter gain level equivalent to input #1 alone).

Apply some clever gain-structure thinking through each stage of your sound chain and you'll find that, rather than being a crunch-and-beyond machine, your thicker-voiced guitars will reveal a broadness and versatility of tone that you previously couldn't have imagined. Clean it up and you can always crank it from there.

the multidimensional sonic picture that we think of as a great amp sound. It adds harmonics and other sonic layers that thicken the note, making it so much more than that thin tone you hear when you strike a tuning fork or pluck an unplugged solidbody electric guitar. This distortion factor comes into play with tubes more crucially than with any other amplifier component. Groove Tubes founder Aspen Pittman is fond of saying that tubes are not amplification devices at all—he thinks of them as distortion generators, and there's a lot to be said for that. Certainly tubes are the devices within the amp that are responsible for amplification—in simple terms, the signal goes into one side of the tube at x voltage and comes out the other side much bigger than x—but there are other devices that can amplify a signal. The beauty of tubes as conduits of amplification is that they don't only make a sound bigger, they do it *with style*.

A circuit as simple as that within a small, single-ended Vox AC4, for example, certainly amplifies a guitar signal, but if you wind the dial up anywhere past the early numbers you'll soon know that it adds plenty of distortion—and very sweet distortion, too. Construct a simple, transistorized amplification circuit involving similarly few components, and it will also clearly make your signal louder, but any added distortion —and there will be plenty when you crank it up—will very likely be of a rather nasty, jagged variety. I have already discussed, in terms of pure tonal integrity, the virtues of a simple tube amp circuit as opposed to more a complex layout, but this is where tube amplification really shines. Compare the simple tube circuit with a basic transistor version and you soon realize that any designer of a solid-state amp is going to need to put in a whole lot of extra sound-shaping just to make the 'simple,' featureless circuit sound remotely pleasing for guitar amplification. They can do so, certainly, and plenty of solid- state amps today can sound pretty damn good. But they're not simple affairs, by any means. All of which begs a question: why labor over something that requires 50 parts and intensive design efforts in order to make it sound *almost* as good as a thing made with 14 parts wired up to a 60-year-old schematic?" The answer is, of course, cost.

Tubes distort and that's why devotees love them. We know the sound of a maxed Deluxe Reverb, JTM50 Plexi, or Vox AC30, and we lust in our sleep over the addictive thrill of the high volume distortion that is at the core of their gorgeous tones. But even at low volumes, tubes are introducing an element of distortion, and it is this which is largely responsible for livening up even what we think of as a clean tube amp sound. Lower levels of distortion in tube amps set to 'clean' levels are producing mainly second-order harmonics, which don't have the dirty, crunchy, or fuzzy character of extreme distortion, but do contribute to a richer and more multi-dimensional tone than would be achieved without that slight edge of distortion. Essentially, we have two types of distortion produced by tube guitar amps: the obvious, intentional distortion that is part of the classic rock lead sound, and the subtler distortion that is always with us, making clean sounds a little warmer and more multi-dimensional.

We are probably all aware of the age-old debate that pitches the relative merits of tube and transistor distortion and the received wisdom about tubes easing gradually and smoothly into breakup as more of the signal is applied, while transistors tend clip off their output harshly when finally pushed too far. Such explanations are usually accompanied by two diagrams: the smooth if slightly off-balance sine wave of a clipping signal through tubes (usually with some shading toward the tops of the waves to indicate distortion), and the angular square wave of a signal clipping through transistors.

Beyond a lot of deep science that is more than we need to get into here, that's all you probably want to know about the basic function of tube distortion compared to that of transistor distortion; more importantly, you probably already know that the former can sound very, very good. What is worth knowing, however, is that it sounds so good thanks to the types of harmonics generated by that distortion, as mentioned above, and by the smooth swell and sustain that comes naturally to tubes.

The addition of harmonics relative to the fundamental note is what makes any instrument—acoustic guitar, piano, oboe—sound like more than just the thin tuning-fork tone of a pure pitch. These harmonics are present even when you pluck the string of an unplugged electric guitar; you just don't hear them as readily. Plug in, and these harmonics are amplified, along with others added by the distortion of the amp itself. The louder the amp gets, the greater the balance of these distortion-generated harmonics compared to the pure fundamental of the pitch, and the thicker your sound, up to the point of heavy clipping, when the tube's ability to keep amplifying starts to shut down and we just get mush when notes are hit hard, rather than more volume. We have already encountered the term 'harmonic distortion,' and this is what tubes do so well, and why they make our guitar amps shine. At this point it is worth introducing the notion that different tubes produce distortion differently, and they definitely have their own tonal characters—voices from which you can pick and choose to tailor your own sound.

The tubes we encounter in guitar amps are generally divisible into preamp tubes, output (or power) tubes, and, occasionally, rectifier tubes. Even more so than with other amp components, tubes present a multi-dimensional variable. Different types of tube clearly account for different sounding amps—an EL84 verses a 6V6GT, for example, while they are different makes of the same tube type, have characteristics that differ to an extent that is sometimes surprising. I'll follow this section with a tube-by-tube reference guide to some of the more popular types and their characteristics, but for now let's move on to consider the major differences between preamp and output tubes.

Preamp tubes are easily identified as the smaller bottles that usually correspond in position to your amp's inputs and early gain and tone stages (although be aware they are sometimes covered by metal shields, which are easily removed). Since the mid 50s, these have mostly been of the smaller, nine-pin variety, with the 12AX7 being by far the most common type (also known by the European designation ECC83, or the high-grade US alternative, 7025). Others that occasionally make an appearance are the 12AY7, as found in original tweed Fender and Gibson preamps, the 12AT7, which sometimes appears as a reverb driver or phase inverter, and the rarer 12AU7. All of these are 'dual triodes,' which means they have two independent tubes in a single bottle. The only pentode preamp tube found in guitar amps today is the EF86 (or 6267), which first appeared in a few early Vox amps, and more recently in models from Matchless, Dr Z, 65amps, and a few others. The EF86 fits into the same nine-pin bottle, but operates with entirely different circuit requirements. Another less common pentode, the 5879, is known mainly for its

use in the beloved Gibson GA-40 Les Paul Amp, the Maestro GA-45, and also for its recent reappearance in Victoria's Electro-King model. Many amps of the early 50s and before also used larger, eight-pin octal preamp tubes, such as the 6SC7 and 6SL7 dual triodes that appeared in early Fender, Gibson, and Valco amps, and the lesser-seen 6SJ7 pentode.

All of these small tubes can be driven into distortion, just as their big brothers in the output stage can, and any amp's overall tonal breakup is usually a combination of distortion from both of these stages, and sometimes the driver/phase inverter too. The character or quality of preamp tube distortion is quite different from what you will find with output tube distortion, however, as we have already seen.

Makers of effects or 'hybrid' amps that carry a single 12AX7 tube in the preamp (and usually a lot of added diode clipping and other solid state tone and distortion-enhancing stages to help create that 'real tube' sound) are fond of praising these little bottles for the warmth and smooth distortion they add to such products. Truth be told, when a 12AX7 is driven into distortion, the resulting sound is frequently bright, edgy, and a little harsh—which can be a real asset in some circumstances, but shouldn't be confused with genuine 'warmth.' Cascading one triode gain stage after another from a series of 12AX7s running into each other can create a classic high-gain preamp rock sound, one that has become the signature tone of countless shredders, grungers, metalheads, and other wailers. A great sound it may be, but it is surely not the 'real tube warmth and classic rock tone' that so many marketing departments would have you believe it is.

What these preamp tubes really excel at—for many tone purists, at least—is amplifying a signal up to a point just short of heavy preamp distortion, and passing it on to an output section that can be driven into the kind of juicy, fat breakup that is responsible for most of the classic rock tones we all lust after. Once again, both categories of tubes can be responsible for distortion created within the amp, but the distortion produced by preamp tubes is by no means simply a lesser version of that produced by output tubes. They sound different and suit different sonic requirements.

In most amps, the output tubes will appear as the larger pair, or quartet, of identical-looking bottles placed furthest from the input section. A few, mainly EL84s, are of the same diameter as preamp tubes and fit in the same nine-pin sockets, but are clearly longer and thus easy to identify. The other popular types—the 6V6GT, 6L6GC, 5881, EL34, and 6550, and, less commonly, the KT66, KT77, and KT88—all fit in larger, eight-pin sockets. While they might appear interchangeable in terms of socket size, most have different circuit, voltage, and bias requirements, and they cannot simply be substituted one for the other in most amps. An exception to this rule is the single and dual single-ended 'tube swappable' amps that are popular today, models such as THD's UniValve and BiValve, and Victoria's Regal II and Two Stroke, all of which will run on 6V6, 6K6, 6L6, 5881, EL34, or KT66 output tubes without complaint. As such, any of these amps make great test beds for 'tube tasting' and provide an excellent means of allowing you to hear the inherent differences between these output tubes, while all other factors remain equal.

As the final amplification unit before the signal is converted by the OT back into a form of voltage that can drive a speaker, it's obvious that the output tubes have a major bearing on an amp's overall sound. That said, plenty of amps that use precisely the same output tubes sound nothing like one another, so there's also a large element of the output stage shaping and amplifying whatever signal it is presented with from the preceding stages. As we discussed earlier in this chapter, an amp's signature sound is the sum total of a large number of variables that sit along the signal path, and whatever the signature sound of a 6L6 or an EL34, a change in preamp biasing levels or coupling-cap values from one amp to another will significantly alter what either of those tubes presents us with.

TUBE TYPES
Preamp Tubes
12AX7

Also known by the European designation ECC83, or as a 7025 for its high-grade US variant, this is by far the most common preamp tube type of the last 45 years. Quality 12AX7s are clear and open sounding, relatively uncolored when used within specifications, and offer a high target gain of 100, although many will fall below that, and a few rise above it (by which I mean tubes from the same make and from the same batch, because consistency is very hard to achieve even in the manufacturing of quality tubes—greater inconsistencies and failure rates apply to the lesser brands).

Throughout the late 80s and much of the 90s, 12AX7 production was in a pretty dire state. Affordable current-manufacture tubes consisted mainly of the fairly reliable but characterless Russian varieties or the less bland but less reliable Chinese options. Players seeking real quality in both construction and tone went in search of 'new old stock' (NOS) American and European tubes made by GE, RCA, Telefunken, Mullard, Brimar, and others, and supplies of these dwindled rapidly. Some of these NOS versions are still great items to get your hands on if you can find them at a reasonable price, but be aware that the small batches that turn up now and again are generally less likely to be reliable than the more plentiful stocks of a few years back. Supplies are so short now that seconds and substandard units are coming out of old reject boxes and onto the market, and some unscrupulous sellers aren't testing them in the slightest before taking $50 or more for a single little glass bottle.

Other good suppliers do test thoroughly and offer guarantees, too, at a price, and the little extra is worth it if you're laying out for NOS tubes in the first place. If you're exceptionally lucky, you can occasionally find an old radio spares supplier who has a few of these to sell at a fraction of what the big guitar-amp suppliers are asking.

Fortunately, some great new 12AX7 types are being newly manufactured. Recent designs from Sovtek, JJ/Tesla, Ei, the Chinese factories, and others offer both good-sounding and reliable tubes that can even rival some of the US and European examples of old. Large distributors like Groove Tubes and Germany's Tube Amp Doctor are even pitching in with their own designs; GT notably funded the retooling of a Chinese factory in order to begin reproducing an ECC83 very close in spec to one of the original Mullards—many players' idea of the best 12AX7 type preamp tube ever produced.

Whatever you pop into your preamp, there are certainly still variables in sound between both the quality newer units and any NOS tubes you can lay your hands on. It really pays to invest the going rate of $7–$15 per unit in two or three really good, properly tested new 12AX7s of different makes and even to try and scrounge a few NOS examples (pulled from used/junked audio gear, if necessary) and try them in the first and second positions of your favorite amp. One could fill pages on the subtle differences between Mullards, Brimars, GEs, JJs, and so forth, but by the time a player has absorbed all of these nuances, the NOS units in question might have become impossible to find, and the new production units may well have been modified again. It's sufficient to know that enormous variables do exist, and that it is really worth the time and money required to test them for yourself.

12AY7

When Fender moved from old-fashioned eight-pin to newer nine-pin preamp tubes in the late to mid 50s, this was the one that appeared in the first gain stage of most of their wide-panel and then narrow-panel tweed amps. The 12AY7 (also designated 6072) has a lower gain factor of 44, but is otherwise virtually a direct replacement for the 12AX7, although the tubes have different impedances and would ideally want different bias resistors to be tweaked to perfection. The 12AY7 is responsible for the smooth, crisp performance of many tweed Bassman, Super, or Pro amps, although as supplies gradually began to dry up, many players popped in a 12AX7 instead. The more powerful preamp tube yields a hotter sound in these tweed amps, and the fact that so many vintage examples have been equipped this way has probably led to some misunderstanding of the 'true' tweed sound, which is rounder, more open, and offers a slightly wider frequency response than many tweed amp owners have ever experienced from their equipment (that, and the fact that Leo Fender didn't really design them to be played with the volume at 12).

A 12AX7 can sound great in these amps if you want to achieve earlier breakup for blues or rock'n'roll, but for the authentic experience (which can definitely include blues and rock'n'roll when you crank up), locate an NOS 12AY7, which are still fairly plentiful. Alternatively, you could try the following.

5751

This tube is another direct replacement for the 12AX7, but also with a lower gain, something close to that of a 12AY7. A lot of guitarists, Stevie Ray Vaughan for one, used these for years; it's a 'secret weapon' in position one, used to ease past preamp distortion and generate juicy output tube distortion. The fact that plenty of great NOS units were available at a reasonable price made them an excellent find. Similarly, Dr Z uses a 5751 in the PI of several of his amps, including the Z-28 and Carmen Ghia, to evoke a slightly smoother signal delivery to the output tubes and, in the case of the latter model, to reduce that 'splat' you can occasionally get when driving EL84s too hard. Enough guitarists have apparently cottoned on, because NOS examples are becoming both more expensive and short in supply, but they are still worth seeking out. With a little hunting and some luck, you can probably still track down a few great GE/JAN versions of these for not a lot more than double the price of a new-manufacture 12AX7, and if it's a tested tube it should last you for several years. Sovtek also makes a current version of the 5751. If you feel any stage in your amp carrying a 12AX7 could use a little taming—in an effort to pass a somewhat truer and less distorted signal on to the next stage—try one of these. Good ones have a full, clear, clean sound that plenty of great players swear by.

12AT7

Found in some preamp positions, but most commonly as a phase inverter or reverb driver in black and silverface Fenders, this tube has a lower amplification factor of 60 and a somewhat different character than the 12AX7. It is often referred to as a lower-gain direct replacement for a 12AX7, but that is misleading. The 'AT' has considerably different impedance to the 'AX,' and while many circuits will work with one in place of the other, they won't work at their best, and might play other tricks besides. I recall popping a 12AT7 into the hot-modded (that is, 'modified hot-rodded') normal channel of a Super Reverb years ago to tame its too-quick distortion, only to find that when I plugged into the vibrato channel there was nothing happening. The 12AT7 in the first channel was robbing the 12AX7 in the second channel of the voltage it needed to operate. Changing the AT for a 5751 instantly fixed the problem.

These tubes can provide an alternative to 12AX7s in many positions, but in some cases you will want an experienced tech to change the cathode bias resistor to make everything play together nicely. Otherwise, instead of more headroom and a cleaner sound, you might find yourself with less headroom and a flattened frequency response. The exchange can work the other way, too, and plenty of players like the sound of a 12AX7 in the phase inverter position of black and silverface Fenders, especially when they seek to drive the output tubes hard.

12AU7

Found in some vintage amps and Ampegs in particular, this has an extremely low gain of around 18, compared to the 12AX7's amplification factor of 100. This tube is seen more in the hi-fi world, but can occasionally be useful in guitar amps where you really want to knock down a fierce overdrive stage or tame your signal in some other way.

EF86/6267

Here we part company with the dual triodes that are all close relatives of the popular 12AX7, and venture into the world of pentodes. In very simple terms, the added elements in a pentode (as detailed above) allow them to develop more power, which in terms of preamp tubes means higher gain. The added goings-on inside an EF86 can mean extra handling noise (microphony), too, and these tubes have to be used carefully in preamp circuits. Some classic early Vox designs used this tube—the AC15, AC10, and earliest models of the AC30 for example—but it wasn't seen much in the guitar-amp world through the later 60s, 70s, or 80s until Matchless revived it for the DC30. Dr Z, Bad Cat, 65amps, TopHat, Gabriel, and many others have employed this tube, but its tendency toward microphony has put off other potential users. Those that capture it in the right circuit find it makes for a fat, rich, full-frequency preamp with lots of gain as

required. As used by each of the aforementioned makers, the EF86 allows for a simple but powerful preamp with just one pentode gain stage and no further gain make-up stage required before the PI. Among NOS supplies, the really prized EF86s are those made by GEC and Mullard, and they command extremely high prices these days.

5879

This pentode preamp tube, best known for its use in Gibson's GA-40 Les Paul Amp of the late 50s (and the similar Maestro GA-45), and modern reproductions of these, has similar characteristics to the EF86, but is perhaps a bit warmer and rounder, with a thick, creamy tone. The elements within it are also connected to different pins, so one isn't a direct substitution for the other.

6SJ7

This octal pentode preamp tube is found in some of the vintage Gibson BR-series amps, a couple of very early Fenders, and a few other oddballs. It is a warm and rich sounding tube with a lot of gain—much like an EF86, although a little smoother if anything. The scarcity of most NOS octal preamp tube types makes it an unlikely candidate for broad use in any mass-manufactured tube amps today.

6SC7, 6SL7, and 6SN7

These are the octal preamp tubes that you will find most often. They are all dual triodes that were generally replaced by nine-pin 12AX7 types over the years, and appeared variously in vintage Ampeg, Fender, Valco, and other lesser-seen amps. A few newer builders of hand-made tube amps, notably Alessandro, have indulged in octal preamp designs, with some great results. Some players find that these sound smoother and more rounded than many nine-pin preamp tubes. As they required entirely different sockets and circuits, however, it is impractical to make direct comparisons.

Output Tubes

6V6

This is the archetypal smaller American tube, which powered all of the classic sub-25-watt Fenders until recent years, when EL84s were introduced (on Pro Junior and Blues Junior models) due to a scarcity of good, new 6V6s. It also appeared in countless models from other great American amp makers: Gibson, Valco, and occasionally Ampeg among them. The 6V6 is often touted as the 'little brother' of the 6L6 and fits the same eight-pin socket, although a lot of players actually prefer junior to the more powerful 'L' tube. The 'V' develops less power, so it is easier to push into distortion when volume levels are restricted at your club gig or in the studio, and it is a little smoother and 'browner' sounding along with it. Good 6V6s in a well-designed amp should sound open, rich in frequency, and well defined, but often with a nice little edge of grit and a throaty roar when pushed hard. The 6V6's bottom end is inherently a little softer than that of some other, larger output tubes.

This tube usually puts out a little more than half the power of a 6L6 in the same circuit, although it can't take the higher DC voltages that the 'L' can handle. A pair will usually generate around 15–18 watts in push-pull, and up to around 22 or maybe even 25 watts when pushed hard in a fixed bias, class-AB output stage. Most amps with 6V6s feed them somewhere between 330 and 360 DC volts, which at the higher level is approaching the maximum spec for the tube (which you will sometimes see cautiously rated at a maximum plate voltage of just 315). A few amps push their 6V6s way beyond spec: the Fender Deluxe Reverb, for example, puts a whopping 415 volts on the plates to generate about 22 watts. Sturdy, American-made 6V6s of the 60s and 70s handled this surprisingly well, but Deluxe Reverbs became good at popping weaker Russian and Chinese 6V6s in the 90s.

NOS 6V6s are still plentiful and not as expensive as other popular NOS output tube types, and some popular makes come from Britain and France, as well as the USA. Fortunately, new 6V6s are being made today that are far better than those that were available from Eastern Europe and China for many years. Some good ones currently carry the Electro-Harmonix and JJ brands. The resurgence of this tube has led a number of makers to design around it once again.

6L6

Here is your big Fender output tube, the bottle that powered everything from the tweed Bassman and Twin Reverb to the Showman, and all the 25-watts-plus models in between. It offers full lows, generally even mids, and pronounced, shimmering highs. This tube was also frequently seen in the form of the rugged 5881 variant in the 50s and 60s, but newly manufactured tubes labeled 5881 are generally just 6L6s in all but number. The 6L6 is often described as bright, crisp, even a little harsh, but in the right circuit these can be very smooth, with a great, aggressive bark and roar when pushed. The fact that they have been seen most in fixed bias, class-AB designs has probably helped to determine their overall sonic image, but I have a pair in a very nice cathode-biased amp with no negative feedback loop that generates around 30 watts, and at some settings you could mistake the sound for a sweet and juicy AC30. This is a great tube, and fortunately there's a pretty broad range of decent, newly manufactured 6L6s available today, and good, tested NOS pairs can still be found, too, at a price.

A pair of 6L6s in class AB, fixed bias, usually puts out a maximum of around 50 watts, although many amp manufacturers using them will claim 60 watts. These tubes can vary quite a lot with make and model, so if you have a favorite amp that carries them it is in your interest to try pairs from a number of different sources to discover what you like best. A little taste-testing of 6L6s can yield tubes that offer greater or less compression and breakup, a tighter or looser sound, recessed or pronounced mids, and so forth.

EL34

Here is the British colleague to the US 6L6, the quality and sonic character of which is underscored by Marshall's move from the 6L6/5881/KT66 in the JTM45 to the EL34 in the plexi models of the late 60s. This tube is a little crunchier and crispier sounding than the 6L6 when pushed, sometimes with more breakup in the lows, but with a fat, ballsy bass response

nonetheless, especially when roaring through the 4x12 cabs that frequently accompany them. Good EL34s were also in short supply in the 80s and 90s after the majority of stocks of excellent Mullards and other British and European makes started drying up. Eastern European makes of the period often couldn't handle the high voltages applied to these tubes by some amps. A good EL34 should be capable of handling a fair bit more than a 6L6, and of putting out more wattage along with it: 60 watts is no stretch at all for a pair, with up to 70 watts possible when handled properly. As with 6V6s, the tables have turned recently—to the benefit of Marshall players everywhere—and some of the Eastern European factories are turning out great EL34s again.

EL84

This tall, slender, nine-pin bottle has been one of the most popular output tubes for smaller and medium sized amps of the past couple of decades. Many makers turned to EL84s (also known as the 6BQ5 in the USA) when the quality of new 6V6s began to suffer, and the tube has won a lot of fans among players just for its sound. It is a bright, harmonically rich tube at lower volumes, with a juicy crunch, raunchy mids, and shimmering, even glassy highs when cranked up. The archetypal EL84 amps are the early Vox classics such as the AC15 and AC30, but Marshall used them in its 18-watt and 20-watt heads and combos, they frequently appeared in Gibson amps, and they have been a favorite of the boutique-amp revolution.

A pair of EL84s in cathode bias usually puts out around 15 watts, or up to 20 watts in class AB, fixed bias. True class-A performance should keep them down around 12 watts or so. Most amps run these at between 320 and 350 DC volts on the plates, although the Matchless Lightning pushes them to about 365 volts, and some versions of Traynor's Guitar Mate had these little tubes dealing with as much as 390 volts on the plates. Voltage levels like these require sturdy, reliable tubes; fortunately some very good newer makes are widely available, and matched pairs of NOS examples can often still be found. If you have a good EL84-based amp and can get your hands on a tested pair of Mullards or Brimars, you are in for a treat. I have also used US-made Philips and GE EL84/6BQ5s that sounded out of this world.

KT66

This big, Coke-bottle-shaped tube is a direct replacement for the 6L6 in guitar amp circuits, but has a beefy, succulent sound all its own. The European tube is best known for its appearance in Marshall JTM45 heads and Bluesbreaker combos after the US-made 5881s that were initially installed in these amps started to become scarce. KT66s were extremely hard to come by for many years, but a couple of newer versions have proved to be great-sounding and reliable tubes, particularly Groove Tubes' GTKT66-HP. If you have a reissue Marshall JTM-type model, pop in a good set of KT66s and feel the amp come alive. The all-time classic version of this tube was manufactured in Britain by GEC, and NOS examples of these fetch extremely high prices these days. A few newer amp-makers have latched onto the KT66, and models such as the Mojave Plexi 45 and the Dr Z Route 66 feature them to excellent effect. THD recommends them as a good tube to use with its UniValve and Flexi-50 amps, which can handle a wide range of output tube types.

CHAPTER 2

6550

Late-70s and 80s US-distributed Marshall amps boasted big, sturdy 6550 output tubes retrofitted to them as a substitute for the original British EL34s, which were failing at unusually high rates at that time. This tube is related to the 6L6, but will handle more voltage, puts out more wattage, and offers a bolder, firmer sound, too. The 6550 has usually been the choice of amp makers seeking a big, loud, clean amp.

Ampeg put six of them in the revolutionary SVT bass amp to generate around 300 watts, which really put the stadium bass rig on the map. Rugged, US-made Sunn amps used these tubes in a big way, too.

A few makers have put the firm, loud, 6550 to sweeter use, most notably George Alessandro who uses them in his larger amps such as the Bloodhound, Greyhound, and Redbone. A number of usable makes from Eastern European factories have become available in recent years.

KT88

A seriously powerful tube, in an impressively large bottle, the KT88 fits the standard eight-pin socket, although you might not think so at first glance. Marshall used four of these to generate 200 watts in its massive Major amp, and two of them put out around 75 watts in Marshall's accurately named Park 75. This tube had become extremely hard to find (and prohibitively expensive if you do), but decent new versions are now coming from both China and Slovakia.

6973

Used in several Valco-made amps from the late 50s to mid 60s, including the Supro Model 24 and the Gretsch Playboy, this tube is famed as one of the secret ingredients in Jimmy Page's studio tone from the early days of Led Zeppelin. Although it looks much like an EL84 and fits the same nine-pin socket, it is actually a very different tube. The 6973 is rated to handle up to 440 volts on the plates (whereas the EL84's limit is nearly 100 volts fewer), and has a thicker, chunkier, slightly darker tone than its slender look-alike, and is capable of a meaty crunch when you push it hard.

This tube is also wired and biased differently to the EL84, so don't think you can simply pop one into an EL84-based circuit and give it a spin! Good, properly tested NOS examples are becoming hard to come by, but Electro-Harmonix manufactures a new version that works in the same old circuits.

7591

The reappearance of this tube, courtesy of Russian factories, comes on the heels of severely dwindling NOS supplies and has put a smile back on the faces of many Ampeg owners. Favored for its ability to produce a bold, firm, round, open guitar tone at medium output levels, this erstwhile 'jazz tube' also gives up a sweet, smooth overdrive tone when pushed hard enough—something most Ampeg designs that used it tried to avoid. Newer designs, such as 65amps' Stone Pony, wring a little more breadth out of this bottle. Volume-wise, it puts out something between a 6V6 and a 6L6.

C H A P T E R 2

CRANK IT DOWN

Amp makers from the late 50s through to the end of the 60s were generally bent on achieving more power, more clarity, and more punch from their designs. On big stages, before PA systems reached anything like today's capabilities, a guitarist's amp was responsible for getting the instrument heard, often without any additional amplification. Today, guitar amps are all about generating tone. Get that tone just the way you want it and the considerably advanced contemporary sound-support systems can offer an efficient means of carrying it to the masses. With this in mind, I want to devote a chunk of this chapter to considerations of wattage and amp size in general, and ways of achieving satisfactory tone without creating the kind of excess volume that will get you in trouble.

The Right Amp for the Job

I'm the first person to admit that there are few feelings as powerful as standing in front of a cranked, raging, 100-watt stack. You just can't achieve that wind-in-the-hair, thump-in-the-gut feeling from a small amp, and the hovering, edge-of-feedback immediacy and totally 'alive' playing feel of a big rig is hard to replicate in any other way. While it's fun to fantasize about an occasion when such wattage might be justifiable, let's consider a more common gigging scenario. The average music venue is a compact 80 to 120-capacity club, one which, for example, your 15–22 watt, 1x12 tube combo suits just fine (although you are still likely to be asked to it turn down). Every once in a while, a booking in a 250-capacity room comes along up and you briefly consider bringing a 45-watt amp, before deciding instead to take the opportunity to crank the smaller amp, without any complaints. Does it suffice? Of course it does, in spades (and the sound engineer will still probably interrupt your sound check to make you turn it down a little).

The fact is, given the capabilities of modern sound reinforcement systems—with good mixes running in both the mains and the monitors—you really don't need any more volume than you could comfortably tolerate in a room the size of the stage you're on; and with monitor levels set appropriately, you can get away with even less.

In reality, the oversized amp often just leads to the heartbreak of unsatisfactory tone. It's not just that everyone else in the room will be your friend if you use a smaller amp, but you'll enjoy your own playing experience a lot more because you'll be able to hit that sweet spot where shimmering clean tone segues over into succulent distortion at the thwack of a pick. Err on the side of too large, on the other hand, and you'll almost certainly be forced to reduce your volume, either by a hoarse lead vocalist or a furrow-browed sound person, leaving you fatally short of the golden tone zone. In the unlikely event that they leave you to crank up your beast, the chances are you will obliterate the room with excessive volume anyway—a sure-fire show-spoiler. All of these considerations are doubly pertinent in the recording studio.

So why do the 50 and 100-watt stacks and combos even exist? As discussed at the top of this section, they used to be a necessity. Way back in the early 60s, when rock'n'roll was still evolving toward the technologically advanced monster it is today, successful bands found themselves on an inexorable trajectory from basement clubs to dance halls and theaters (and, ultimately, stadiums)—venues whose routinely inadequate PA systems meant progressively larger guitar amps were a prerequisite simply to get the instruments heard. Thus, Leo Fender designed the Showman, initially for surf guitarist Dick Dale, while Dick Denney created the Vox AC50 and AC100 for The Beatles, and Jim Marshall sealed the deal with the JTM100 for Pete Townshend (who quickly jumped ship for Hiwatt amps, in fact) and, before long, just about every other rocker in the UK.

While these are events that were relevant 40 years ago, if you grew up with the sound of Eric Clapton, Jimmy Page, Jimi Hendrix, or Paul Kossoff playing through a Marshall stack, it's hard to get that tone—and that image—out of your head even today, and it's understandable why you'd want the rig of doom, even if the world won't let you play it. Of course, certain scenarios that allow, or even encourage, the use of a big amp do still exist. As a rule of thumb, if you're touring with a signed act that plays stages larger than the footprint of your house or apartment, and you have someone to carry the road cases for you (and your band name has some association with Satan, darkness, heavy machinery, or evil in general), you can probably still get away with the stack. However, for many contemporary, professional acts—country artists in particular—massive stage volume levels are old news; they prefer running amps behind Plexiglass shields, or even under the stage, and monitoring everything with in-ear units. On the other side of the coin, if you're a country or jazz player who needs 100 watts in order to obtain the clean headroom that 40 per cent of your amp's potential provides you, or a seven-string metal thumper who wants to project pure punch and crunch with a lot of low-end rumble, you might very well need the power. Also, the player who uses a lot of pedals to achieve overdrive and distortion, or who uses a channel-switching amp's high-gain lead channel coupled with appropriate master volume levels to rein in output, might also find a 50 watter is appropriate, or even vital. The majority of bar and club regulars, and especially those seeking organic, rootsy, amp-generated overdrive, must forget the old dreams of macho-looking amplification and instead embrace the new dream of consistently excellent tone.

In order to wean ourselves off excessive amplification, let's take a look at how power ratings actually equate to volume. The peculiarities of the human ear and the logarithmic nature of our perceptions of volume mean that output ratings don't correspond directly to volume levels. While a 100-watt amp might have five times the power of a 20 watter, its perceived volume is really only around twice that of the smaller amp (this is an imprecise science, since it involves so many variables and considerations of frequency perception). What the higher-wattage amp *does* increase is its headroom and the ceiling for the onset of breakup, which means that players who use amp distortion as part of their tonal palette have to push hard to get into the juice.

Before moving on, let's examine another scenario. Have you ever wondered why your bass player with the 200-watt head and 4x10 cab is always grumbling that your 15-watt, 1x12 combo is too loud? There are a couple of considerations here. Firstly, it takes a lot of wattage—that is, more tubes and a bigger output transformer—to adequately reproduce the low frequencies that bass guitar requires. Secondly, human hearing is more sensitive to midrange and high frequency sounds than it is to lows, and the nature of these perceptions changes as an amp

TONE TIP   Gig Tone versus Home Tone

The vast difference between 'home tone' and 'gig tone' is something that experienced performing musicians know intuitively, but which often slaps newcomers to live work right in the face. While 'good tone' is a holy grail fanatically sought by innumerable guitarists these days, more often than not that obsessive pursuit is undertaken in the isolation of a player's living room, bedroom, home studio, or some other 'home alone' environment. That's absolutely fine: these are the places where we practice, learn, discover, and sometimes record the results. But honing our ultimate tone in these objective environments can often lead to disappointment when we get out into the entirely subjective world of the concert venue.

Among web-boarding tonehounds, there seems to be a lot of emphasis on guitar and amp sounds that are 'smooth, warm, round, and organic.' This might run to everything from the general preference for neck-pickup tones to a love of the round, thick, early breakup of heavily worn-in vintage speakers. Certainly, any of these can bathe the ear in their juicy goodness when enjoyed without distraction, and sound a lot more pleasant than anything that hints at a 'harsh' or 'cutting' sound. However, what the ear perceives from a solo electric guitar and from a guitar blended into the mix of a full band are two entirely different things. In the latter, that smooth, warm, round tone can simply get lost.

The fundamental notes—meaning the pure, fretted notes, without any consideration of overtones (harmonics)—of guitars with 22 frets cover the frequency range from 82 Hz at the low E to a high D at 1,174 Hz. It so happens that the human voice has a range from approximately 85 Hz to 1,100 Hz. The human ear can detect frequencies from around 20 Hz (a further octave below the low E on a bass guitar) to around 20,000 Hz (20 kHz), but the average human's hearing is biased toward detecting sounds in the midrange frequencies (these frequencies are perceived more readily, in other words), while upper-mid and high-frequency sounds will also stand out in a blend of frequencies, even if they are not louder in the pure sense. Midrange frequencies encompass the human voice as well as the guitar. As it happens, they also define a lot of what a drum kit produces (although drum frequencies trample all over the spectrum), anything your bassist will create above his first octave or so, and lots of what a keyboard or horn section will produce. In other words, without some clever tone-shaping to distinguish the note production of each instrument, you can be left with sonic mush.

Meanwhile, thanks to the range of harmonics that any plucked guitar string also produces, the guitar's frequency range is actually extended far above the frequency of its highest fundamental note, and it takes up a lot more space in the sonic stew than just this

segues into distortion. Therefore, the frequency range and distortion content of any given amp will also skew our perception of apparent volume. Stand your 15 watter and your bassist's 200 watter side by side, set her volume at noon and yours at ten o'clock, and you'll almost certainly find that you are still cutting through just fine.

All of which brings us to the issues of speaker type and efficiency, and how cab design and speaker complement one another, all of which is addressed thoroughly further on in this book. For now, it's worth bearing in mind that a more efficient speaker will make any amp louder, so

C H A P T E R   2

chunk of around 1,000 Hz, located toward the center of the midrange. Put the guitar through an amplifier, especially a semi-distorted one, and these harmonics are accentuated further.

Analyze the 'warm, smooth, round' tone that seems so easy on the ear at home and you'll discover that it achieves this quality by minimizing some of the aural spikes, or strong harmonic overtones, in the upper frequency range. Transfer it to the stage, however, amidst all the other sonic information, and this spike-free tone is often about as effective as a rubber crutch. Stand back from the stage, and—in a large, loud band, at least—such a tone will often be all but obscured when everyone is playing, contributing more to the general sense of low-end presence and midrange body of the band's sound than it does establishing a distinct, ringing part in its own right. Of course, that may be just the sound you are aiming for. Equally, if you're playing in a small blues combo, with a fairly minimalist drummer and no extremes of volume, your smooth, rich tone might be delightful just as it is. In so many other, less minimal live scenarios, however, you are going to want your rhythm and lead parts to shine through.

Often, the 'warm, smooth' tone essayed in an unforgiving context will mean a lead player repeatedly increasing their overall volume in an effort to get heard, which duly inspires the rest of the band to crank up, too, ultimately accentuating the mush. To get that tone heard properly, you'll want to dial in some upper-midrange cut, some attention-getting shimmer in the highs (although without creating an ice-pick-in-the-ear for anyone in the first few rows), and a firmer low end. This might involve simply tweaking your amp's tone and gain controls, or selecting a different pickup, but it might also require a total rethink of your rig before the next gig.

Having said all this, it is important to remember that the guitar's voice still exists in the midrange frequencies. That is still where you will get your punching power and your body. You will cut through better by retaining firmer lows and more appealing, harmonically rich highs, but too much of either will defeat the purpose. As Victor Mason, of Mojave Amplifiers, puts it: "If you let [the guitar] breathe in the bandwidth in which it was created to work, you'll get the best sound from it."

It's also important to realize that your tonal requirements will vary from night to night, room to room, and to remain flexible in all gigging situations. All of which is not intended to say that you should entirely scrap that warm, luscious, ear-candy tone that gives you goose bumps in the bedroom, just that you should prime yourself against being too precious about it in the real world.

When you get 'your tone' set up and ready to go in sound check, only to find that it's lost in the ether once the band kicks in, don't be too proud or stubborn to change the settings, or to do whatever you have to do, to get that tone heard by the ears that really matter: the audience's.

let's consider all of the above as if rendered on an equal playing field, speaker-wise. While a big, 4x12 speaker has a lot more surface area, and will therefore pump more air than a diminutive 1x12, I have run the same amp head through both types of cabs side by side, and on some occasions found the efficient, open-backed 1x12 to have a higher perceived volume level than a closed-back 4x12. Remember, a 40-watt amp doesn't pump 40 watts through each speaker in a 4x12 array but divides the total into ten watts each, while all 40 watts are being pumped through the single driver in a 1x12 cab.

Taming the Volume

If you mostly play smaller bar and club gigs but are steadfastly attached to a larger 50 or 100-watt amp, for cold financial reasons, or out of sheer infatuation, there are ways to tame its output level somewhat and therefore get it to sing and break up somewhere short of ear-splitting volume. Note that none of these solutions will yield exactly the same tone as when running the same amp flat out, as designed, but they might make acceptable compromises in some instances.

Attenuators

One popular cure for an amp that's too powerful for any given room is an output attenuator. Attenuators have been around for some time, but they have become more popular in recent years, perhaps due to improved design and reliability as much as the trend for lower stage and studio volumes. Some early units from the 80s had a reputation for burning out their elements and, as a result, frying essential components within the amp they were attached to, but design advances in these units have greatly improved their dependability and the safety of the amps running into them.

In brief, an attenuator is a device placed between a tube amp's output and the speaker (or speaker cab input), connected with proper speaker cables in both instances, carrying large resistors that 'soak up' some of the amp's power before it gets to the speaker, thereby lowering the overall volume, regardless of the amp's control settings. Some of the more complex designs include additional circuitry designed to compensate for the tonal loss of an amp working at reduced volume.

The obvious function of the attenuator is to bring big amps down to the volume levels of the kinds of small amps that I discussed above. This opens them up to the same kinds of recording applications, enabling their use in smaller studios, with sensitive microphones, and so forth. Many players have also been using them for live work—to knock off 6dB or so from a larger amp's output, for example, in order to tailor it to a smaller room, or to rein in levels early on in an evening, when the room is empty and bright, before restoring full output with the flick of a switch or twist of a knob (and without dramatically changing the amp's sound or distortion character) when the venue becomes fuller and bodies are absorbing more sound.

Alternatively, if you are gigging mainly in large rooms and don't need to reduce your volume for shows, an attenuator can help you get something close to your full output 'live sound' in smaller rehearsal room situations, where you might be getting a set together with just a vocal PA, no mics on the drums, and so forth. There are a lot of uses for the things, there's no doubt, and if you don't own one already, I'm sure almost every player reading this can imagine a situation in which a good attenuator would be handy.

By the very nature of their operation, however, these devices have inherent quirks that can make tonal alterations to your rig that go beyond merely ameliorating a full-output sound. The first of these occurs as a result of driving your speakers at different levels—making them perform in different ways. The interaction of speaker with amplifier is a major constituent of any amp's overall sound, and speakers sound quite different when driven hard than when driven gently. The second, perhaps less obvious factor is that the human ear responds differently to the frequency spectrum at different volume levels. In short, even if the attenuator is allowing your amp to pump the same output-tube distortion portion of its overall tonal palette to your speakers at a lower volume level, the lessened volume will inevitably alter the way your ear perceives the frequencies that make up that sound. Even in a rig that doesn't produce any speaker distortion at full volume, the amp's tonal and harmonic spectrum will still sound different to you at 96dB than at 112dB—and 'different' in more complex ways than simply quiet versus loud.

Some players worry about attenuators damaging their amps, and the jury is still out on that subject. On paper, the better models seem to have nothing in their own makeup and function that is inherently detrimental to an amplifier. The simple fact that you are likely to be running your amp harder with an attenuator attached means that all components will be under more stress—tubes in particular—and will be liable to burn out faster. This is also the case if you play in large auditoriums every night and habitually turn the amp up to the same higher volume, without an attenuator. The amp is still pumping as much voltage through its system and running its tubes and transformers as hot as it would be when normally cranked, but the attenuator is converting a lot of that energy to heat to be dissipated through a large heat sink, or other means, rather than sending it all to the speakers. As far as the amp itself is concerned, however, it's a case of same volume levels, same wear and tear. If that's where an amp sounds best, many players conclude that replacing output tubes more frequently is a small price to pay. The fact that the amp doesn't *sound* as loud can make it easy to forget that you are nevertheless driving those tubes and components pretty hard, so anyone using an attenuator on a nightly basis should be extra vigilant about maintenance issues.

That said, however, I have occasionally experienced premature output tube failure when using output attenuators. One pair of quality, tested NOS tubes died far sooner than would have been expected. I have spoken with some respected amp manufacturers who have voiced their concerns in this regard, too. Still, the definitive verdict has yet to be heard.

Ultimately, many players who use attenuators on a regular basis maintain something of a love-hate relationship with these devices: the majority would rather play their amps at full blast, with nothing in the way, but acknowledge the expediency of the attenuator when it comes to maintaining cordial relations with bandmates, sound engineers, and the first few rows of their audience. Attenuators can definitely be a useful part of any well-rounded guitarist's tool kit— even if matching the right-sized amp to the right-sized room might still be a preferable route for total tonal satisfaction, whenever possible, at least.

Master Voltage and Power Scaling-style Circuits

Several amp manufacturers today are including some form of voltage-based output reduction system in their designs, thus reining in these amps' volumes in ways that are purported to be more tonally sensitive than the traditional master-volume control, or even an output attenuator. While such claims are very often true, most such circuits are generally bespoke, proprietary designs which are included only in the amps of the manufacturer that has developed them. So, for example, should 65amps' Master Voltage control or Mojave's Power Dampening system

appeal to you, you'll only ever get to use them by investing in the respective Mojave or 65amps model. There is one exception, however: Canadian manufacturer London Power has developed a popular circuit called Power Scaling that goes into its own amplifier designs, but which is also available under license as an add-on to other appropriate amps.

Although all of these circuits—and a few others like them—are somewhat different (each maker claims them to be totally original), and are usually closely guarded, they all tend to function by allowing the player to govern the operating voltages delivered to the tubes, thereby decreasing the tubes' actual outputs, rather than merely clamping down the full natural output of the tubes with a potentiometer, as most master volumes do. As such, they provide a means of volume reduction that works with the tubes, rather than against them. While all of these circuits also promise to deliver 'the exact same tone at lesser volumes,' each that I have tried is taking slight liberties with such a claim. Reducing the tubes' DC voltages, even if you do it right across the board, to preamp, PI, and output stages simultaneously, inevitably alters their sonic behavior somewhat, as it does the way in which they interact with the output transformer; so tone is bound to change slightly as a result. Having said that, I find the better of these circuits do offer a more satisfactory volume reduction, from the perspective of tone preservation, than many of the better output attenuators I have tried, so they are certainly to be welcomed to the fold.

Half-Power Mods

Several amps come with switches to reduce output power by half, or sometimes more. Many of these use simple circuits that can be added by a qualified tech to existing amplifiers to affect a useful reduction in power. One of the simplest power-reduction techniques can be achieved with fixed-biased amps carrying four output tubes in two push-pull pairs. By removing one tube from each side of these pairs (that is, removing either the two inside or the two outside tubes, but never two from one side), the power of the amp can be approximately halved. Removing two tubes also changes the impedance relationship between the remaining output tubes and the speaker, however, as seen via the OT, so ideally you will make another change here, too. On amps with multiple output impedance options, drop the impedance setting by half when continuing to use the same speaker or speaker cabinet. For example, if you are running a 16-ohms cab and you pull two tubes, switch your selector to 8 ohms; if you're running an 8-ohms cab, switch it to 4 ohms, and so on. Rather than a selector, some amps have dedicated outputs at different impedance ratings, so just re-plug the speaker connection to the output jack, rated at half the one you were previously using to get the same result. If the amp has just one output impedance, as is often the case with older Fenders, you can either run different speakers to create the desired load, or just tough it out. In truth, most Fender OTs will easily tolerate an impedance mismatch of either double or half the rated impedance (one step up or down). Frequency response and power might change somewhat, but that's what you're trying to achieve by pulling two tubes, anyway. If the result works for you, sonically, without an impedance switch, you are probably OK to go with it. Marshall amps are reputedly not as happy with an impedance mismatch, but fortunately the larger Marshall models generally carry impedance switches to match 4, 8, and 16-ohms loads.

C H A P T E R   2

Given the ability to compensate impedance-wise, this technique still doesn't instantly create, for example, a 50-watt amp that is exactly the same as the four-tube, 100-watt version in every regard other than power. The two remaining output tubes are now feeding a much heftier OT than most 50-watt amps would normally carry, so even when the amp is cranked up high there is likely to be less OT saturation in its overall distortion character. Again, if you try this technique and the sound really works for you, don't worry about the 'OT saturation' factor. The other side of the coin is that this bigger-than-standard '50-watt' OT (meaning the 100-watt iron) should give you fat lows and a firm response overall.

A trick achieved with a little more intervention is the pentode/triode switch, already used by a number of amplifier makers in the form of a 'half-power switch.' It doesn't halve the power exactly, but gets close, and changes the output tubes' tonal character in some other ways besides. Those caveats being understood, it is at least a relatively simple modification, and certainly offers a faster path to output-tube distortion, with a definite drop in volume levels.

The pentode/triode switch involves some fairly simple rewiring of the output tubes to make the pentode tubes think they are behaving as triodes. It doesn't actually turn them into triodes, but instead produces what is effectively a 'mock triode' performance. In any case, this triode mode makes the amp break up a little more quickly, and also induces a creamier, smoother, more midrange-dominant sound in the tubes. This can also be heard as a lack of sparkle and chime, with noticeably attenuated highs, so it won't suit every player's taste. Fortunately, the mod is simple and easily reversed, so things can be undone if you find you don't like the result (it always includes a switch, too, so you can select either pentode or triode settings). Be aware that this—like any internal modification—involves working around high voltages, so it should only be undertaken by a qualified amp tech. The work simply involves installing a sturdy DPDT on/on toggle switch, using one half of the switch for each side of the push-pull set (a single switch functions for two, four, or six tubes, since the significant connections will be tied together), lifting the output tube screen grids' connections to their DC voltage supply, and switching between that supply (standard pentode mode) and a new connection made to the plates of the tubes (triode mode).

The work should take a good amp repairer about 15 minutes to complete, plus the time it takes to drill an appropriate hole to mount the switch. This can sometimes be located in the opening meant for the spare output jack, which you are not using. If you aren't entirely sure you will like the results, see if the repairer can safely wire up the switch in a 'free floating' configuration first, so you can hear the results, then drill and permanently mount it if you are happy with the new sound. Ensure your tech uses a switch rated for the kinds of voltages likely to be seen here (which are DC rather than the AC for which most such toggle switches are rated; a high rating in the 240-volts ballpark with the ability to handle five or six amps of current should do the trick).

Tube Converters

Another means of reducing your amp's output involves converting to a lesser-powered output tube. Usually referred to as 'tube converters,' these were all the rage when they first hit the

market a few years ago, and most commonly take the form of a direct plug-in adaptor that changes 6L6 or EL34 output tubes to EL84s without any further modification to the amp—there are even variants for converting 6V6s. In addition to including internal wiring that matches the connections between the adaptor's nine-pin socket and eight-pin plug, tube converters contain a small network of resistors to bring the voltages down to those required by the lower-powered EL84, and a bias resistor to change the format from fixed to cathode bias. In doing so, makers of such converters universally claim that they change an amplifier's output from 'fixed bias class AB to cathode-bias class A.' As discussed earlier in this chapter, that claim would need to be verified on the bench with the kind of accurate measurements that most players can't make for themselves. It is certainly worth knowing that such converters contain a preset cathode-biasing resistor intended to be used with a wide range of amps, which can include designs running their output tubes' plates at 400VDC, 425VDC, 475VDC, or whatever. Given what we have already learned about true class-A performance being critically tied to bias point with relation to an output stage's operating voltages, it's hard to see how a single resistor value could manage this 'class-A conversion' across such a broad range of amps. Also, these converters do nothing to alter the decision to include, or omit, a negative feedback loop (which, admittedly, has nothing to do with class distinction either, but is a major factor in the associated sounds of different class types).

Whether or not you feel the claims of instant conversion to class A are a bit far-fetched, tube converters can indeed be useful as volume-reduction devices, and also provide a handy means for achieving a more 'British' EL84-based tone in many amps not originally designed for these tubes. The overall results achievable from these units are pretty impressive given their relatively low cost. A 50-watt Fender or Marshall amp, with a pair of 6L6 or EL34 output tubes, will yield an output of around 20 watts with a pair of THD Yellow Jackets or TAD Tone Bones in place. This can obviously bring a large-room amp down to bar-gig and studio levels. Be aware, however, that the relationship between wattage and apparent volume isn't a direct correlation. If sonic character, speaker performance, and cab type are close to equal, a 20-watt amp will still sound significantly *more* than half as loud as a 50 watt amp. The alteration afforded by the converters definitely offers a quicker onset of output tube distortion, and that is the more often desired goal, anyway. For the cost of a pair of converters, it's a fast-track to a significantly different sonic signature. I have tried these in some excellent 6L6 and EL34-based amps, however, which resulted in a fizzy and overly compressed tone. In others, the Yellow Jackets offered an excellent alternative. Do not expect a magical AC15-conversion in any amp you care to pop them into, but they can make an interesting and useful volume-dropping, tone-altering option in many cases.

If you are really looking for a smaller amp with what is generally characterized as 'the class-A sound,' and find yourself playing your larger amp with the Yellow Jackets or other converters installed all the time, I'd argue that you probably ought to sell the thing and get the amp that's designed from the ground up to do what you're looking for. The general principle of good, solid tone is to travel the simplest and most direct road that gets you there. On the other hand, if you love the sound you get with converters in place and wouldn't want to change it one jot, that's fine; or if you can only afford one amp, but have the need of cranked-up sounds at very different volume levels and with different output tube signatures, that can work, too. Either way, tube converters can be a lot of fun.

Volume-Reducing Speakers

As I will discuss in greater detail in the next chapter, I have always favored moving to less-efficient but great sounding speakers in order to reduce the overall volume of an amp for use in smaller clubs. Now, a new speaker design that allows the player to manually determine, and instantly adjust, its efficiency makes this procedure effortless. A piece of patent-applied-for technology from Eminence called the 'Flux Density Modulation' speaker (FDM for short) is a simple yet ingenious design. While my aim in this book is to avoid anything that might be perceived as a direct product plug, the FDM speakers really are, to my knowledge, the only such product available at the time of writing, and are, I believe, worthy of consideration while the topic of reducing output is under discussion. The FDM comes in the form of two types of standard 12-inch guitar speakers—a US-style Maverick and a British-style ReignMaker—with what look to be, and indeed are, big industrial plastic dials mounted on the back of their magnet structures. The dial allows the player to adjust the precise relationship between the voice coil and the magnet, and thus alter the efficiency of the speaker itself, without using any external circuitry or intervening attenuation. Turned fully clockwise, either speaker offers its maximum sensitivity of 100dB (as measured at one meter, with an input signal of a single watt, or '1W/1M'); fully counter-clockwise it's an inefficient 91dB.

The perceived change in volume between the two is dramatic, and brings a 40-watt, dual-6L6 combo down to the level of a dual-6V6 Fender Princeton or similar. As such, it's a potential game-changer for many players, making larger amps entirely viable in smaller clubs and studios. No mere gimmick, this is actually a rather elegant technological solution which simply takes advantage of the physical factors that have made different speaker types more or less efficient since the inception of tube amplification, and is no more of a strain on your amp than playing through any standard speaker. Reducing efficiency does alter the overall tone slightly, giving you a little more warmth and compression as you wind down, but these are often characteristics of less efficient speakers. To my ears, they are perfectly decent-sounding speakers to begin with, even when approached as standard drivers with their output levels set to maximum.

Isolation Cabinets

The isolation box provides another moderately popular solution to issues of excessive volume. These units are akin to shrunken studio vocal booths: a crate of the minimum size necessary, rendered as close to soundproof as possible, and loaded with a speaker and a microphone. Connect amp to speaker and crank up to whatever levels said speaker will handle, and the microphone inside the box picks up everything, while noise levels outside it are reduced to a whisper. Sounds simple, and in many ways it is. Commercial examples exist, or you can build your own with readily available and fairly obvious materials.

Isolation boxes don't offer much of a solution for practicing (unless you mic them into a

mixer and play in the headphones, which seems a pretty convoluted way around it), but they can provide a great recording tool in some situations. If you really need to record your amp, cranked up high, unattenuated, and miked-up through a roaring speaker, this is one way to do it. Of course, that roaring speaker is unlikely to be the same one mounted in the cab the amp usually plays through, and these rigs offer several other additional drawbacks. They can be both boomy and over-compressed, because there is rarely enough air around the speaker to let the sound really breathe; they are difficult to either plan out or to acoustically tune, until you have built one, tested it, and perhaps discarded it for a larger or smaller box which itself will be just another trial-and-error effort; and they make everything sound much like a closed-back cab, so a classic Fender or Vox combo sound, for example, is difficult to achieve.

They do, however, generally present high-saturation overdrive or over-the-top grungy amp filth pretty well, and usually work fine for hot rock leads or chunky, bottom-heavy rock power-chord rhythm parts. Another advantage of the isolation cab is that, in addition to keeping all the noise inside, they keep unwanted external noises out. In other words, while not bothering the neighbors, you can also record without them bothering you, or at least your mic—the same thing applies to intrusive street noise, screaming children, ringing telephones, and so forth. Because you are not attenuating output level, merely containing it, you need a tough mic inside the box; so this volume-squelching solution doesn't allow the use of sensitive ribbon or condenser recording mics the way small amps or attenuators do. You also need a very high-powered but guitar-voiced eight or ten-inch speaker (not something much in demand design-wise, although a few of the latter exist), unless you can build a box big enough to hold a 12-inch speaker and its internal baffle (some do exist). The bigger the speaker, however, the more air space you need around it for even a semi-natural sound. As simple as it is, the isolation cab is a tough item to get sounding perfect, but perhaps perfection isn't absolutely necessary. A rough-shod DIY job is usually good enough for rock'n'roll, and will soon have you laying down some wailing, cranked tube amp sounds on your formerly anemic tracks.

Demeter has offered an isolation box for many years, the SSC-1 Silent Speaker Chamber, as has Randall in the form of its unambiguously-named Isolation Cab. Newcomer AxeTrak provides the most compact version of the breed that I have encountered, and it comes loaded with both speaker and microphone. Players have made their own versions over the years by using either temporary solutions, like locking a cab in a closet full of blankets, pillows, and other padding, or in a large flight case, or by building their own containers. Avoid putting an entire combo in an enclosed space, however, as this is an easy way to quickly overheat and burn out your output tubes.

Since like-rated speakers in a parallel set-up divide an amp's power output in half between them, you can also use the box as a load for all sorts of applications. You can also employ it as a 'semi attenuator'—to drop the wattage reaching a particular standard speaker cab or combo speaker by half, for either recording or live use, place it in parallel with an isolation cabinet carrying a speaker with the same impedance rating. Mic up the 'open' cab, which can now be cranked a little higher, and you'll find you've taken a little of the excessive volume off the overall level. A little creative thinking should reveal other useful applications for the isolation cab.

In addition to bringing big-amp volume down to small gig and studio levels, all of the avenues to quieter cranked sounds have another major benefit: your hearing is precious, and the less aggressively you assault it, the longer you'll have it. Plenty of great volume-reducing solutions exist, many of which retain all or at least an appreciable portion of an amp's original voice and distortion characteristics, and as such these products and techniques render sheer volume a purely quantitative phenomenon. When the quality of your tone is preserved—but at lower volume levels—you will most likely be a happier player in the long run, and, hopefully, one who can hear the playback, too.

C H A P T E R   2

CHAPTER 3
SPEAKERS AND CABINETS

- Vintage (low-powered) speakers
- Modern (high-powered) speakers
- Speaker distortion
- Magnet types
- Speaker cabinets

For many years, the majority of guitarists gave little consideration to the speakers that came with their amps from the factory. They played through them for the life of any given amp, thought little about how the components affected their tone, and only replaced them if there was a functional problem. In recent years, however, plenty of guitarists have come to the realization that their speakers, and equally importantly the cabinet those speakers are mounted in, play an enormous part in shaping their overall sound.

Of all the inaudible electric-current-producing and shaping gizmos that lie between guitar string and amp output jack, the speaker is the first constituent that actually puts your tone back into the air—the first element that makes it *sound* again. It is the speaker which carries your tone to the human ear, and that is what really matters.

Guitarists strive for that illusive 'ultimate tone' by making pickup swaps, changing bridges and hardware, upgrading nuts, tuners, and more. But one of the biggest sonic alterations achievable, short of getting an entirely new guitar or amp, can be accomplished by changing out your speaker(s). It's usually even simpler than changing a pickup, costs approximately the same, and, arguably, has a more immediate impact on your overall sound, yet the simple speaker swap is overlooked by countless players. Many struggle to perk up an inadequate tone by trying new pickups, different strings, and innumerable effects pedals while completely neglecting what may simply be a worn-out speaker; unbolting that tired driver and slapping in something that has some teeth will often provide an instant fix.

Swapping to a more desirable speaker, or replacing a faulty one, is not always simply a matter of installing a 'better' unit, however, so knowing a little about the general characteristics of different speaker types can prove invaluable in your quest for improved tone. Obviously, speakers vary enormously in size and power-handling capabilities, but also in resonant character, construction, make-up of cone and magnet, efficiency (that is, loudness relative to power input, also referred to as 'sensitivity'), and so on. In order to work toward some understanding of what's available, let's divide the different speaker types into more easily digestible genres and then see what each has to offer. In this postmodern age, it isn't entirely fair to rigidly categorize all components in the field—many contemporary manufacturers make speakers that blend a range of characteristics—but this is still the easiest way to get a handle on the subject. For our purposes, let's split drivers into two fairly broad categories: 'vintage' and 'modern'—each of which is subject to two subdivisions: 'US' and 'British.'

VINTAGE (LOW-POWERED) SPEAKERS

In the 40s, 50s, and early 60s, guitar amps rarely carried speakers rated higher than 15 to 30 watts (although we'll look at a few exceptions below). Indeed, earlier guitar amps rarely put out more than the higher figure until the arrival of the 'high-powered' 80-watt Fender Twin of the late 50s, and a few others. These speakers were just fine when used singly in small venues or recording studios, or in multi-driver cabs at dance hall volumes. Push them hard, however, and they started to break up, adding a degree of speaker distortion to the amp's own distortion when

pressed anywhere close the peak of their operating capacity. As rock music boomed, and guitarists found themselves performing in increasingly large venues requiring increased 'clean' volume levels, amp makers sought out more robust speaker designs to facilitate them. Those that they found, however, were generally more expensive than the lower-rated drivers, so they weren't universally employed. And that's probably a good thing. A lot of players who weren't seeking absolute 'clean-clean' tone enjoyed the added grit, bite, edge, and compression that a touch of speaker distortion adds to the sonic brew. Lower-powered speakers, therefore, with all their inherent 'flaws,' became a big part of the rock'n'roll and blues sound, and have retained this role for more than 50 years.

In the USA, Jensen was the big name in (low-powered) speakers in the 50s and early 60s, and their drivers retain their reputation as the hottest vintage American make. Jensen's P10R and P12R (15-watts output, 10 and 12 inch respectively), P10Q and P12Q (20 watts), P12N (30 watts), and a few others, played a big part in the signature sounds of great, US-made 50s amps from Fender, Gibson, Ampeg, Magnatone, Premier, Silvertone, and others. Their respective ceramic-magnet descendants (with similar designations—a 'C' prefix replacing the 'P') were likewise the voice of many 60s classics. Each of these models has some distinctive characteristics, but they are broadly characterized by bell-like highs, somewhat boxy but rather open, transparent mids, and juicy, saturated lows (to the point of flapping, farting, and general freaking in the lower-rated units when pushed too hard). Whatever adjectives we apply to them, these performance properties combine to yield sweet, tactile, 'clean' sounds when driven a little, and gorgeous, rich, chewy overdrive when driven that little bit more.

Depending on availability, many of the same amp manufacturers also used speakers from makers such as Utah, Oxford, CTS, and others, which usually shared some of the vintage Jensen properties, but are not generally as revered. The original Jensen Loudspeakers company ceased trading long ago, but Recoton of Italy manufactures a vintage range based on the most popular Alnico and ceramic models of the 50s and 60s. These capture at least some of the originals' tonal characteristics, although not all the materials used are precise matches for those in the old units. Major US manufacturer Eminence—a development of the CTS speaker company—also makes a number of vintage, American-voiced drivers (broadly defined by the snappy lows and crisp highs of many Jensen speakers of the 50s and 60s), including the popular, long-running Legend series, and the newer Patriot range. The smaller Indiana-based manufacturer Weber Speakers offers a range of highly regarded vintage-style units, many of which are based on Jensens from the company's Chicago era (1950–65).

Across the pond, Elac, Goodmans, and Celestion were manufacturing speakers in the 50s that had broadly similar characteristics to their American cousins. Using pulp paper cones and Alnico ring magnets to achieve power handling conservatively rated in the 12–20-watt ballpark, the most common were Goodmans' Audiom 60 and, more famously, the Vox Blue—a Celestion G12 relabeled by the amp manufacturer. The Celestion, which is still available today in an excellent reissue known as the Alnico Blue, is famous for its sweet, rich, musical mids and its appealing highs, coupled with a slightly rounded low-end response, and plenty of aggression when it's pushed.

The 'Blue' has always been a highly efficient speaker, too, which is to say it translates a relatively high proportion of the wattage pumped into it into volume. The G12 has a sensitivity rating of 100dB (measured at a single watt from a distance of one meter), compared to figures of 90dB to around 97dB for similar styled, vintage Jensen speakers. Such sensitivity means, for example, that a pair in a 2x12 Vox AC30 can produce a lot of noise from that 35-watt tube amp, even making it sound as loud as a 60 or even 100-watt amp with less efficient speakers. Higher efficiency might sound like a universally good thing, and for some players it is, but remember that louder isn't always better, and in some circumstances you might want to tame a little volume in the name of dynamics and easy breakup—but more of that later.

In the mid 60s, Celestion evolved its cornerstone guitar driver into the ceramic-magnet G12M 'Greenback' (rated 20 to 25 watts). Typically found in multiples of four inside closed-back Marshall cabs, this speaker set an early standard for the rock guitar 'amp stack' sound. The Greenback is warm, gritty, and edgy, with a bottom end that isn't particularly firm, but which can still pack plenty of oomph when doing its thing in fours or eights in a closed-back cab (or cabs). This speaker, as much as any amplifier, typifies the 'Brit-rock sound' sought by so many classic-rock and blues-rock players. In the late 60s, the slightly higher-rated G12H-30 took on a heavier magnet and a slightly more efficient design to offer a bigger low end and a little more volume and punch. Today, Celestion produces variations of the Greenback and G12H-30, one each in the British-made Heritage Series and Chinese-made Classic range. Eminence covers both sides of the Atlantic by also offering a wide range of Brit-voiced drivers in its Red Coat line, and California maker Tone Tubby pays homage to the original Alnico G12 with its hemp-coned speakers. Similarly, Weber Speakers offers many units based on the most popular classic Celestion models, and Austin Speaker Works has made inroads with several highly regarded variations on these themes.

MODERN (HIGH-POWERED) SPEAKERS

As already mentioned, the quest for increased onstage volume had amp manufacturers developing speakers that could handle the escalated power. Increasing a driver's power-handling capabilities usually brings other performance changes along with it, however, so we can broadly characterize 'modern' speakers as those that are not only able to take more of a beating but which also exhibit a tighter, clearer voice, usually accompanied by firmer lows than those offered by the typical vintage speaker.

The first such driver to be widely used by a major amp manufacturer came into play a lot earlier than might be imagined. In developing the loud Showman amps of the early 60s for surf guitar sensation Dick Dale, and the unusual ported and closed-backed speaker cabinets that accompanied them, Fender sought a sturdy, efficient driver, and came up with the JBL D120F and D130F (12 and 15-inch speakers, respectively). Based on the JBL D120 and D130 models used in the hi-fi audio industry—the 'F' added to denote Fender OEM units—these speakers had enormous Alnico magnets, sturdy cast-metal frames, large voice coils, and, as a result, power-handling capabilities like practically nothing else available in the world of early-60s guitar amplification. Fender succeeded in making the Showman a hellaciously loud amp, and the later

addition of JBLs to Twin Reverb combos also helped to make these iconic amps both unfathomably loud and excruciatingly heavy. The JBL's classic voice, defined by firm lows, a rounded midrange with an edge of bark and a slightly nasal honk, and ringing, occasionally piercing highs, meant that this was a speaker to use when you needed to play loud and really cut through.

Two other makers of advanced, modern-style US speakers, Electro-Voice (EV) and Altec, started appearing in guitar amps in the 60s. Early examples employed big Alnico magnets, although EV's most famous guitar driver, the EVM-12L, was a ceramic-magnet speaker that came to fame in many Mesa/Boogie and other big rock amps of the 80s. Rated at 200 watts, and still available today, it is famed for its ability to stand up to incredible punishment and keep pumping out pristine clean tones and rich, detailed overdrive (a Zakk Wylde signature Black Label EVM-12L is actually rated at an awesome 300 watts). Altec's most popular rock speaker was the 417-8H. No longer available, these were also optional equipment in Mesa/Boogie amps and a key ingredient in the mid-period Santana tone, as well as being favored by the likes of Randy Rhoads and other big stadium-rock wailers. These 100-watt drivers are known for their powerful, full-throated clean tones, able to translate cranked-amp overdrive tones while adding a minimum of speaker distortion to the brew.

Many big names in vintage speakers survived to produce designs that fit more easily into the modern category. Celestion, for example, also offers the G12T-75, G12H-100, and Classic Lead 80—all of which are popular—among others; all powerful rock drivers with big voices and serious power-handling capabilities. Several other speaker makers blur the lines between vintage and modern. Eminence carries robust speakers in its Legend, Patriot, and Red Coat ranges, which boast impressive power-handling specs but achieve tones that fall more into the vintage-voicing camp—namely the Legend V128 (120 watts), Swamp Thang (150 watts), and Man O War (120 watts). Even a couple of Celestion's most popular speakers of the past couple of decades, the G12-65 and the Vintage 30, could be classified as somewhat vintage-sounding drivers in more robust packages capable of handling 65 and 60 watts respectively. Similarly, the recently introduced Celestion Alnico Gold seeks to capture the tone of the 15-watt Alnico Blue in a sturdier 50-watt speaker. Another British manufacturer, the oft-overlooked Fane (whose speakers powered many a Hiwatt and WEM amp in the late 60s and 70s), still manufactures an Alnico speaker, the AXA12, that looks for all the world like a vintage driver but handles a whopping 100 watts.

SPEAKER DISTORTION

By this we generally mean a form of distortion—distinct from amplifier distortion—that is generated when a driver is pushed near to its operating limits. At these levels, the voice coil and paper cone begin failing to translate the electrical signal cleanly, and as a result produce a somewhat (sometimes severely) distorted performance. Put simply, the voice coil begins to saturate, the paper cone begins to flap and vibrate beyond its capacity, the magnet's performance compresses, and the entire electro-mechanical network that makes up a speaker conspires to bring its own measure of fuzz to the tonal picture. The concept of such distortion is sometimes confusing, because it often occurs in addition to any distortion that the amplifier unit is already producing. The distortion produced by a high-gain preamp stage, or a floored output stage, can occasionally be heard on its own, however, when an amp is played through firm, high-powered speakers that refuse to distort (or distort very little) even under high-output conditions. In most cases, however, when an amp is raging you're hearing a little of both.

ALNICO VERSUS CERAMIC, AND NEO MAGNETS

Alnico magnets enjoy a certain reputation in the speaker world, as they do in the world of guitar pickups, and are considered by many to be the most 'musical' of their ilk, revered for their sweetness and dynamics. Alnico is an alloy of aluminum, nickel, and cobalt (blended with a quantity of iron). Thanks to the relative scarcity and expense of cobalt, it's a costly alternative to the ceramic magnets that are also employed in speaker manufacturing, and was all but dropped from use in the 70s and 80s. While this description of Alnico implies superiority, be aware that several classic speakers, even many vintage models and those that remain the drivers of choice of countless major players and tonehounds, employ ceramic magnets. Celestion's G12M Greenback and G12H-30 are both ceramic speakers, as are several great units from Eminence and plenty of revered, early-to-mid-60s Jensens. Magnet material can have an effect on tone, but other elements of the speaker's design and construction play an equal (occasionally greater) role, so it would be shortsighted if you were to make your decisions based on magnet preference alone.

Neodymium magnets have also made considerable inroads in the speaker market. A 'rare earth' magnet, neodymium is expensive but very powerful, so relatively little is needed to create the magnetic strength (gauss) required to drive a speaker. Some of the first guitar speakers using neodymium magnets arguably sounded a little hard and brittle, and were perhaps simply too efficient for the best tonal results. Over the past few years, however, Eminence, Celestion, Jensen (as reissued by Recoton), Weber, and others have learned to work very well with this powerful material to make great-sounding speakers. And, whatever the magnet's innate sonic properties, many players are happy to welcome 'neos' as viable guitar drivers because of the considerable lessening in weight that such speakers bring to their load.

WHEN LESS IS MORE

You will hear a lot about how you to make an amp louder, and how to render a small amp gig-worthy where it just couldn't cut it before, simply by swapping an inefficient speaker for a more sensitive one. That's certainly true: changing a speaker with a 95dB rating for one with a 100dB rating can sound like you're suddenly using a much more powerful amp. Sometimes, however, you want to go the other way—so let's also consider the issue from that perspective.

These days, there's a greater consciousness of onstage amp volume than ever before, and a general move toward maintaining great tone at moderate volume levels. With this in mind, let's consider the fact that, as well as using a more efficient speaker to make a small amp louder, you can use a less efficient speaker to make a great but too-loud amp quieter, and therefore better, since that decrease in volume will let you hit the amp's sweet spot more easily. In essence, you

make your speaker choice work something like an attenuator. Mark Sampson, of Star Amplifiers (and formerly of Matchless), puts it succinctly: "Speakers always sound best when they're pushed, so if you can push the speaker and cut the dB level at the same time, you end up with a better tone at a lower volume." The less efficient the speaker, the more you are able to push it with an amp, in circumstances when the ultra-efficient speaker might have you backing off your volume levels to avoid punching the audience in the face.

Of course, you still want good, all-round tone, and choosing a speaker according to its sensitivity rating can limit you somewhat in that respect. Swapping in a new speaker is always a little bit of a crap-shoot anyway, if you don't have the privilege of trying it with your own amp before buying it; but by reading the reviews, checking out the speakers your guitar-playing pals and bandmates are using, and always keeping an eye out for well-regarded speaker makes that carry slightly lower specs for efficiency, you can at least narrow down your selection.

Many vintage Jensen speakers typically have lower sensitivity ratings, and some of the new ones in the Italian-made Jensen Vintage Reissue series, or similar models from makers such as Weber, follow suit in this regard. The reissue Alnico P12R and P12Q are both rated at 95dB, which is fairly inefficient by today's standards. Their ceramic counterparts, the C12R and C12Q, are even lower, at 93.8dB and 94.6dB respectively (consider these against the 98.4dB-rating of the P12N and C12N). Also, the new Jensen Jet Tornado neodymium-magnet speaker has a good all-purpose tone with plenty of warmth and roundness, and rates at 97.3dB, while handling 100 watts of power.

Celestion is perhaps best known for two great-sounding, classic, high-efficiency speakers: the Alnico Blue and G12H-30, both rated at 100dB, and if you like that tone you might just have to make do with a loud amp. Nonetheless, the British company does produce a range of great, if different, sounding drivers with lower ratings. The legendary G12M Greenback comes in at 98dB in the Chinese-made Classic Series and a mellower (and more authentic) 96dB in the English-made Heritage Series. It's a fantastic rock lead and rhythm speaker and an undeniable classic, although it doesn't have the firm lows or snappy high-end twang that some players also look for in a guitar driver—and it handles only a relatively meager 25 watts. The Heritage G12-65, however, offers much of the Greenback's sweet midrange grind, but has a fuller bass response, clear, sweet highs, and handles 65 watts with an efficiency rating of 97dB (original examples from the early 80s are also often readily available on the used market, frequently the result of players breaking up the 4x12 cabs they came in).

Many of Eminence's speakers have extremely high sensitivity ratings, but—unless it's just my ears failing—I find that a lot of them don't sound quite as loud as their three-figure ratings might imply, although they are usually aiming for higher sensitivity specs than the speakers I have focused on so far. Their Red Fang Alnico speaker is rated at a whopping 103dB, for example, but it sounded no louder than other 98–100dB speakers I tested it against; so something like their 98.8dB Legend 1218 or 99dB Texas Heat might not be quite as blasting as you would expect. Also, Eminence now offers the ReignMaker and Maverick models that feature their new 'Flux Density Modulation' technology, as discussed in the previous chapter, which allow the player to dial in an efficiency setting from 91dB to 100dB.

C H A P T E R   3

Dr Z's 'Speaker in a Box' Trick

While I was writing *The Guitar Amp Handbook*, I spoke with Mike Zaite of Dr Z Amps, and he passed on a great tip which is worth reiterating here. What Zaite suggests is a fantastic way to perk up the sound of your amp by 'reconditioning' its speakers—or, more accurately, 'reacclimatizing' them—without doing a thing other than giving them a short vacation from the dampness, moisture, and humidity of your current environment. Here's what the doctor has to say. "Speaker cones are weighted and measured in grams. It doesn't take a whole lot of weight difference to really throw a cone off from sounding the way it should sound. Now, when you store an amp, the worst thing you can do is put it in a damp basement or in a situation where it's going to be able to wick up moisture. It's amazing how a speaker can do that, and now all of a sudden you have a dull, dud-sounding speaker, because it doesn't take much water to throw it off … just a few drops can really change the response and characteristic of a speaker. So, what I do when I store speakers is get the little silica bags that come with electronics components, throw one of those in the box, close it up, and put that speaker away for a little while to let that silica soak up all the moisture of the cone. You'll be amazed how wonderful that speaker sounds after the moisture's been taken out. It's nice and dry and reedy sounding, and now you've got a cone that responds the way it was supposed to, with this earthy tone to it that's just unbelievable. People use hot guns, they do this, they do that, and boy, you just never really get them right. But just put a couple of those little silica bags in and leave it be … it's such a natural way of wicking the water out and drying the cone out nicely, without overheating the surround."

Zaite adds that this isn't just a good way to store speakers you aren't using: it's also a great fix for any dull-sounding amp—especially one that you know has been stored in potentially moist conditions, or one you have just acquired. Carefully remove the speakers and box them up with some silica bags for a week or so as per his instructions; the chances are the newly dehydrated speakers will bring the whole amp to life.

Ultimately, of course, tonal consideration should still be the key criterion when it comes to selecting your speaker. If the driver sounds right and also drops your output just a little, allowing you to play right in the sweet spot without attracting the ire of half-deafened bandmates or sound engineers, that's surely a double bonus. If you are trying to tame a too-harsh amp for use in smaller clubs on a regular basis, a less efficient speaker (or speakers) can be a simple, efficient way to go about it. Or, if you can maintain a couple of different speaker cabs to use with one amp head—one 1x12 with a G12-65, for example, and a 2x12 with a mixed pair of G12H-30 and Alnico Blue—you could find the exact same amplifier fitting the bill perfectly in both 60 and 150 capacity venues.

CHOICES, CHOICES

Selecting the speaker to best meet your tonal requirements, as upgrade or replacement, is a sort of soul-searching process, one in which you navigate between all the characteristics described

C H A P T E R 3

above, considering them in the light of power-handling requirements and desired sensitivity/efficiency. Remember, too, that you can summon some distinctive and outstanding sounds by employing unlikely speaker choices in unexpected places; so don't let the US/British categories discussed here imply any rigid rules. I have heard great results with a Brit-voiced Eminence Red Fang in a vintage, tweed-style US amp, and an American-voiced Weber 12A125 in a British class A-type amp. And if you are trying to record the perfect 50-watt 'plexi' tone without blowing down the studio walls—or your ribbon mic's element—that old brownface Fender Princeton pumped through the dusty Greenback-loaded 4x12 in the corner might be just the ticket. Experiment as much as time, budget, and your local guitar store allow; take tips from friends' rigs and those of name players whose tone you admire; and, as ever, discover what works for you.

SPEAKER CABINETS

If relatively few players give much thought to their speakers, you can bet fewer still meditate on ephemeral matters such as speaker-cabinet design, materials, and construction. This is an enormous variable in your painstakingly conceived tone, however, and definitely deserves some thought. Try this if you ever get the chance: keep your amp settings at peak output and plug that setup first into an open-back 2x12 cab made from finger-jointed solid pine with a 'floating' baffle, then afterward into a closed-back, 2x12 made from 11-ply Baltic birch with a fixed baffle—both, ideally, with exactly the same speakers. They will sound remarkably different.

The speaker cabinet makes an enormous contribution to the very last link in the sound chain, and is responsible for shaping those sound waves that the speakers themselves finally put back into the air. Every subtle difference in the way two cabs are made will make them sonically distinct. I have a great little brown 1962 Fender Princeton, for example, equipped with a replacement baffle to hold a 12-inch speaker instead of its original 10-inch, making it more suitable for small club gigs. It sounds great as it is, but plugging it into a slightly larger 1x12 extension cab made from the same solid pine, with a similarly made and mounted baffle, and carrying the same speaker (a vintage Celestion G12-65 in both cases) makes a big difference. In short, it sounds like a whole new amp: through the extension cab its sound is rounder, fuller, more transparent, and has more breadth and depth. By comparison, switching back to the original combo cab makes the amp sound a little boxy and constricted. It's the same amp, the same speakers, with just a different size and shape of cab—and the difference is startling.

Aside, of course, from the speakers that you mount in them, other major variables include the size and particularly the depth of the cabinet, the type of wood used to build it, the way that wood is fixed together, the type and thickness of the baffle (the sheet of wood to which the speaker is mounted), and the way this baffle is mounted to the cab. One of the biggest variables depends on whether or not you close off the entire back of the cab or leave it open. As ever, it isn't a matter of one approach being empirically better than the other, but of obtaining the results that best suit your playing style.

To examine the open-back cabinet let's consider Fender's classic tweed and blackface guitar combos (correctly speaking, most of these are actually only partially open-backed, since upper and lower panels still enclose between a quarter and three-quarters of the rear side). The most noticeable sonic characteristic of such cabinets is their 'surround-sound' projection, which, while pumping the greatest volume out front, also disperses sound from the open back of the amplifier and, to a lesser degree, from the sides, too. This can be a virtue on club stages where your band uses just a vocal PA and there are no mics on the guitar cabs, because it helps your drummer and the other musicians on stage hear what you're doing. An open-backed cabinet also provides interesting miking opportunities in the studio: a mic aimed at the back of the cab captures a tone that is slightly more raw and more ragged than it would be if it were directed toward the front.

Sonically, the open-backed cab presents a broad, transparent soundstage that might be considered more 'realistic' than many closed-back cabs. High frequencies are shimmering and multi-dimensional, and the midrange avoids being over-aggressive, while lows generally pack a little less 'oomph' than with the close-backed cab. When the sound emanating from the front of the cab, created by the speaker pumping forward, blends with that from the rear (the speaker pumping backward), a degree of out-of-phase frequency cancellation occurs—this softens up the low frequencies in particular. As a double-whammy, backless speaker cabs make the speakers work harder to produce the low notes, because they remove the supportive cushion of standing air that is present in the closed-back cab. The open back also helps to open up the highs and make them feel airier. Thus, if you want to achieve thundering lows, you'll get there quicker with a closed-back cab.

Aside from emphasizing the lows by keeping those out-of-phase sound waves inside the box, closed-back speaker cabs offer one other advantage. While they lack some of the transparency and wide sound-dispersal of the open-backed cabinet, they score by emphasizing a muscular midrange and a real kick-in-the-gut low end, with, of course, superb directionality, and this makes them extremely punchy out front (and relatively quiet in back, a boon to some sound support situations).

Most of you are probably already picturing a Marshall 4x12 cab, a classic of the closed-backed genre. When Marshall arrived on the scene in 1962, Fender had already been using closed-back cabs, in the shape of its 'Professional Series' piggyback amps, for more than a year, and Vox had begun using closed-backed cabs with the AC30 Super Twin in July 1961, but Jim Marshall created the most emulated template for the breed when he crammed an unprecedented *four* Celestion G12 speakers into one chunky cabinet. The box that became the model 1960 speaker cabinet (that's its designated number, *not* its year of birth) was devised simply as the most logical container for the array of Celestion G12 speakers required to handle the JTM45's power. These speakers were rated at just 15 watts originally, and were prone to flapping out on low notes when hit hard. Putting four together gave them a fighting chance of handling the amp's power surges, and enclosing the cab's back created natural damping—a sort of air-pressure suspension—helping to support them by limiting extreme cone travel. As an interesting side note, and further proof of a speaker cab's contribution to any amp's overall sound, consider the fact that a late-50s Fender Bassman and an early-60s Marshall JTM45 share almost identical circuitry—and, initially, Marshall even used the same 5881 output tubes. These amps sound

quite different in large part because one is an open-back 4x10 combo with a lightly mounted 'floating' baffle, while the other uses a closed-back 4x12 cab with a rigidly mounted baffle. By the same token, an open-back 2x12 Bluesbreaker, which is the combo version of the JTM45, and a tweed Fender 'low-powered' Twin—both of which put out around 45 watts—sound astoundingly alike.

The majority of closed-back cabs manufactured today still follow Marshall's example to some extent, although there are many different approaches to the format. Some makers also seek to achieve a low-end response that approximates that of a closed-backed cab by making their open-backed units deeper than the average. A cab's size influences its tone, too, with larger boxes allowing more room for bass notes to develop (make it too big, however, and you risk creating boomy, overbearing lows). One way to increase lows and maintain relatively compact overall dimensions is to extend the depth of the cabinet: boutique maker TopHat, for example, extended the depth of its 1x12 Club Royale combo from 9.25 inches (235mm) to 11 inches (279mm) a few years back, and as a result these ripping little amps have offered a much bigger bottom ever since, even in their open-backed cabs.

Although we generally think of the 'ported' cab as a thing of the hi-fi world, and sometimes an ingredient in bass cabs, some guitar amp manufacturers also use porting to help tune a cabinet's response. A ported cab contains some form of opening (sometimes called a 'vent') other than that into which the speaker itself is mounted, which lets a portion of the sound waves produced by the back of the speaker cone exit the cabinet. Rather than the random blending of the open-back cab, the port's design is calculated to fine-tune the overall sound without severely squelching the cab's low-end response. This is usually achieved by feeding a determined amount of reverse-phase sound back into the overall sonic picture at a slight delay to that which is coming from the front of the cab, either by letting it pump out through a relatively small hole in the otherwise closed-off back panel, or by sending it through a tube or internal reflection baffle that carries it through an opening in the cab's front speaker baffle. Fender used these principles in its early-60s Showman, which used elaborate, ported double-baffles to help maximize the performance of its 12 and 15-inch JBL speakers. A number of contemporary makers do something similar. Dr Z, for example, uses a sturdy double-baffle system in some of its punchy Z Best cabinets whose effect is described in terms of 'lens technology' by maker Mike Zaite. "If you think of the idea of a front-loaded horn, you've got a driver and then you've got a distance through that horn that makes for a specific projection of sound," he explains. "That lens focuses the sound and allows it to project a little bit further before it disperses. Fender would use a 15 inch and add a Tone Ring to it, and boy, the speaker would sound like an 18-inch, then. So basically, that's what I do. I take my 10-inch, and use a lens baffle over the baffle [a second baffle to increase the overall thickness of the structure], and I basically add about an inch and a half to each; they kind of sound like 12-inch speakers."

Of course, classic open-backed and closed-back cabs often sound different for reasons other than what's happening on their blind sides. For illustration, let's take the early Fender and Gibson cabs on one hand and early Marshall and Vox cabs on the other. The cabinets in 50s tweed and 60s blackface Fender amps were made from glued, finger-jointed, solid-wood boards, usually yellow pine, red cedar, or a similarly sturdy softwood. The timber generally contributes a warm, round, slightly soft resonance to the sound of the speaker itself, and while the exact effect can be somewhat unpredictable, it *can* become a major constituent of an amp's voice. 50s Fenders had thin, 'floating' plywood baffles mounted in their cabs—baffles that were bolted in at their four corners only (with extra bolts center top and center bottom in the larger amps) rather than firmly across all four sides. When these amps are cranked up, the floating baffle vibrates considerably and contributes its own resonance to the resultant tone.

An expert at high-end tweed amp reproductions, Mark Baier, of the Victoria Amp Company, recognizes the contribution that cabs make to the 'tweed mystique.' "I'm not going to say it's an inferior cabinet," says Baier, "but when you take a look at the tweed cabinet construction next to a blackface cabinet, it's pretty obvious that the blackface is a little stouter and a little sturdier. That makes a difference, sonically, as well—so the relative 'looseness' of the tweed cabinet is responsible in part for the amp's sound. It acts as a passive radiator of sound in some ways: it vibrates a lot more."

Using quality plywood and more rigid construction techniques, which often include a fully secured baffle, creates a more braced structure in which the wood itself contributes less resonance. Don't equate this with the acoustic flat-top guitar model, however, in which a resonant solid spruce or cedar top is preferable to the stiffer laminated top; numerous top-notch boutique makers use plywood cabs these days (usually made from high-grade 11-ply Baltic birch or similar) in order to produce consistent and predicable results in a punchy, powerful speaker cabinet. The more rigid box allows the speaker to project its sound a little more immediately, and to retain its own character while doing so, and is often the choice of amp makers who favor muscle, articulation, and a quick response over a compressed and somewhat velvety vintage tone. Plywood construction was the Marshall and Vox standard, although modern makers often update the format with deeper cabs and, in some cases, thicker woods. Decent 'firm-sounding' cabs have even been constructed from MDF and particle board, although these are usually considered low-budget options.

The numbers of speakers loaded into any of the above cabinet designs will also affect the resulting tone. The purest, simplest format is, of course, the single-speaker cab, in which the lone driver presents no interference with its own tonal character. No two speakers of even the exact same make and size sound *exactly* the same (these are, after all, electromechanical components with multiple moving parts and numerous inherent variables), and putting two or four speakers into the same cab will introduce a degree of phase-cancellation that affects the sound the cab produces as a whole. Multi-driver cabs remain very popular, so this effect is clearly not perceived as a negative by many players, but it is a factor to be aware of. Some makers even emphasize this effect by mixing and matching entirely different speakers in the same cab. For years, Matchless used slightly modified versions of the Celestion G12M Greenback and G12H-30 in their DC30 cab. Mojave, 65amps, and TopHat are all enamored of the G12H-30 and Celestion Alnico Blue pairing in their 2x12 cabs. When mixing speakers in this way, however, amp designers put in a lot of thought and testing to find pairings that complement each other, rather than conflict. Celestion's famed Alnico Blue has gorgeous sweet mids and highs, for example, but a rather soft low end, which the G12H-30 fills in perfectly. In more extreme cases, even two speakers of different sizes can sometimes work well together—a firm 12 inch and a more vintage-sounding 10-inch, for example. The wrong mismatch, however, could create a sonic blur far worse than the sound of even two identical but mediocre speakers paired together. The slight out-of-phase quality presented by cabs with two or four identical speakers often works to improve a cab's overall performance by smoothing out any harshness or 'flabbiness' that the same speakers present individually (Celestion Greenbacks are shunned by some makers in open-backed 1x12 cabs, for example, but can sound incredibly good in a closed-back 2x12 or 4x12).

As often as not, of course, amp manufacturers use multiple speakers simply to help the cab handle more power. The speakers in a cabinet divide the amp's output power between them equally, so two speakers that can only handle 30 watts individually are together enough to blast the full fury of a cranked 40-watt amp, while four can handle a 100-watt half stack. The ways in which multiple speakers are wired together also influences a range of factors in their performance. Many players will be aware that wiring two speakers in parallel yields a total impedance half that of each of the individual speakers, and four in parallel results in a load a quarter that of each speaker (thus, two 8-ohms speakers equal 4 ohms and four 8-ohms speakers equal 2 ohms), while wiring two in series yields a load double that of each individual speaker (two 8-ohms speakers equal 16 ohms).

Fewer players are aware of the fact that these different wiring schemes contribute to different-sounding cabs, too. Wired in parallel, speakers in a pair or quartet will dampen and restrain each other somewhat, yielding a slightly tighter response and a smoother breakup. Multiple speakers wired in series (usually no more than two) run a little looser, giving a slightly rawer, open, edgy sound. Some cabs with four speakers often feature pairs of speakers wired together in series, the two pairs then wired in parallel to achieve a total load that is equal to that of each individual speaker. This also yields a smooth and open performance.

There is, needless to say, no 'best approach,' and what works for you depends on what you seek to achieve. If you have an easily rewired 2x12 speaker cab with two 8-ohms speakers and an amp head with 4, 8, and 16-ohms outputs, you can try wiring it in series with your amp set to 16 ohms, then wire in parallel with your amp set to 4 ohms, and see which you prefer.

Test several cabs of different sizes and construction types if you have the opportunity, and see how different they can make a single guitar amp sound. You might find that an amp which you were lukewarm about comes to life in a different cab, and save yourself the dissatisfaction of never quite finding that 'perfect tone machine' simply because you failed to account for the wooden box that your speakers were mounted in.

CHAPTER 3

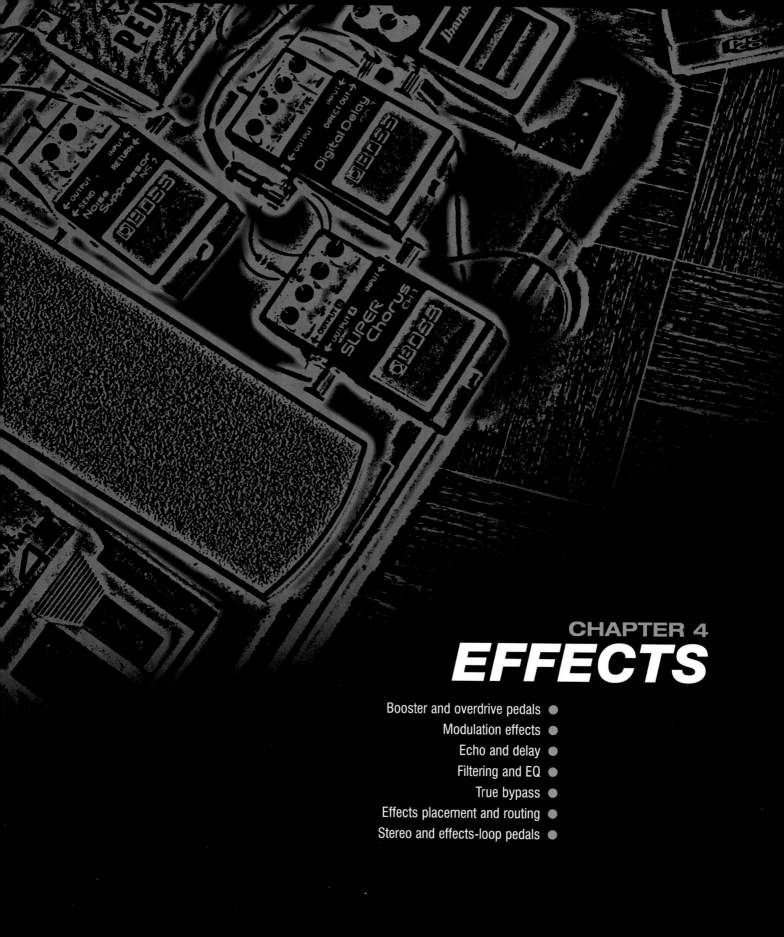

CHAPTER 4
EFFECTS

Back in 2003, when I was writing *Effects Pedals: The Practical Handbook* (Backbeat 2004), we were still on the cusp of the pedal market boom, and while I may have missed a few, it still seemed possible to detail the majority of the significant makes and models available, old and new. Now, as we enter the second decade of the 21st century, things are quite different. There are so many units available, and so many new ones hitting the market every day, that documenting them all is simply impractical.

What is still worth attempting, however, is an assessment and analysis of many of the general types of pedals available, most of which continue to fall into discernible categories. Understanding what different types of pedals do, and how they do it, can greatly simplify your search for specific effects-laden tones, so a little knowledge here can go a long way.

For all the fretting that currently goes on when it comes to the nuances of hand-wired tube amps and hand-crafted guitars, many of us are still willing to accept pedals that function using circuits that are decidedly *not* hand-made. Others, however, insist that the kinds of stellar build quality and components used in amplification electronics are also applied to the construction of the compact circuits within their small but significant effects boxes.

In fact, incontrovertibly different standards apply to these two sources of tone creation. Circuits that use 350–450 DC volts to do their thing have very different requirements to those that use 9–18 DC volts, as is common in the average effects pedal. Quality counts in all arenas, certainly, but the conditions that might make carbon comp resistors and signal caps as big as your thumb contribute to superb tone in a hand-wired tube amp are simply not present within that little metal pedal enclosure, and such components are as likely to get in the way as to enhance your tone.

In other cases, the 'best' part available might not always be the greatest part for the job. In all things electric guitar-related we are dealing with an element of distortion, after all, and it's distortion that helps to make even our 'clean' sounds shimmy and dance. Fulltone's Michael Fuller discovered this early on in his own manufacturing adventures. "I remember when I first started making a wah-wah," he says. "I thought, 'I'm going to use WIMA capacitors and polypropylene caps and that's going to be great.' Then, when I first hooked a couple of them up, I thought, 'Oh my god … .' You know, a wah-wah's such a raw circuit … when you try to put a tuxedo on a homeless guy it might not fit. It's just not the way to do it."

Ultimately, as long as what comes out the other side of the box is acceptable, sonically, and does the tone tricks you are looking for—and resists depleting your dry guitar signal when switched off—there really is very little to object to. Whether an effects unit is hand-made or factory churned, there are still certain immutable principles of what we might call 'tonal virtue' that should be adhered to in order to achieve pure results, even when those results are slathered in fuzz, modulation, or delay. One of the cornerstones of this set of principles says that, unless you are seeking an entirely synthetic sound, you want the effects unit to preserve as much of your guitar's natural character and dynamics as possible. Roger Mayer, the effects designer and manufacturer and former tech to Jimi Hendrix, expresses this notion succinctly. "You want a tone that's organic … [but] you've got many boxes that, to be frank, you put a guitar into it and you wouldn't know what type of guitar it is. The whole tonal quality of that guitar just disappears. It's got 'brick wall' processing in it, and this is ever so true of some of these cheaper multi-FX processors."

The 'brick wall' in Mayer's metaphor is the circuit that uses the guitar signal at the input merely as a trigger to a synthetic sound that results at the output, and relates to the input only so far as following the notes that appear there while squelching the original dynamics, harmonic content, and tonal depth in general. There are degrees of such 'brick wall' processing—in Mayer's book, any is too much—but it doesn't apply merely to 'guitar-synth' effects and extreme filters and modulators. Even simple distortion or fuzz can run the gamut from human, organic, and expressive to generic and synthetic. Mayer expounds: "All that stuff that was done with Jimi [Hendrix] on all the records, even the stuff that was very distorted, it was very human sounding. If you listen to the classic 'brick wall' effect of a fuzz box on something like, say, 'Summer Breeze' [by The Isley Brothers], that's got one tone on it and that's it. You might like what it's playing, but it's got no human quality to it."

Pete Cornish, the British maker who is known for the large effects rigs he creates for stars like Brian May and David Gilmour, has similar feelings about a pedal's transparency. "My first consideration is not to lose the tone and dynamics of the guitar when one of our effects is used," he says. "The tone and 'playability' of an instrument/amp combination is something that's often ignored by other designers, which is why everyone can end up sounding the same. My effects allow the musician's personality to show through, but with added tonal enhancement."

This second virtue expressed by Cornish illustrates another of the important principles behind any good effect: namely, that it should interact well with both the guitar and the amp, rather than dictate how these larger elements in the rig will sound. Naturally, you expect the guitar to interact with the pedal—it comes before it in the sequence, after all, and you play the darn thing. But the kind of interaction that Cornish is talking about, the kind that any thoughtful maker or player talks about, is the kind that produces a different feel and response from the pedal according to your touch, technique, and dynamics on the guitar. This can most obviously be heard with good booster, fuzz, overdrive, and distortion pedals, those that clean up as you pick lightly and then bring on the full filth when you hit the strings harder. Similarly, the more dynamic of these still allow you to achieve great clean tones with the unit 'on,' simply by rolling down the guitar's volume control, a setting that will, in the cases of many better units, give you a thicker, smoother clean tone than that achieved with the guitar on full, going straight to the amp, with the pedal switched 'off.'

The ways in which a pedal interacts with an amp might seem less obvious; after all, the amplifier comes after the pedal, and so the pedal—being *input* into the amplifier—obviously imposes its sound upon that of the amp. That's not quite the full picture, however. The right kind of dynamic, transparent chorus, phaser, or vibe pedal, for example, will often sound its best when its modulation also gooses the amp's own distortion content slightly, and melds with it. While doing so, it simultaneously retains the dynamics and tonal signature that are inherent to the amp, yet enhances them, too. These are the elements that make an effect 'playable,' to quote

Pete Cornish; and those that make it 'organic' and 'human,' according to Roger Mayer. Few players would argue against the idea that for pure, clean tone, your guitar is likely to sound best going straight into the amp through a relatively short cable of a good quality. Yet, even among purists, there are some who will tell you that adding a little something in front of the amp can actually maximize your clean tone. I'm not necessarily talking about chorus, reverb, or delay here—effects which a lot of players use to enhance their clean tones. But even with 'dry' tones, in some cases a booster, compressor, or another even more unlikely candidate can tease your signal into giving a little something extra.

From the 'unexpected' camp, several Uni-Vibe-style pedals are known to add some perceptible juice to clean tones, even when the effect part of their circuit is dialed out of the mix. If you get the chance, try a Fulltone Deja-Vibe or a Roger Mayer Voodoo-Vibe with the intensity control set to minimum: the signal still passes through the opto-coupler (the light cell responsible for the modulation function), resulting in some warming and fattening that gives a truly luscious enhancement to some clean tones (the Fulltone Supa-Trem achieves similar results). Plenty of players use a compressor switched 'on' for most of their clean playing, even with the squash and sustain properties of the pedal set quite low, and this can also add thickness and shimmer. Some more cumbersome units, like the tube and solid-state versions of the Maestro Echoplex, have been found to carry gain stages that dish out the juicy goodness, and both Jimmy Page and Eric Johnson are both fond of using a solid-state EP-3 Echoplex as a buffer/driver stage that is left on at all times (Xotic Effects offers an emulation of this preamp circuit in its compact EP-Booster pedal). An even more obvious candidate for 'upgraded clean' is found in the BBE Sonic Stomp, a pedal unit which houses a simplified rendition of the BBE Sonic Enhancer designed for studio processing.

Whether any or all of these provide a truly 'better' clean tone than your straight-to-amp tone is a tough call. The enhancement they provide can be addictive, and playing through any of them for a while and then taking them out of the chain can feel a little like throwing a heavy wool blanket over your amp. And yet, on some occasions, I almost find my ears tiring of such augmentation, as if the added aural dimension they provide makes things sound *too* lively, *too* titillating, if that is possible. Try one or more of the above enhancers or signal processors when you get the opportunity, and see if they do anything for you.

EFFECTS TYPES
Booster and Overdrive Pedals

If you've only got one pedal in your arsenal, the chances are it is some sort of overdrive. Populating the broad category that we'll label 'OD' for short, fuzz, boost, overdrive, and distortion pedals are the most popular stomp boxes out there, and for good reason: if you don't have the luxury of being able to crank up a great tube amp to excessive volume to get the world's sweetest lead tones—and few of us do—you need one of these machines to dirty up your sound a little (or a lot), and to help generate the singing, saturated, sustain sound that so many styles of guitar playing require.

Despite their popularity, however, the distinctions between the different pedals in this category are easily blurred. While all of them help you get 'cranked up' at the stomp of a switch, each type works its magic in a different way, and many from within the same type also function very differently. So, in this section, let's break down the OD category to define, dissect, and demystify each of the effects in the group and provide a better understanding of what they do and how they do it.

Boosters

The booster is among the simplest and the oldest types of overdrive-inducing pedals. At its heart, the booster is just a straightforward preamp that is placed in front of an amp's input. These are used to increase the guitar's signal, either to create a louder but relatively clean volume lift for solos or, more often then not, to kick the amp into overdrive. Many types of boosters first became popular in the mid 60s, and remain so today mainly because elements within their design—flaws, you could argue, in terms of creating a truly linear gain stage—made them imperfect as clean tone enhancers but instead induced tonal qualities which players came to love.

Early examples such as the Dallas Rangemaster Treble Booster, Vox Treble Booster, and Vox Bass/Treble Booster, owed their creamy, thick sound to a single germanium transistor, an archaic component that is still used as the magic ingredient in many current boosters (and fuzz pedals, as we shall see). These models didn't merely boost the higher frequencies, as the name might imply. While they did help highs push through, they also boosted other frequencies, and, besides, the 'treble booster' tag was partly just a selling point in an age when players wanted something to counteract guitar tones muted by high-load cables and murky live mixes. In addition to boosting the signal, the germanium transistor also added a little midrange girth and high-end sweetening, elements that became crucial to the signature lead tones of Eric Clapton, Jimmy Page, Brian May, and many others. These players used their germanium boosters to hit the front ends of Marshall or Vox amps with a little extra oomph, kicking them into a singing and more harmonically-saturated tube overdrive.

As such, pedal and amp work together as one instrument: few boosters are used purely for their own inherent tone, but rather for the way they perform in conjunction with a particular amplifier. Both mass-manufacturers and 'boutique' makers offer contemporary versions of such vintage-style boosters, but a different breed, the 'linear' or 'clean' booster, is also popular. These purport to retain the full frequency range of the guitar signal that is put into them, and simply make it louder. In the process, they can also help to overdrive a tube amp in the same way that many vintage units do. Many, in truth, are not entirely linear, and still fatten up the signal somewhat, even at lower settings.

Compressors

These generally contain a boosting stage as well, but are designed as compact versions of large studio compressors—leveling devices that smooth the attack and decay of a signal by softening the front edge of the note and amplifying its tail, to put it simply. Part of the compressor's original appeal to guitarists was its ability to replicate the natural compression, or sag, of a tube amp run at medium to high levels, thereby sustaining a held note in the process. Whether

induced by a pedal or by the amp itself, compression is often as much a 'feel' thing as a tonal element, making the guitar seem more tactile, touch-sensitive, and playable. Many favor compressors as sustainers, and some players also use them as booster pedals, by turning down the 'compression' or 'sustain' control and winding up the 'gain' or 'volume.'

More than just the intended squashing and sustaining effect, however, certain compressors have been attributed with magical tonal properties, especially the gray Ross Compressor, MXR's Dyna Comp, and Dan Armstrong's Orange Squeezer—some or all of which have been upgraded by contemporary makers like Analog Man and Keeley. The first two in particular are frequently mimicked (and sometimes even improved upon) by boutique builders and hobbyists alike. In addition to softening the attack of the note and sustaining its decay, each of these adds its own characteristic thickening of the tone, often with a little appealing grit thrown in as a bonus. Plenty of players go their entire careers without using a compressor pedal; others give one a try and fall for its appealing swell and fatness so much that they rarely switch it off from that day forward.

The compressor has long been considered an essential weapon in the Nashville session-player's arsenal. It helps to smooth out snappy chicken-pickin' runs or to thicken up otherwise thin, clean rhythm and lead parts. But the effect can be heard in the work of guitarists across all genres—from LA session player Jay Graydon to British Strat-picker Mark Knopfler and alt-rocker Trey Anastasio of Phish. While even a good compressor's range of settings is far narrower than those of, say, a fuzz pedal (which might go from mild distortion to freakish buzz) or a chorus (which can shift from gentle swirl to nauseating wobble), great players manage to carve their own individual sounds with the units. In fact, guitarists with no first-hand experience of a compressor's sound and function can often hear a great part played through one and simply attribute the results to 'great tone'—some magical combination of guitar, amp, and touch.

While a compressor pedal's function is somewhat akin to a large studio compressor/limiter, in miniature, many guitarists use the effect for rather different purpose than would a recording engineer—although these applications do cross over in certain respects. Compression as a studio tool is usually intended to be transparent: a means of keeping sonic peaks from overloading the desk or the tape, or causing digital distortion, while boosting quieter passages to give an overall impression of greater loudness and presence in a particular part, or even an entire mix. Guitarists, on the other hand, turn to compressors for sustain, punch, thickening and, as described above, to increase the dynamic feel of their set-up. Compression applied too heavily in the recording environment can kill off dynamics, but guitarists, conversely, often treat compressor pedals as a tool to increase the dynamics in their playing and tone. In the truest sense, however, over-used compression from a guitar pedal will also level out the peaks and troughs of a part, and will therefore literally decrease its dynamic range.

In their infancy, rack-mounted or standalone studio compression units were made with fairly complex tube circuits, or used equally intricate solid-state circuits based around an opto-cell, as in many classic designs of the 60s. Most pedal compressors use far simpler circuits based around fairly basic opamps ('operational amplifiers,' chips that are at the heart of many electronic products), or sometimes slightly more complex integrated circuits (ICs), as well as the usual transistors, resistors, and capacitors which enable them to function in the desired manner.

Original models of the Dan Armstrong Orange Squeezer used a single JRC4558 dual opamp, just like that used in the most revered versions of the Ibanez Tube Screamer, along with a pair of JFET transistors. Demeter's Opto Compulator, one of the more advanced compact compressor pedals, is an exception to the rule, and is built around an opto-cell, just like many revered studio units. Another that follows the studio-compressor format is Maxon's CP9 Pro+, which uses a circuit licensed from dbx. The more complex units often boast about their 'transparency'—that is, their ability to color the signal very little, or not at all—while other desirable but more basic models make a virtue of the way they liven up and enrich the guitar's straight sound.

Fuzzes

The real godfather of dirty effects, the fuzz pedal arrived even before the booster, and was initially intended as a unit that would let a guitar player mimic the raspy, reedy tone of a saxophone. Legend has it that one of the most famous fuzz-guitar parts of all time, the signature riff to The Rolling Stones' '(I Can't Get No) Satisfaction,' was originally recorded by Keith Richards as a 'holding track' for a horn section that would eventually replace it. The 'Satisfaction' riff, recorded through an early Maestro Fuzz-Tone, is an archetype of the fuzz pedal's sound, as are many of Jimi Hendrix's legendary solos, often recorded through a Dallas-Arbiter Fuzz Face.

Each of these pedals and others like them, old and new, owe their tone to a pair of the hallowed germanium transistors mentioned above. These components, along with a simple network to govern their functions and connect them to a pair of potentiometers for volume and fuzz (or some form of level and drive controls), can be combined to unleash all manner of ungodly sonic mayhem on your tone, but mayhem with a smooth, warm, furry heart. Yet the very best fuzz pedals are also loved for their 'playability,' the extent to which their response and dynamics can be controlled by your pick attack and your guitar's volume control. Silicon transistor-based fuzzes followed germanium units, and these are known for their slightly harder and more crisply defined tones, which often appeal to players seeking more contemporary rock tones.

Unlike linear boosters, fuzzes slather a wealth of their own stink all over your signal (that's precisely the idea), but they can also be used to drive a tube amp into clipping. Ultimately, most great guitarists with definitive fuzz tones are using their pedals in both these ways simultaneously, creating a larger, interactive instrument out of the individual components in their rig. Listen to the way Jimi Hendrix, Jimmy Page, or Jeff Beck used their fuzz pedals back in the late 60s and early 70s, and what they create is far from a 'brick wall' tone, while contemporary artists from Buckethead to Queens Of The Stone Age's Josh Homme also employ fuzz with dynamic results.

Overdrives

Like it says on the box, an overdrive pedal seeks to replicate the sound of an overdriven tube amp. In the course of doing so, it often facilitates the real thing a little more quickly, too, by pushing your amp into clipping a little earlier, just as a booster and fuzz will frequently do. In

C H A P T E R   4

truth, most lower-gain overdrive pedals (which is the majority) sound appalling when played through a high-fidelity driver such as a solid-state audio or PA amp, for example, and really don't sound in the least 'sweet and tubey' in that context. Most, therefore, work hand in hand with the tube amp into which they are injected, and used as such, some can be just the ticket for drawing delectable crunch and lead tones from your amp at a range of acceptable volume levels.

While fuzz pedals of the 60s and early 70s sound inherently dissimilar to an overdriven amplifier—other than an amplifier in bad need of attention, perhaps—it occurred to many players, and pedal designers, in the late 70s that it would be useful to have a box that sounded more realistically like the warm, 'tubey' crunch of a mildly-pushed amp. The granddaddy of overdrives is the Ibanez Tube Screamer TS808 (and its Maxon equivalent), manufactured for Ibanez by the Nisshin company from 1979–81 (both small and large-box versions). The TS808, TS-9, and TS-10 that evolved from it were adored by players who wanted something a little less than the extreme hair of the fuzz pedal but more than the pristine clarity of a clean amp; their warm, round voices and midrange hump helped to give the sonic impression of a semi-cranked amp, even at lower volume levels. Several name players, Stevie Ray Vaughan and Eric Johnson among them, also used Tube Screamers for their amp-boosting functions, and the low-gain/high-volume control settings that facilitate this have become popular with many guitarists.

DOD, MXR, Boss, and others issued seminal overdrives, and the genre continues apace today as probably the most popular single breed of pedal. Maker after solder-dazed maker has chased the ultimate in transparent, tube-like, dynamic overdrives, with units such as the Crowther Hotcake, Fulltone Full-Drive and OCD, Jacques Tube Blower, Barber LTD, Klon Centaur, Blackstone Mosfet Overdrive, Visual Sound Route 66, and plenty more receiving high praise from various quarters. Many of these achieve their overdrive tones quite differently. Some players eulogized the 'vintage' JRC4558D dual opamp (as used in the most lauded of Tube Screamers), while others regarded any opamp to be the death of transparency and dynamics, and favor instead the discrete circuit route. Whichever way you go, a good overdrive can be one of the cornerstones of any comprehensive pedal board, and an extremely useful tone-gooser.

Distortion

Like going from a ball peen to a sledge hammer, a distortion pedal seeks to reproduce—in and of itself—the full stack-like tube-distortion rage that the kinder, gentler overdrive pedal barely hints at. In doing so, most distortion pedals also emulate the high-production-value version of this sound, rather than merely the overdriven vintage amp that such tones were originally born from, and do so complete with scooped EQ curve and liberal helpings of compression. There are many flavors of distortion available, of course, but by its very nature this pedal aims to achieve a 'sound in a box,' rather than merely create the tone enhancements of the overdrive, fuzz, or booster pedals which also frequently need to be partnered with a good tube amp to sound their best.

Although the Boss Distortion DS-1 preceded it by a year or so, and is also a great pedal in its own right, the ProCo Rat, released in 1979, is usually considered the seminal heavy distortion pedal (the MXR Distortion+, released in 1973, is really more of an overdrive pedal).

Fuzz Power

One thing that a lot of players don't consider when faced with the sea of fuzz unit options available today is how to *power* the things. On contemporary units with AC/DC converter inputs, many guitarists just hook up their wall-wart with daisy chain and forget about it. In the past, however, players in the know understood that, in addition to the fuzz interacting with the amp, it also interacted very directly with the battery installed inside it. Many guitarists still believe that a lot of fuzzes, and the vintage style units in particular, are happier with batteries than with power converters, and that they might actually sound better with an old-style nine-volt carbon-zinc battery installed, too. Zachary Vex, of Z.Vex Effects, one of the more creative 'mad scientists' among the new breed of pedal designers, has some very specific views about batteries. "Carbon-zinc batteries have got a very high start voltage. The start voltage in a carbon-zinc battery can be 10.5 volts. I've seen them at 10.6 or 10.7. You don't see that so much any more—Rockets used to make them that high … I can't seem to get Rockets any more, but I can get ones that are 10.2 or 10.3. At that higher voltage, you seem to get a little more 'zip' out of a fuzz."

That extra 'zip' puts a little more bite and edge on the tone of a fuzz unit that is affected in this way. Modern alkaline batteries, on the other hand, tend to start at around 9.2 or 9.3 volts at the most, a whole volt lower than the average carbon-zinc battery, so they also don't give you the crucial 'zip' at the top of their life span, if you're looking for a fuzz tone with more cutting power to it. "Batteries have an output resistance just like a circuit does," says Vex. "For carbon-zinc, the output resistance is much higher to start with, and it gets terrible toward the end of its life. It becomes so saggy that if you try to pull any power out of it, it just goes *ppphhhh* … ." And while that might sound like a *bad* thing, it can yield another soft, squishy fuzz tone that really appeals to some players under certain circumstances. Vex elaborates. "Alkalines, even toward the end of their lives, never have such a high resistance, so you never experience them going through the same sort of phases of output resistance; and you also don't see a big spread of voltages over the lifetime of the battery. Alkalines are much more stable, so they're kind of nominal. You see a lot more changes in fuzz pedals over the lifetime of a carbon-zinc battery: you'll hear pretty oscillation things you've never heard before and you'll notice a roundness to the waves [on an oscilloscope] that you'll never have with an alkaline battery."

Get your hands on a selection of different carbon-zinc batteries, check them with your little Radio Shack voltage meter to see what they are actually putting out, and see how they perform in your pedal. You might find a voltage 'sweet spot' that is actually somewhere above or below the so-called nine-volt battery's supposed power rating.

Marshall's Shred Master has been a popular latter-day unit, and every major pedal maker on the market today offers their own rendition of a distortion—or several, in the case of Boss and a few others. Most distortion pedals employ a combination of opamps and silicon diodes to do their dirty work, some using the latter in asymmetrical circuits to produce a jagged and edgy form of clipping that has more sonic depth than smoother, symmetrical clipping.

C H A P T E R 4

If you don't have the luxury of being able to play a 200-watt Marshall Major set to eleven, a good distortion pedal can give you that thump-of-doom rhythm and lead tone for all occasions, and in any setting. Of course, being a preamp of sorts, and including a hefty amount of gain in most cases, a distortion pedal will also interact with a cranked tube amp—large or small—to create an interactive overdrive; so it can do many of the tricks of an overdrive or booster pedal when required, too.

Modulation Effects

'Modulation' is a broad church, and includes phasing, flanging, chorus, vibrato, tremolo, rotary speaker effects, and in this case, because I'm not sure where else to put them, octave dividers. Later analog versions of the first three above do, in fact, use much of the same technology as echo and delay units, using bucket-brigade chips with shorter delay times, but it makes sense to include them here because their obvious sonic characteristics are of a type with other units made from very different kinds of circuits. Most such effects were developed in an effort to add depth, dimension, and movement to the guitar's natural sound without necessarily distorting it, strictly speaking. A few noteworthy types also evolved from effects that were in use on the electronic organ.

Phasing

We call these boxes 'phase shifters' because they split the guitar signal and shift one path out of phase by amounts that range from 0 to 360 degrees through the entire range of the frequency spectrum, and blend it back with the dry path so that the moving in-phase/out-of-phase relationship can be heard. The two signals are totally out of phase at 180 degrees—or, technically, 540 degrees or 900 degrees, and so on, because the shift keeps moving beyond the standard 360-degree cycle, reversing its phase every multiple of 180 degrees, depending on how many stages the circuit allows for. When that happens, they cancel each other out, creating what is called a 'notch.' In fact, a number of factors interact to give a phaser its characteristic 'swooshing' sound. I will explain them in relatively simple terms, but in many units some pretty clever and complex electronics go into making all this happen.

When a notch in the frequency response is swept across the spectrum, the most dramatic sonic effect occurs at the peaks *between* the notches, where both paths are completely in phase, and where there is a full-strength signal. Leaving it there, however, would repeatedly emphasize the same low, middle, and high-frequency notes—and delete the same notes at the notches—so the phaser circuit also employs an oscillator to continually move (or 'shift') the point at which these notches and peaks occur; thus, different frequencies are emphasized and de-emphasized at each pass, at a rate determined by the unit's 'speed' or 'rate' knob.

I say "from 0 to 360 degrees" because that's the simplest way to envision the 'full circle' of the phase relationship. In reality, of course, you can't walk further around anything than a full circle—unless, that is, you're a phase shifter. For these pedals, designers talk in terms of a continual shifting of the phase relationship from 0 to, in theory, infinity, depending upon how many shifting stages the circuit contains. The phase shifts by 180 degrees for each stage, so for the typical simple phaser with four stages, we're talking from 0 to 720 degrees, with three peaks and two notches along the way. Phasers with six, eight, and even ten stages have been built for use with guitar. But for many, the simple four-stage circuit is most appealing.

Preference for the relatively simple four-stage phaser is probably down to the famous Univox Uni-Vibe. Despite the name, and its two famous functions labeled 'Chorus' and 'Vibe,' the Uni-Vibe is more akin to a four-stage phaser than what we would today consider to be a chorus pedal. The deception is forgivable when you remember that the Uni-Vibe's intention was to reproduce the chorus-type sound—or 'chorale,' as it was often labeled—produced by a Leslie rotating speaker cabinet used with a Hammond organ. Also, the unit existed before there was much categorization of such things: it was a guitar effects foot pedal, it had its own sound and that was all anyone needed to know. The Uni-Vibe—and the better clones that have followed down the years—is based around a discreet transistorized circuit with four sets of light bulbs and light cells, and a low-frequency oscillator (LFO) that shifts the peaks and notches. Unlike the drawing-board phaser discussed above, however, the frequencies of each stage of the Uni-Vibe are set differently, so it could be argued that there is indeed more of a chorusing of the sound.

Other early phase shifters deployed field effect transistors (FETs) to control each phasing stage in place of the light bulbs used in the Uni-Vibe, and later units employed opamps with variable resistors (six TL072 dual opamps or similar in the MXR Phase 100, for example). Electro-Harmonix's Small Stone, on the other hand, has a more unusual design that employs five CA3094 type operational transconductance amplifiers (OTAs). The results are similar, but subtly different. Many phasers—such as MXR's Phase 45 and Phase 90, and the aforementioned Small Stone—carry nothing but a speed control, plus a 'Color' switch in the case of the latter. Others feature depth, mix, and resonance controls. Resonance controls appear on many units with internal feedback loops (the Small Stone and most phasers before it lack this circuitry), and allow the player to tweak the degree to which the portion of the fed-back signal enhances the frequency peaks.

The gray area between different types of phasers and chorus pedals—and phaser-style chorus pedals versus delay-based chorus pedals—probably arises because designers and manufacturers really have followed two distinct paths in this field. Some phasers have sought to approximate the Uni-Vibe's approximation of a Leslie cab, and some so-called choruses have done much the same. Other phasers have been designed from the ground up using the purer principles of phase shifting itself, rather than making an effort to sound like a whirling speaker or any other electromechanical device that has come before. The result means the field is broad and varied, and different phasers (or their related effects) can often have different voices with characteristics more distinct than, say, two delays from different makers.

Flanging

Usually considered the phaser's big brother, the flanger is indeed a relative, of a kind, although it achieves its heavier, some would say more oppressive, sonic results by imposing more control over its placement of the notches created by the phase relationship, rather than spacing them evenly, as the phaser's sweep does. Much of the basic circuitry that produces flanging effectively follows this template, but some complex engineering is needed to take it where it's going. Pedal-sized units designed to replicate the sound of two large reel-to-reel tape machines sliding in and

out of sync weren't made possible until larger, more complex ICs became available to help get the job done. This extra technology is needed to harmonically tune the out-of-phase notches, and, relative to these, the peaks, and it's this harmonic spacing of the spread that can make a genuine flanger pedal sound almost like it's actively participating in the note selection of a sequence you are playing. Whereas phasers have from four to ten stages, the individual chips within a flanger may carry hundreds of stages.

Not the first commercially available flanger pedal, but probably the first that really worked properly with the full sonic depth of the effect, the A/DA Flanger was made possible by the advent of the SAD1024 chip (others were used through its lifetime, depending upon availability). It hit the shelves in 1977, and was shortly followed by Electro-Harmonix's equally beloved Electric Mistress, and MXR's big, gray Flanger. Nearly every big pedal maker slapped its own flanger on the butt and sent it toddling down the pike within the next few years. These were serious pedals in their day, the big boys requiring their own regulated, onboard AC power stage to run all that thirsty silicon. Most required a serious investment on behalf of the impoverished guitarist, too. A/DA's unit retailed at $199.95 when introduced, and others went for even more. Hardly a steal, when you consider that the US minimum hourly wage was $2.30 in 1977.

The sound blew away guitarists when units first popped up in guitar stores. If the dizzying harmonic swirl didn't make you nauseous, it really sent you tripping. Interestingly, many tired of it a lot quicker than they did the phaser's subtler, less imposing 'swoosh,' and consequently it is difficult today to name too many great guitar tracks with flangers slapped all over them.

The same cannot be said of phasers. Examples of the latter include 'Shattered' by the Stones (or just about anything from the *Some Girls* album) and The Clash's 'Lost In The Supermarket,' from *London Calling,* not to mention a whole host of tracks on the follow-up, *Sandinista.* Heavier rockers from early Van Halen right up to Foo Fighters have also demonstrably favored the phaser. As for flangers, there's The Pat Travers Band's 'Boom Boom, Out Go The Lights,' the intro lick to Heart's 'Barracuda,' and, well, most of the others get a bit heavy-handed. Zachary Vex says this extreme quality is seemingly inherent to the flanging sound. "There was one bad, bad use of it: 'Sky Pilot' [by The Byrds], from the 60s. You were positively queasy by the end, like a bad carnival ride. I think that's the difficulty with flanging that goes up and down: every time it comes up again you feel you've been through this: let's hear something else, please! It's not that pretty, it's kind of grating, and it gives you that inside-out kind of queasiness. It's too similar to having something shooting toward you and moving away from you."

All of which is not intended to chastise flanging out of hand; it can be an impressive effect. It's just that, used heavily—where it best shows off its massive harmonics-plinking capabilities— it can become too imposing a sound for a guitarist to easily play with, which consigns it to the realm of background effects and early-80s electro-pop. Still, the more creative among us will no doubt find stunning and artistic uses for it.

Chorus

While modified four-stage phasers like the Uni-Vibe and its predecessors had sought to evoke a chorale-like sound, the chorus pedal as we know it today didn't arrive until affordable, short-delay 'bucket brigade' chips became widely available in the late 70s. This in itself implies that chorus is a type of delay, and indeed it is, but the ways in which chorus transforms these short delays locates the effect firmly in the modulation camp, so it's easiest to consider it as such (we'll examine the function of these delay chips in more detail a little later).

IC-based chorus effects work in a manner very similar to flangers, as detailed above. Put simply, the main difference between them is that the short delays used to create harmonically-spaced notches and peaks in the frequency spectrum are manipulated to modulate more tightly above and below specific frequency ranges, rather than being shifted to swoosh broadly up and down the entire spectrum.

The result, and the intention, is a sound that is akin to a group of singers or a cluster of similarly-toned instruments, all performing at the same time and with some of the voices or tones inevitably wavering slightly up and down in pitch from those beside them. This all sets in motion a quivering clash of harmonics that evokes space and dimension, when used subtly. Chorus is possibly best heard—as a pure effect, at least—in stereo, and chorus undoubtedly lends itself most readily to stereo outputs. The broad sound stage and the Doppler-like movement that a good stereo chorus unit can spread before you between a pair of widely-placed amps (or on headphones) make it one of the most space-evoking, three-dimensional effects available.

The Boss CE-1 Chorus Ensemble was the first of these effect units to be made commercially available, and is the best-remembered of the company's now archaic-looking early range of die-cast metal pedals. The CE-1 was an instant success when it hit the market in 1976, and was quickly seized upon by a number of major players. Andy Summers used the CE-1 with The Police in the late 70s and early 80s, and it's probably most famously heard on the band's 1979 hit 'Message In A Bottle.'

Shortly after the CE-1 was launched, Electro-Harmonix offered both its Memory Man Stereo Echo/Chorus—which featured a very good, spacious chorus setting which a lot of players loved—and the smaller, stand-alone Small Clone chorus. Like the Small Stone phaser before it, the Small Clone had a softer, subtler sound than many of the chorus pedals that would soon flood the market, and it too was a huge hit. Kurt Cobain's use of the pedal on 'Smells Like Teen Spirit' and Chris Novoselic's bass part on 'Come As You Are', from Nirvana's *Nevermind* album, show off the pedal's facility for adding a rich, moving, liquid texture to both clean and distorted parts. MXR, DOD, and Ibanez all offered popular IC-based analog chorus pedals, and practically all mass-manufacturers nowadays offer such a unit.

Subsequent technological developments would lead to the advent of digital chorus pedals. The effect might sound broadly similar, but it is achieved quite differently from that created by analog circuits. Digital chorus pedals double a signal and add delay and pitch modulation to one path, the latter wobbling below and above the pitch of the unadulterated signal, producing an audible out-of-tune quality when the paths are blended back together. It's hard to fault the power and range of control that digital technology affords, and this version of the effect has been hugely successful, although many guitarists still prefer the subtle, watery shimmer of the analog version. For some, the sound of the digital chorus is just too queasy.

C H A P T E R   4

Vibrato

True vibrato, as distinct from the volume-chopping tremolo effect often mislabeled as such, is an actual wavering of the note above and below pitch to create a sort of harmonious 'wobbling' effect. Singers do it, and guitarists do it when they wiggle a finger against string and fingerboard or manipulate the arm of a vibrato tailpiece. Heavy 'true' vibrato can induce similar seasick qualities to those produced by heavy digital chorus or flanging, but subtler implementations of the effect can add movement and gently trembling beauty to a guitar part.

Electronic vibrato was initially achieved using a relatively complex circuit that usually required at least two preamp tubes, and even then the effect was usually not 'true' vibrato in the pitch-altering sense but a watery and sweet-sounding approximation of it. The effect was most often installed in amps but occasionally built as a standalone unit, such as Gibson's GA-V1 Vibrato Box. Fender was guilty of mislabeling many amps with a 'vibrato' channel which actually only carried opto-controlled tremolo (and compounded the felony by simultaneously calling its guitars' vibrato tailpieces 'tremolo units'), and the company did build a few of its initial, front control-mounted, brown and blonde Tolex amps of the very early 60s with a subtle form of vibrato. Despite its name, the earlier, tweed Vibrolux actually carried tremolo, produced by a circuit similar to that used in the slightly larger Tremolux. As it appeared on the 6G8 Twin and 6G5-A Pro Amp of 1960–61, the vibrato effect drew on two and a half of the preamp's total of five 12AX7s—excluding the phase inverter (the vibrato circuit 'wasted' half a tube, which was left unused). It also required about as much circuitry again as the rest of what was used for the two channels combined, and was clearly laborious to build. It sounds fantastic, and has made true addicts of plenty of trem-o-philes. Apparently, however, all the effort just didn't pay off, and the circuit was dropped after just a couple years of production. Gibson, Vox, Magnatone, and a few others also offered amps with so-called 'true' vibrato.

The effect is achieved today in solid-state guitar pedals with circuits similar to those used for analog chorus units, or sometimes, in high-end pedals, fairly complex, discreet transistorized designs that are modified variations on early phasers. Discreet vibrato pedals really haven't developed a major following, although when included as a setting on other pedals—the Electro-Harmonix Deluxe Memory Man or several Uni-Vibe clones among them—the subtle vibrato sound still gets an occasional airing. A few companies, notably boutique amp builders Matchless and Victoria, have also offered tube-powered units that work along the lines of the shortlived Fender vibrato circuit. When used judiciously, it's a lush, moody effect that adds thickness and motion to any guitar part, just like the better analog modulation effects.

Tremolo

Simply put, tremolo achieves its modulation of a signal by switching it on and off at a designated rate, using any of a number of means. Among the more common—and better sounding—early amp-based tremolo circuits was one whose name bears testament to this process: bias-modulating tremolo. This creates its on/off pulse by altering the bias of an amp's output tubes or a preamp tube in the signal path, bringing the signal in and out at the desired rate. Tremolo first appeared in the form of a number of add-on units (often too large to be called 'pedals'), and the first bona fide standalone effect of all was a tremolo unit made by DeArmond, the Model 800 Trem Trol ('tremolo control'). By the mid 50s, the effect was included on amps by Gibson, Premier, Danelectro, and, shortly afterward, Fender. The early bias-modulating tremolo effect that most commonly appeared on such amps is difficult to accurately replicate in a pedal, since a major constituent of its sound is produced by modulating signal level within the amp circuit itself.

The opto-cell circuits used in many amps from the 60s onward, on the other hand, with their atmospheric-sounding, lopsided triangular waveform, can be adapted to fit into a pretty small box. These circuits are based around a photo-coupler made from a small neon lamp and a light-dependent resistor (LDR) coupled together in a small, opaque tube. An oscillator makes the lamp pulse at a speed determined by the effect's 'speed' or 'rate' control, and the LDR injects this pulse into the guitar signal with an intensity determined by the 'depth' control. While most amps of the 60s and 70s that carried this effect used a tube to drive the oscillator, most pedals use a photo-coupler to convert the drive section to a transistorized stage. Demeter's Tremulator and Fulltone's Supa-Trem are two units that achieve excellent renditions of this effect, as do several other models.

Most budget-to-mid-priced units, however, do things even more simply. As with the majority of pedals, they use ICs to accomplish all oscillation and modulation tasks, usually with transistorized input and output-stage buffers. While purists will argue vehemently for the tonal purity of discrete transistorized circuitry in most applications (that is, without opamps or ICs of any sort), it is probably harder to make the case for a basic dual opamp-based tremolo pedal that effectively pulsates volume on and off—without corrupting tone along the way—and is significantly inferior to a discrete opto circuit. As ever, you must use your ears and decide what's best for you. In any case, pedal-based tremolo will still be inherently different to amp-based tremolo, since the former modulates the guitar signal on the way to your amp, while the latter modulates it within an amp stage itself.

Tremolo dropped from fashion in the late 70s and remained something of an underdog throughout the 80s and into the 90s (aside from its use at the hands of a few hip guitarists: Johnny Marr of The Smiths, R.E.M.'s Peter Buck, and erstwhile Television leader Tom Verlaine among them, all of whom understood that it was perhaps the finest, most 'organic' effect available). To many at the time, it just sounded old fashioned when compared with long digital delays, digital chorus and flanging, and all the rest. As with so many sonic colors from the early days of rock'n'roll, however, the effect has built a major modern following (Angelo Badalamenti's tremolo-laden soundtrack to the *Twin Peaks* television show from the early 90s certainly reminded a lot of people of its haunting power). Many great guitarists now keep a tremolo pedal on their board, or play through an amp with an onboard effect, and many will argue vehemently over the merits of different designs.

Octave Divider

This is a relatively simple effect, but also one of the freakiest when used properly—sometimes more so when used 'wrongly.' Like a surprising number of classic guitar sounds, this effect

arrived courtesy of Jimi Hendrix—specifically, a custom-built Roger Mayer Octavia which was used on several iconic Hendrix tracks.

Mayer developed an octave divider with fuzz specifically for Hendrix, following experiments in which Mayer doubled the frequency of a signal in order to make it appear to add a note that was an octave higher than the original, although he never offered his original octave-dividing unit as a commercial item. This left the door open for the Tycobrahe Sound Company of California to offer its own Octavia copy, and that unit was followed by clones from a host of other makers.

The circuit itself is fairly simple: three transistors, a couple of diodes, and an impedance interstage transformer, along with the usual caps and resistors. Primitive stuff it may have been, but it had a wild effect on a guitar signal. Roger Mayer explains how a simple circuit pulls off such a substantial aural trick. "It [the Octavia] doubles the number of images of the note, and that, apparently, makes it sound twice the frequency—whereas it really isn't. Because the signal's going up and down twice as much, even though you've changed the relationship of it, the ear perceives it as twice the frequency, though it isn't. It's much like putting a beer mat up to a mirror [our conversation took place in a London pub] and you see two of them, but there's still only one."

Octave effects are among the trickier pedals to play, because the circuit only tracks well if a single, pure, cleanly-played note is introduced—and honks into total freak-out if it sees an interval. Also, the fewer harmonics the better; so firm picking on a neck pickup does it the most favors. Again, Hendrix's own playing offers a good lesson in how to use octave fuzz: hear how he cleans up his technique—simplifying the blues slurs, trills, and bends that are otherwise plentiful—in order to make the most of the effect.

The octave divider's prevalence in heavy rock of the late 60s and early 70s has rendered it somewhat dated—and a genre-tied sound, too (you don't hear it a lot in country music). A few adventurous players continue to apply it creatively to more experimentally inclined modern music, and it can still be an extremely powerful effect.

Ring Modulators

These units come to the guitar from the world of analog synthesizers, where they enjoy far more applications. However, they can still be useful for the guitarist who needs some wild, whacked-out, non-guitar-like sonic obliteration every so often. The ring modulator's signature is close to the octave divider's percussive, synthesized, octave-up sound, but with a jagged, atonal, random-interval performance. This is another of those tools that travailing guitarists took up in the early 80s in order to compete with the then pervasive synthesizer. For a time, it looked as if guitarists had lost the battle, but I'd like to think we won the war.

The ring modulator takes its name from the simplest of its transistorized topologies, consisting of a ring of four diodes and two transformers. Most are considerably more complex than this. In any case, a ring modulator takes the signals from two sources—either from two separate inputs, or one input and one internal oscillator (called a "carrier frequency")—and multiplies them to produce a new signal that is totally different from either of the two sources.

The result is a little like an octave divider trying to handle two notes at a time, rather than the single, pure note that it's more readily able to deal with, and coughing up a dissonant mess as a result. The ring modulator is designed specifically to cope with this pair of disparate signals, but their multiplication produces a new signal with notes as both the sum and difference of the two source signals' frequencies. Consequently, this output offers a mathematical result, with no harmonic relationship to the original notes. That could make for a messy sound—and perhaps, sometimes, it does—but most units that are designed for guitar (or other tonal instruments) generally tap off a portion of the main signal at its input and feed it forward to the output to retain a degree of the original note. This blend of the original guitar signal and the sum-and-difference signal produced by the ring modulation circuit is percussive, jagged, dissonant, and sometimes extremely effective. Early, basic ring modulators designed for the guitar generally had a single input and generated their carrier frequency internally, occasionally with user-selectable variations. Some more elaborate modern models—such as Lovetone's Ring Stinger or Frantone's Glacier—allow for internal oscillation selections and add an extra input to make provision for an external control signal such as a mic, drum machine, separate line level source, or whatever. What does the sum and difference of your own funk guitar riff multiplied with a garage drum loop sound like? Chaotic, probably, but, just possibly, like a major hit.

Echo and Delay

These effects are among the earliest efforts to add something to the guitar picture other than the pure sound of vibrating strings amplified through a speaker. Such units do everything from replicating the natural sound of playing in a dry, hard-walled room to creating space-aged and entirely unnatural aural effects. Echo and reverb are often versions of the same thing, although the term 'echo' was used more often in the early days, and is sometimes used today to refer to the distinct and distant repeats of a signal, while 'delay' can refer to anything from the short multiple repeats heard as reverb to the long, complex, manipulated repeats of an intricate digital delay line.

Analog Delay

The transmogrification of bulky, fiddly tape echo units into transistorized analog echo pedals in the late 70s was an undoubted boon for delay-loving guitarists. Players addicted to anything from slap-back to the hypnotic sonic cloning of their Echoplex, Copicat, and Space Echo units breathed a sigh of relief when Electro-Harmonix and MXR introduced relatively affordable, portable analog delay pedals. By the early 80s, there was barely a rocker who stepped on stage without a delay pedal, and every major effects maker offered a model or two.

Over time, many players decided that their old tape echoes actually sounded better than the transistorized alternatives, but for convenience, the majority stuck with their stomp-boxes for live work. Opinions on the tonal superiority of tape echo—and especially tube-powered versions—have become even more vehement in recent years, spawning inflated prices in the used market and new models like the Tube Tape Echo from boutique pedal maker Fulltone. For most, however, tape remains impractical.

Like so much else, analog delays were first made possible by a shift in available technology—specifically, the mid-70s advent of affordable delay chips. Techies call these 'bucket brigade delay chips' because they pass the signal along in stages from the input pin to the output pin, through anywhere from 68 to 4,096 stages. Inject a signal, govern the speed at which it gets passed from stage to stage, tap the output and, *voila*, you've got echo. The more stages in the chip, the longer the delay the circuit can achieve. The longer the delay, however, the greater the distortion and loss of fidelity in the wet signal, so most makers compromised to keep maximum settings within acceptable delay/noise ratios.

The Electro-Harmonix Memory Man and Deluxe Memory Man are two of the most popular solid-state delays ever made. Even with its meager delay time of between 5 and 320 milliseconds, the original unit was little short of revolutionary when introduced in 1976. At around $150, it was a relative bargain, although hardly dirt-cheap when you consider that at the time you could buy a new Stratocaster for a little over three times that figure. The Memory Man was launched with Reticon SAD1024 chips, but E-H switched to quieter, better sounding, and more adaptable Panasonic MN3005 ICs when these became available. The latter is also the chip found in the better known Stereo Echo/Chorus and Deluxe models. Early analog delays from MXR, Ibanez, Boss, Maxon, and others were, and remain, extremely popular, too.

Similar bucket brigade delay chips, differently manipulated, were also at the center of the more advanced chorus and flanger pedals that emerged in the late 70s. With ICs that were capable of creating a controllable time delay in any given signal, the job of harmonically modulating part of a split, delayed signal to produce a warbling chorus or swooshing flanger sound became a lot easier.

Digital Delay

The digital delay arrived on the pedal board in the early 80s. Its capabilities seemed vast: lengthy repeats, clean signal reproductions, and the endless fun of 1, 2, or up to 16 seconds of looping delay. In many cases, in the early days, reproductions weren't really all that clean (and while they were cleaner than analog, they were often colder and harsher), and many delays were prone to digital distortion if pushed, or poor resolution on the decay of the signal. Even so, the power of the new technology stomped all over the bones of the old analog delay units, and for a time threatened to bury them entirely.

The nuts and bolts of digital delays are complex, too much so to be entered into here (I assume you will know at least the basic principles behind binary encoding by now). But for the uninitiated it may be useful to think of digital delay as a form of sampling: the unit makes a small digital recording of your riff, and then plays it back at the time-delay you have set, with depth and number of repeats also more or less selectable. The higher the sample rate, the better the sound quality. Early, affordable 8-bit models really did leave a lot to be desired sonically, but as 16, 20, and 24-bit designs began to emerge, the reproduction of the echoes dramatically increased in quality.

As with so many elements of guitar sound, once the novelty of digital delay wore off, players became less awestruck by its sound—and, in many cases, came to realize that there was little use for 2 seconds, or even 800 milliseconds, of delay time—and many began to miss the warm, pliable sound of the old analog pedals.

The jury is still out on the digital versus analog delay issue; there are plenty of great players who favor one or other of these pedal types—and, as ever, the music you make with the technology remains far more important than the type of technology you choose to produce it. Played in isolation, at the same delay settings, digital and analog units would sound just a little different to a guitarist with keen ears. At the back end of a pedal board, with eight or ten other effects, three or four of them running at a time, the differences are likely to be less apparent—but different players have different preferences, depending on what makes them feel good about their tone.

Reverb

Originally achieved using springs or plates, reverberation is a distinct sonic effect on its own, even if it has been bracketed with the delay camp in recent years. The same bucket brigade analog or digital technology that is used to create long delay-pedal echoes can be manipulated to produce a reverberant sound, too. Tap the multistage analog delay chip at a very short delay and layer these repeats with other such short delays, and a reverb effect is produced. It has something in common with the spring reverb in guitar amps—or old studio plate reverb units—in that both approximate the reverberant sound of the instrument when played in an empty, reflective room.

While many players make good use of reverb pedals, anything from units like Danelectro's new Far East-built pedals to classic Electro-Harmonix and Boss models, most consider the amp-based, tube-driven spring reverb to be the pinnacle of the breed. There are, however, many great guitar amps out there with no reverb onboard—so, for your tweed Fender Bassman, Marshall JTM45, or Matchless DC30, an add-on unit is the only option.

You couldn't really call it a pedal, as such, but Fender's tube reverb, in its original or reissued form, has always been widely considered one of the finest spring reverb units there is, and it can be added at the front end of any amp (although this isn't ideal if your overdrive sound comes from a channel-switching overdrive preamp placed after the reverb). Other US and British amp makers have offered standalone reverbs, plenty of which can sound totally fabulous, and Dr Z's new Z-Verb provides a contemporary, hand-wired means of achieving this sound. Fender was actually a little slow getting onboard-reverb into its amplifiers, and it was makers such as Gibson and Ampeg who in fact first offered combos with fantastic sounding built-in reverb in the early 60s.

A spring reverb unit is really a small amplifier in itself, one that sends the guitar signal through a tube circuit to a small output transformer (or through a transistorized circuit) and from there to one end of the springs housed in a 'pan' rather than to a speaker. This signal vibrates the springs, is picked up by a transducer at their opposite end, and from there is blended back with the dry signal by degrees determined by a 'depth' control, and sent on to the output (or the power tubes, if part of a guitar amp). As you can imagine, it's a bulky effect when achieved in this way, requiring at least a couple of transformers, two or three tube sockets, and

C H A P T E R 4

the spring pan, but the circuit itself is fairly simple. While most players consider reverb to sound its best when emanating from an all-tube/spring-pan circuit within an amplifier, many others feel that adding such a circuit to a good tube amp can slightly impede that amp's natural tone.

Digital reverbs, like their sibling delays, offer more power and a greater variety of settings. In addition to approximating spring reverb sounds, digital units usually offer more 'lifelike' reverberation as heard in anything from an empty room to a large concert hall. If you want to add a synthesized 'natural' room sound to your signal rather than merely replicate the classic *sproing* of springs, then digital is the way to go. A few pedals do this very well, but many such devices are rack units that are best used in an amp's FX loop. For all the power of digital reverbs, however, there are plenty of guitarists who just don't warm to them, and the tube-driven, analog, spring reverb effect remains hands-down the favorite for guitar.

Filtering and EQ

Occasionally overlooked in the realm of effects, a relatively simple manipulation or filtering of the frequency spectrum in which the guitar operates is capable of producing some of the most emotive sounds heard in music. We know this category best in the form of the wah-wah pedal—an effect whose deployment is practically an art form at the hands (or rather feet) of guitarists such as Jimi Hendrix, Eric Clapton, Slash, or Zakk Wylde. Filtering also gives us voltage-controlled envelope-follower auto-wah sounds. Down at the simpler end of the scale, plenty of guitarists seek the aid of an active tone control in the form of a graphic EQ.

Wah-Wah

Wah-wah pedals are often described as a tone control with a rocking pedal attached, but there's a lot more to this iconic device than that. In truth, the wah-wah circuit is a 'sweepable' peaking filter: that is, a band-pass filter that creates a peak in the frequency response that the player can manually (or 'pedially') move up and down the frequency spectrum. When that peak is swept through the portion of the spectrum that contains the notes being played, it emphasizes those frequencies and produces the 'wah' sound. Differing amounts of resonance produced as this peak is swept also contribute to the characteristic sound of any given wah-wah pedal, and this is something that can vary considerably from model to model.

Because the wah-wah is (usually) dealing with guitar, its frequency spectrum typically runs from around 400 Hz to about 2.2 kHz. This is well within the range of the average sweepable midrange control on a standard mixing desk, and a look at one of these can help you better understand the function of a wah-wah pedal. A popular, affordable home-recording and PA desk such as the Mackie 1604-VLZ Pro, for example, has an EQ section with a mid frequency sweepable from 100 Hz to 8 kHz. Set the mid-boost control to maximum (most wah-wahs don't allow manual control over the extent to which the peak is boosted, it is preset in the circuit design), find the range between 400 Hz and 2.2 kHz on the frequency sweep knob, and twist this rapidly up and down between those levels while a friend vamps some guitar riffs through the channel. You should hear a dramatic emphasis when your frequency range hits that of the notes being played—in short, something like the sound a wah-wah pedal makes.

Of course, the bandwidth in this mixing desk EQ control is broader than that of the peak produced by most wah-wahs (1.5 octaves on the Mackie, in fact), so the pedal's frequency emphasis should be more focused, and therefore more dramatic. Some wah-wahs offer control over this bandwidth—Dunlop's Cry Baby 535Q and the Boss FW-3 Foot Wah, for example.

The most revered wah-wahs of all time, the Vox Wah-Wah and Cry Baby of 1967 and 1968, respectively—and Thomas Organ's Clyde McCoy Wah-Wah which preceded them by a year or so—do their thing with circuits that consist of just a couple of transistors, a coil inductor, a few resistors, and a capacitor, and, of course, a potentiometer with a gear on its shaft to enable a rocker treadle to set it in motion. It seems like pretty simple stuff, and in principle it is, but there's plenty of magic and mystery associated with good wah-wah circuits, and it can take a lot of effort to get the things sounding just right.

Many players rave about early Italian-made Jen Vox wah-wahs with Fasel inductors in the circuit, and claim that nothing made after them has sounded as sweet or expressive. Some flaw in these early Fasel inductors—probably a result of their cheapness—has been credited with enabling them to achieve asymmetrical clipping with some even-order harmonic content, as opposed to the spikier-sounding, odd-order harmonics produced by other types of inductors when clipping, and this could indeed be responsible for any 'magic.' Dunlop has reissued a Cry Baby Classic wah-wah with a Fasel inductor, but this is apparently a new generation of the component and I have yet to hear whether it performs similarly to the original. Plenty of guitarists also swear by the silver metal 'trash-can' inductor found in early Cry Baby wah-wahs.

Tweaking and tuning wah-wahs is considered something of a black art, and a number of modifications exist—some user-installable—to help players make the most of both vintage and new models. Many vintage wah-wahs also have a less than ideal input impedance for use with guitar, and can be guilty of severe tone sucking, even when the wah-wah circuit is switched out, so some guitarists also modify them to eliminate this. The boutique effects maker Fulltone also offers wah-wah mods, and its own Clyde Wah is a clone of the original Thomas Organ Clyde McCoy wah-wah.

While the Vox/Cry Baby wah-wah remains the classic template, makers have offered a range of variations on both the circuit and the mechanical operation of the pedal. Morley offers designs, popular with several notable players, which use quiet photo-resistors instead of potentiometers for sweep control. Roger Mayer's Vision Wah is also a potentiometer-free pedal, with low-profile housing and a treadle positioned ergonomically for a more comfortable action while standing. For pure, wild inventiveness, it's hard to beat Z.Vex's Wah Probe, which uses a Theremin-type antenna in the form of a copper plate mounted to the sloping front face of the pedal for totally contact-free wah-wah action.

Auto-Wah

The sovereign of the treadle-free wah-wah is the envelope follower (aka voltage-controlled filter, or auto-wah). These effects contain a sweepable peaking filter much like that of the traditional wah-wah, but use the intensity of the incoming signal—in other words, the guitarist's pick attack—to generate the control voltage that sends the peak up and down the frequency

spectrum. With most such devices, pick lightly and the sound remains bassy and muted; hit the strings hard, and brighter wah-wah-like frequencies leap out. Musitronics's Mu-Tron III, introduced in 1972, was the first widely available envelope follower, and it remains one of the best-loved. Electro-Harmonix followed with a range of models such as the Doctor Q, Zipper, Bass Balls, and Y Triggered Filter, and most major makers of the 70s also joined in.

While the treadle pedal is generally considered the rocker's wah-wah (despite the disco-era's clichéd appropriation of the effect), the envelope-follower auto-wah is the archetypal funk machine: think Parliament-Funkadelic, just about anything from bassist Bootsy Collins, or Stevie Wonder's 'Higher Ground' (a famous early use of a Clavinet through a Mu-Tron III). George Clinton, although a singer, has used his 'funk-certified street cred' to endorse recent-era E-H's Tube Zipper envelope follower/distortion pedal. Overall, the effect is probably less expressive than a treadle wah-wah—or, perhaps more accurately, offers less fine manual control over its expressiveness—but is more effective in certain circumstances. Something about the rhythmic way your natural pick attack can induce a pumping feeling in pulsating rhythm parts played through an auto-wah can often sound more natural than the methodical rocking of the typical disco-wah rhythm guitar part. Outside the realm of funk, however, this effect is often consigned to the novelty shelf.

Graphic EQ

The mini guitar-pedal-sized equalizer is not an effect as such, but an inline tone circuit. All the same, it would seem churlish not to acknowledge it here; many guitarists have made great use of graphic EQs over the years. The technology behind these units doesn't need a lot of description. We could delve into the intricacies of circuit and design topologies, but suffice it to say a graphic EQ pedal is a multi-band active tone control with sliders rather than rotary potentiometers and a graph-style presentation of the equalization settings. The frequency bands assigned to the sliders are fixed, and tailored to be useful to the frequency spectrum in which the guitar operates. The bands are logarithmically related to correspond to the way the human ear perceives frequencies and, as such, they provide a simple, intuitive means of tweaking your tone settings.

Graphic EQs were surprisingly popular in the 70s and 80s (when, some would argue, too many contemporarily manufactured guitars and amps were of relatively poor quality and needed severe tweaking to sound decent). Players used them to cure ill-sounding frequency responses, tailor a rig for consistency in different room acoustics, or provide a boost in a specified frequency band for soloing. They were *de rigueur* on amps at around the same time, appearing on Mesa/Boogies and other new makes.

When players chose a graphic EQ in pedal form they chose an MXR more often than anything else. The six-band model was the standard for guitar, but players with a chip on their shoulder sometimes insisted on the ten-band unit (especially those who secretly believed that the guitar was dead and that the synth would soon rule the known universe). All of the usual suspects offered their own versions, and you can still find vintage graphic EQ pedals from DOD, Boss, Ibanez, Electro-Harmonix, and others.

C H A P T E R   4

136

If you've got an unfriendly hump in your frequency response that you just can't eradicate or simply feel your own slice of sonic heaven lies in a ten-band graphic EQ pattern that emulates the waves of the double-helix of baboon DNA, then one of these pedals might be what you need. If your guitar, pedal board, and amp are in sound shape and well connected, with desirable impedance matches and reasonable cable lengths, and you haven't over-egged the signal-chain pudding, you can probably live without a graphic EQ.

True Bypass

A world without true bypass—perish the thought—would be a dark, muddy place, inhabited only by the wan, hollow sound of tone sucking; or so many pedal manufacturers would have you believe. The fact is, true bypass is a great boon in certain situations, but not universally desirable in others. As with so many aspects of music technology, the benefits depend on how and where you use the feature. Let's first take a brief look at what true bypass really is, and what the alternatives are, before exploring its function on a pedal board.

Effects pedal manufacturers use the term 'true bypass' to describe pedals equipped with switching that sends the input directly to the output when the stomp-switch is in the 'off' position, and the feature has become a major selling point. In other words, the circuitry of the effect itself is bypassed, and the guitar signal continues along its merry way as if, in theory, no pedal were even there. This is also sometimes called 'hard-wired bypass,' although I would argue that this is a misnomer, as the input isn't truly hard-wired to the output (it isn't soldered from jack to jack), but is achieved with a switched connection. Achieving true bypass in a pedal where an LED on/off indicator light is also desirable requires a more complicated switch known as a 'three-pole, double-throw' switch (or 3PDT for short). Such a switch has two positions— 'on' and 'off'—but each of those makes three circuit connections within its housing. As such, instead of simply turning the effect part of the circuit on and off, as simpler switches do, true bypass pedals simultaneously switch the incoming guitar signal from effect circuit to output and switch the indicator LED from on to off. Some pedals also achieve true bypass through electronic switching, using a different type of switch to trigger a relay that flips the signal path from circuit board to output. The benefit of the true bypass circuit is that it sends your guitar signal straight along to the amp, or the next stage in the effects chain, without routing it around part of the pedal's circuitry, the way non-true-bypass pedals do. These have switches that simply turn the effect circuitry on and off, while the signal still runs through the remainder of the circuit before reaching the output jack.

True bypass's promise of pure, unfettered tone seems like a great thing, so why would we ever want anything else? When compared with many of the older-style effects pedals which tended to sap tone, even when a pedal was 'off,' courtesy of all their excess circuitry, true bypass is indeed a revelation. But most good contemporary non-true-bypass pedals use a buffers—a small, unity-gain preamp stage—to condition your guitar signal and help it survive the rest of its journey through the circuit, and the rest of the way to the amp, without loss of level or tone. A poor buffer can deplete the signal in and of itself, but a good one has the potential to help your tone make it the rest of the way to the amplifier sounding truer and bolder and more like

C H A P T E R 4

its original self than it would, in some cases, simply by passing unhindered, and un-buffered, down a long guitar cable. If you only use two or three effects pedals, with short cables from guitar to pedals and amp (along with short, high-quality jumper cables between pedals), true bypass pedals might indeed present the best option for uncompromised tone.

Say you use seven to ten pedals on your board, however, which is not an uncommon scenario, a 20-foot cable from your guitar to the first pedal on the board, several feet of cable to get around the board, and another 20-foot cord from the last pedal to your amp. Any guitar cable will impose a load on your guitar signal, and cables of more than 20 feet in length present a higher load that can really start to be heard in a loss of highs and a slight loss of overall clarity. Two of these back-to-back can really muddy the sonic water, and that's without even considering what the cabling on a crowded pedal board must be doing. With eight true-bypass pedals on the floor, your signal has to navigate 16 input and output jacks, 16 internal 3PDT switch terminals, and several inches of internal wiring, in addition to the connecting cables themselves. Add it all up and it can present a significant load to your signal—and mean a lot of tone sucking from a pedal rig that you have carefully assembled with the specific intention of *avoiding* such an undesirable outcome.

If you have even a handful of true-bypass pedals and a couple of long cables you can try this for yourself. Connect it all to the amp, switch all the pedals to 'off,' and play a while; now unplug your first cable and go straight to the amp. You will hear a difference. Now, if you have a good-quality buffered pedal, or a clean, linear preamp that you can set to unity gain (that is, where the output level is equal to the input level), put that in front of your multi-pedal set up and play. In all likelihood, your tone will sound a lot closer to the way it does with one cable straight into the amp.

Another problem with going totally true bypass is that your over-compensation for signal loss at the amp causes further tonal imbalance when you switch on one of the pedals and bring its built-in buffer into play. As British effects and switching-systems maker Pete Cornish points out, many players increase their amps' volume and treble settings to compensate for a tone dulled by dozens of feet of un-buffered cable. "If one of the pedals is now switched on, then its high input impedance—and, usually, low output impedance—will buffer all the output cables from the guitar, and the signal level will rise due to the removal of some of the load on the pickups," says Cornish. "So it's like you're suddenly playing through 17 feet instead of 55 feet of cable. The treble will rise, and the tone will not be as before. If that pedal was, say, a chorus or delay—devices which are usually unity gain—then your overall signal level and tone will vary each time an effect is added. Not a very good idea."

In an ideal world, most of us would love to be able to plug straight into the amp with a relatively short cable for our clean, unaffected tone, then run through just the pedals that are switched 'on' for any effected tones required. This is, essentially, what the big professional switching systems used by many touring musicians do, but these players still use buffers to help drive their long cable runs. In fact, you'll find very few touring professionals working without a good buffer in their signal chain, other than, perhaps, a few diehard, old-school minimalists with only a pedal or two and short cable runs, and these guys are most likely playing smaller venues where such a set-up will work. For most workaday, club-gigging guitarists, a big, expensive switching system that takes up several square feet of precious onstage real estate and requires three or four sliding drawers full of pedals in a backline road case just isn't practical. If such players really do need to run a plethora of effects pedals, they would usually do well to employ a carefully placed buffer somewhere in the chain.

Often a buffer works well in the first position of a crowded pedal board, where it will condition the signal right at the start to help it along its onward path. If you have one particular true-bypass pedal that you like to use first in the chain because of the way it interacts with your guitar's volume control, you might prefer to retain that one un-buffered and place the buffer later in the chain. Also, if you only use a handful of pedals but still want a buffer to help drive the signal run down the final long cable to the amp, there's nothing wrong with placing a buffer stage last, after three or four pedals, and you shouldn't experience any major signal or tonal loss in doing so.

You might find you already have a perfectly good buffer on your pedal board. There are plenty of desirable and perfectly good pedals manufactured these days that are *not* true-bypass, many of which hail from long-established makers. The likes of Boss, Ibanez, and other major names have always built non-true-bypass pedals with small buffer stages, while newer maker Visual Sound swears by the inclusion of a good buffer, and boutique manufacturer Barber Electronics offers a small buffer circuit that can be retrofitted to many of its existing pedals. Various companies offer dedicated buffer/preamp units that will do the job well, and many of the more complicated amp switchers carry buffers, too. Also, if you've got several pedals that you tend to only use one at a time, you can group them and keep them out of the signal path when switched off by placing them in the loop of a good true-bypass loop-selector pedal, another great way of cutting down your cable lengths. Experiment with your buffer placement and pedal order, listen closely to the results, make frequent A/B comparisons with your guitar's straight-in tone, and go with whatever works best for you.

Effects Placement and Routing

Many of us yearn for the simplicity and tonal purity that is going from guitar straight to amp—this is often hailed as the romantic, old-school way of doing things, and guitar chat rooms are crowded with players who swear they never play any other way. If you are playing in anything other than a raw blues outfit, a jazz combo, or a Ramones tribute band, however, you probably require a pedal or two to get the job done adequately. At the very least, few professional players (or serious gigging amateurs) can get away without using a tuner pedal for silent on-stage tune-ups, and once you have broken the straight-to-amp cable connection with one pedal, it usually doesn't hurt to add an overdrive and delay down there, too; and why not a little tremolo, a booster for cleaner lead breaks, and a wah-wah pedal while you're at it? Before you know it you have racked up half-a-dozen pedals and constructed a small board to house them. Now you are confronted with the conundrums that are connecting order and routing, while trying to preserve your much-loved clean tone all the while. There are several ways of doing this, and what works best for you will depend upon where your sonic priorities lie. If you have more than two or three

C H A P T E R 4

pedals on the floor, a compromise will most likely need to be made somewhere, but if you work with your sonic priorities in mind this doesn't need to be something that cripples your tone.

Connecting Order

Nothing discussed here should be taken as a hard and fast law, but it's always worth understanding the standards before exploring the exceptions. The accepted wisdom for connecting pedals says that tone filters and EQs are placed first (that is, the guitar plugs directly into them), gain-producing devices such as overdrive and distortion pedals come second, modulation devices such as chorus and flanger pedals are third, and delay devices such as echo and reverb last (and in that order, if you have both). A common variation on this, depending on the specific pedals you are using and the tones you are seeking, is to swap the middle two of these four stages. Some modulation devices such as vintage-style analog choruses, phasers, or Uni-Vibes, and their clones, do their best work when placed *before* overdrive or fuzz pedals. This is mostly because their function and sound includes an element of filtering-type tone shifting that can sound great going *into* an overdrive pedal but pretty gnarly when working its magic on a signal that is already distorted.

For our purposes, consider wah-wah pedals as EQ or tone-filtering devices, which is really what they are. For most applications, they work best placed first in the chain, with your guitar going straight into them, and that's the option favored by such players as Jimi Hendrix, Eric Johnson, Yngwie Malmsteen, and J Mascis. Others, however, do things a little differently. Carlos Santana places a Tube Screamer before his wah-wah; Brian May puts his treble booster first; and Steve Vai has used wah-wahs both before and after his Boss DS-1 Distortion pedal. The order in which you use such effects depends upon whether you want to distort the frequency-swept tone of the wah-wah (that is, sequence the wah-wah first, with overdrive second), or sweep the frequency of an already distorted tone. The only way to decide what's best for you is to try it both ways.

The placement of a fuzz pedal provides another dilemma: most vintage-style fuzz units interact best with your picking dynamics and your guitar's volume control when they are connected first in the chain. For many wah-wah applications, however, you want fuzz to come afterward. Convention says you should put the wah-wah first, but again, you have to decide for yourself what sounds best.

Delay: The Room Around it All

When working with delay placement, it often helps to remember where this sonic effect came from in the first place. Whether reverb, slap-back echo or long delay, this is an emulation of the sound of playing in a specific room or space. For that reason, delay-based devices will usually go last in the chain so that they envelope the rest of your tone-shapers and paint the final picture of the 'size' and 'atmosphere' of your sound. In other words, you want your fully overdriven and modulated tone to be treated to the spatial effects of echo or reverb—to echo your fuzz, rather than fuzzing your echo, as it were.

Following this prescribed order generally results in the highest fidelity and the greatest depth

C H A P T E R   4

for each effect in the rig. Mixing it up, on the other hand, might create odd and unusual sounds that just happen to produce the sonic magic you are looking for, so don't be afraid to experiment (but do check your effects device manuals first to make sure you won't overload any given delay unit—digital units in particular—by running a hot gain/distortion device into it).

The functions of certain components will also sometimes force you to change the conventional running order of your pedals. For example, if you get your overdrive sound from the lead input in a channel-switching amp rather than an overdrive or distortion pedal, and your reverb and/or echo sounds come from individual pedals or outboard units, you're a little stuck. Many such amps have effects loops that you can run delay-based devices in—that's exactly what they're intended for (again, read manuals to make sure FX loop levels won't overload such devices, and adjust levels accordingly where possible). If your amp has no effects loop but you still want to get your lead sound from its high-gain channel, you'll just have to decide which compromise you'd prefer to make.

In addition, any time you use more than one of each type of effects pedal you will probably have to compromise somewhere. Test, experiment, and work with what you've got to create the best sound for your own music. It helps to know convention, but don't be bound by it if something a little out of the ordinary actually helps to produced the tones in your head. Even Jimi Hendrix had to compromise, and he certainly broke plenty of rules, too. His most legendary pedal set up ran: *guitar—Vox Wah-Wah—Fuzz Face—Octavia—Uni-Vibe*, in that order. That's *filter/EQ—gain—filter—modulation*, in other words. Did it work for him?

Stereo Pedals

Several delay and chorus pedals, and a few others, come with stereo outputs to enable a broadening of the effect's dimensions by connecting to a pair of amplifiers. With only a single amp you will of, course, use only the mono output from such effects (it's usually the left out, if not specified). With two amps and a single stereo pedal on the floor, you simply connect one to the left output and one to the right output, although sometimes it's not quite so simple. Effects chains with multiple pedals might throw up conflicts in connecting order: perhaps you have a stereo chorus or Uni-Vibe-style pedal that you prefer to use *before* your overdrive, but you also want to make use of the width of the stereo field, for example. Ideally, you would connect any stereo pedal last in the chain, but in the above scenario you would have to decide either to run the overdrive after only one of the stereo outputs and keep the other output clean, or compromise your sonic ideal and put the overdrive before the stereo effect. Either that or buy a second overdrive pedal and work out a tortuous tap dance routine which allows you to switch on both simultaneously.

Other conflicts arise when you have two stereo pedals in your setup. Sometimes more complex stereo delays and reverbs (rack-mounted units in particular) will have stereo inputs as well as outputs, and this makes it easy, for example, to connect a stereo chorus pedal before your delay to get the full stereo effect of both, one into the other. Otherwise, you will have to decide whether the sound of stereo chorus, stereo echo, or stereo reverb, whatever the case may be, is most important to you. Try all the alternatives, and go with whatever feels like the least obtrusive compromise.

Split Chains

In some circumstances, it can help to leave linear thinking behind and explore how different effects might be used in entirely different signal paths. Often, a broad soundscape can be achieved by sending differently treated mono signals to different amplifiers. For example, imagine your pedal board runs: *compressor—stereo vibe—overdrive—echo*. With two amps to play through, you could split the left output of the vibe pedal to amp one, and send the right output on to the rest of the effects chain and, ultimately, amp two. Now, when you step on the overdrive, which is placed *after* the vibe pedal, you get crunch and lead tones in amp two, while amp one stays crisp and clean to retain better definition. Alternatively, set amp one to crunchy, to beef up the clean and rhythm tones, then you'll go into a thick, rich lead tone when you step on the overdrive, which will result in pedal-based clipping in amp two, and milder amp-based clipping in amp one.

Parallel Paths

You can even use multiple signal paths going to just one amplifier with two channels, or even, when appropriate, one amp with one channel and two inputs. Consider a scenario where you want to maintain some definition and clarity in your tone, even when you're using overdrive for leads, but you want to try the dirty amp/clean amp blend effect described above. With a two-channel amp (that is, an amp with two independent channels that can operate simultaneously, *not* a channel-switching amp), split your signal before your overdrive or distortion pedal, and run it to channel one set for clean, then send it on to the rest of the effects and out to channel two. This will preserve more of the unadulterated guitar sound in your overall signal and should help you retain more clarity in the resultant tone.

Even two channels in the same amp, each set to different gain and EQ levels, can yield more of a rich, complex tone than one channel alone. When doing this, ensure that the two channels are working at the same phase relationship to each other. If your sound is notably thin and 'hollow' sounding when you try both channels together, the phase of one is most likely the reverse of the other. Some effects pedals will reverse a signal's phase between input and output, so splitting the signal before that pedal could cause such a reversal. Many black and silverface Fender amps of the 60s and 70s have two channels that are reverse phase of each other (because the channel with reverb and/or vibrato carries an extra triode stage). Splitting to different signal paths might cure this, or retain it. You will have to experiment to see what works, and if it's the latter you can also use a decent A/B/Y switching pedal with a phase switch on one output. Also, you can often use input one and input two in a single-channel amp with two inputs to achieve some of the same results described above.

Effects-Loop Pedals

Loop pedals—which are really just signal-chain routing devices with footswitches to select either of one, two, or even more 'loops'—can be very useful if you have a lot of effects on your board and don't want to run your signal through them at all times, thus potentially depleting tonal quality (these loopers should not be confused with the repeating-delay pedals that let you record and 'loop' a riff). If you use pedals that are notably noisy even when switched out, or that result in a loss of highs, lows, or general signal fidelity when they aren't switched in, a looper is a great way of rectifying the situation. And you can use any number of pedals within a single loop to take them out of the signal path when not in use.

To use such a device, run a patch cable from the loop pedal's 'send' to the input of the first pedal in the loop and string the rest together as normal, concluding with a patch cable to the 'return' of the loop pedal. Any pedals that you use frequently and which aren't problematic in terms of noise or tone sucking—a good overdrive or compressor, for example—can still go before the loop pedal (that is, between guitar and loop pedal). If you have just one pedal in the loop, leave it on at all times and let the loop footswitch take it in and out of the signal path. With more than one pedal in the loop, you'll need to switch any effects on at the start of the song that requires it (with the loop still off) and bring it in with the loop switch as needed—or use a looper with multiple loops to leave all the looped pedals on all the time.

Once again, as many supposed 'rules' as there are in the effects world, there are often ten times as many ways of breaking them. If working against type proves the best way to achieve your creative goals—and doesn't prove damaging to your gear—there's no reason at all to stick to the standards. Extreme effects abuse has worked for everyone from Dinosaur Jr.'s J Mascis to Sonic Youth's Thurston Moore and Lee Ranaldo, and Wilco's Nels Cline, and it might just work for you.

C H A P T E R 4

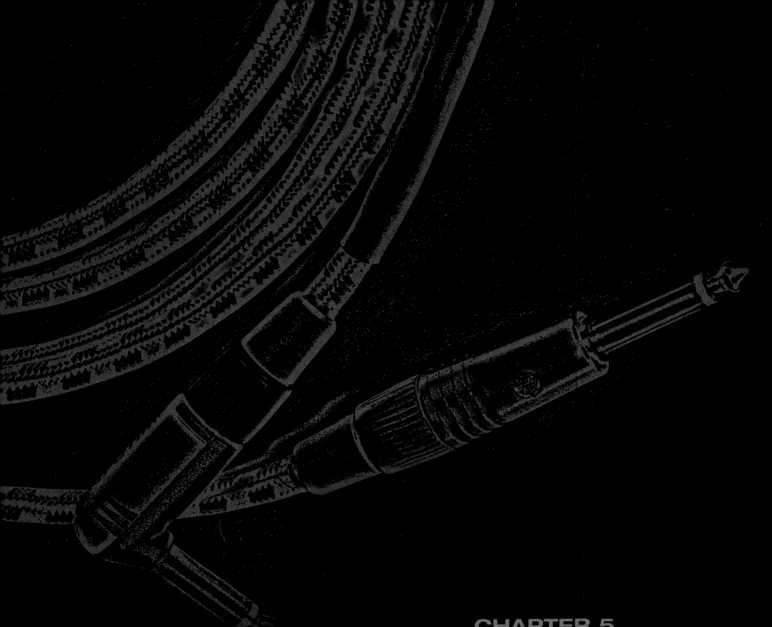

CHAPTER 5

PERIPHERALS AND CONSUMABLES

- Guitar cables
- Speaker cables
- Guitar strings
- Guitar picks

Would you put a set of half-bald retreads on your Ferrari Testarossa? I thought not. Devoting untold time and thought to your guitar, amp, and effects selections only to drag it all down with inferior cables, strings, and other accessories would be a similarly deleterious move. For some guitarists, these peripherals are the least sexy of subjects to contemplate; mere necessities to be acquired then forgotten. For others, the hunt for high-end accessories can be an obsession. There's a healthy halfway point, I'm sure, but whatever your opinion of these bits and pieces, it pays tonal dividends to get them right and to make sure your well-thought-out rig isn't falling flat due to one little tone-sucking link in the chain.

GUITAR CABLES

Whether you call them leads, cords, or cables, it's that thin, stranded wire which carries all of your precious tone to whatever's going to broadcast it to the masses, irrespective of the gear at either end of it. Too many guitarists are gigging and recording with cables purchased somewhat at random (ask, and they might not even remember when or where they came from). As often as not, these cables are in need of urgent attention, or immediate replacement.

As with any piece of music or audio equipment, cords can be divided into qualitative categories, namely: high end, great, satisfactory, and cheap-and-nasty. Your own choice within this realm will have a lot to do with your budget, of course, while also being tempered by your ear and your tonal tastes; but however thin of wallet you might be, always steer clear of the cheap and nasty. The price tag is a giveaway: if it's the cheapest cord in the cheapest guitar store (or cell-phone outlet) in town, you probably don't want it. That's not to say there aren't bargains out there—but if you plug in a cheap 20-foot cord and it dulls your sound noticeably by comparison with another (possibly shorter) cord plugged straight in, or if it's so microphonic that you can easily induce an audible 'thunk' in the amp just by slapping it on the floor, you really don't want it. If you have to sell your grandma (or even just rent her out for a while), you should at the very least acquire and hold on to a satisfactory cord, and ideally a couple if you run effects pedals between guitar and amp.

Beyond that point, while you can spend a lot of money on audiophile-grade cables with mind-boggling specs and impressive write ups, four out of five guitarists will probably get as much service as they're ever going to want out of a merely great, rather than a superb, cord. While many of the pricey (we're talking approximately $100 for a 12-foot cord here), genuinely high end, audiophile-grade guitar cords do indeed let a lot more tone down the pipe, for some guitarists this actually constitutes *too much* tone. We're not used to hearing the highest highs and the lowest lows. All that fidelity messes up our amp and effects settings and ultimately just sounds harsh. That's all there is to it. Arguably, we should readjust our settings and our style and adapt to the fact that cords such as these allow us to hear the big picture. Often, however, it's just easier, and more practical, to stick with the ever-so-slight tone sucking of the merely great cord. For, rest assured, any cord—whatever its quality—will deplete your signal just a wee bit if used in lengths beyond just a few feet. In some cases we hear this as 'warmth,' 'smoothness,' or some other adjective with a positive tonal spin. That's fine, as far it goes. Use

C H A P T E R 5

extremes of cable length, however, and the impedance created by all that wire can really start to dull your tone (see the section in the previous chapter about true bypass and buffers for a more detailed discussion of the effect of cable lengths on tone). Even with great cords, you need to consider your lengths and connections, and if you need to drive long cable lengths for your stage show, consider doing so from the output end of a buffered pedal or preamp, going low impedance to help your signal make the journey undiminished.

How do you select a great cord? Check for low microphony, sturdy plugs, a look—and more often than not, a name—of quality, and a lack of noticeable tone sucking from reasonable lengths: in short, an absence of all the signifiers that tell you a cord is cheap and nasty. Among several respected modern cord makers in the more affordable camp are Mogami, Van Damme, Canare, Gepco, and Gotham, while in the high quality, high-cost category Klotz, Cardas Audio, and Sommer are names to look out for. When it comes to the audiophile cream, Van Den Hul, Evidence Audio, and Solid Cable are revered makers.

Even if you took the plunge and invested in a couple of high-end cables three years ago, the chances are they don't sound as crystal clear to you now as they did during the first few weeks you were using them. While loss of tone might be down to your tubes, guitar, strings, or even your ears (perhaps a combination of all those), the solution may be very simple: you just need to clean the plugs on your cords. UK pedal and control-system maker Pete Cornish is adamant about this. "Clean the plugs and free the tone," Pete once told me; it has become a mantra of his. Over time and use, a thin layer of tarnish builds up on the shafts and tips of those plugs, and that metal needs to be clean to allow an unimpeded flow of electrons from plug to jack, or vice versa. Every couple of months, give them a squirt of a good contact cleaner such as DeOxIt or NoFlash, apply a little elbow grease with a soft, lint-free cloth, and get back to business. The improvement should open your ears.

For truly optimum tone from whatever cable you have, you might consider one other tidbit. It may sound like science fiction, but it's really just science: guitar cords are directional. That means they very often sound a little better when plugged in one way around than they do the reverse. That tip comes from the late, great amp guru Ken Fischer. Ken was a senior engineer at Ampeg for many years and is best known as the man behind the ultra-rare, highly collectable, hand-built Trainwreck amps. To assuage my disbelief, Ken pointed out that most wire, including the type used in the stranded wire which makes up the 'positive' or 'hot' lead within your guitar cord, is *extruded*. That means it is produced by 'squirting' hot metal out of a machine through a hole of the desired gauge, a little like making spaghetti with one of those domestic pasta makers. As such, the metal from which the wire is made flows directionally during the manufacturing process, and that directionality also proves to be the quickest path for electrons to follow when it is cooled, spun, and made into a guitar cable.

Traditionally, quality audio cable has the writing on its outer insulation printed in the direction of its flow. I'm not going to assume, however, that the manufacturer of the average guitar cord had any idea, or paid attention to, the direction in which their bulk wire supplies were extruded (to any who actually do, I apologize). So how do we tell which way round is optimum for any given cord? It's not rocket science, as Ken Fischer explains. "Try it both ways, listen carefully, and see which sounds best to you." Immediately after he passed this info along to me a few years back I checked it out with the half-a-dozen quality guitar cords of 12 to 20 feet in length that were at hand. There was a discernible improvement in four out of the six when deployed one way versus the other. Try it with your own cables and see what you find. Be sure to clean the plugs first, although if they're cheap and nasty to start with you're probably flogging a dead horse.

When you upgrade guitar cords, don't overlook the short patch cables which run between your effects pedals. Once you begin improving anything in the signal chain, any mediocre piece left in place will quickly take on 'weakest-link' status and drag down the purity of your signal regardless, making your other upgrades effectively pointless. The cables between your pedals are much shorter than those between guitar and first pedal and between last pedal and amp, so issues of capacitance aren't a major problem, but their quality, or lack thereof, will still contribute to your overall tone—for the worse if you have spent money elsewhere but ignored these humble little wires.

SPEAKER CABLES

When connecting an amp head to an extension cabinet, or wiring up a replacement connection in a combo amp, you should use a speaker cable—and by that I mean a *real* speaker cable. Getting this right or wrong, as simple as it is, can be the difference between good and bad tone, and getting it right means preventing expensive amp repairs or premature maintenance down the road. When I say 'real' speaker cable, I mean a two-core cable in which each stranded core is of an equal gauge (thickness), and, crucially, *not* a guitar cable, which has one thin, insulated, stranded 'positive' wire in the middle of a braided shield serving as the 'ground' connection.

This might seem obvious: speaker cable for connecting speakers, guitar cord for plugging in your guitar, but the ramifications of getting it right or wrong go way beyond the name on the wire. While a genuine speaker cable of good quality delivers the amp's output equally to the speaker's positive and negative terminals, the unequal design of a guitar cord—to reiterate, one thin insulated signal wire surrounded by one very wide shield—introduces a lot of unwanted capacitance to the connection, which can create an impedance mismatch between amp and speaker. In addition, the thin, positive wire in a guitar cord is of a much lower gauge than you would normally want to use to make an output connection, especially from a powerful amp. The impedance mismatch will strain your amp's output tubes and output transformer and will severely choke and dull down your tone as a result. What's more, if that thin 'hot' wire inside the guitar cord gets *too* hot and shorts, you could blow your output transformer entirely, necessitating an expensive repair.

Trouble arises because many speaker cables made for use with amps often look superficially similar to guitar cables. Most good, modern speaker cables will have their function printed on the outer sheath somewhere, and some will be noticeably thicker than guitar cords; but if it doesn't say, or if you just don't know one way or the other, don't make any assumptions. Confusion can occur when a guitarist buys a used amp-head-and-cab set that comes with a so-called 'speaker cable' which the previous owner has used with it for years; the purchaser

assumes, not unreasonably, that this must indeed be the correct connecting cable. Often it is not. The owner may have been using a guitar cord all along, and while he or she might have had the good fortune to avoid damaging the amp in any severe way, his or her tone will have suffered at the very least, and so will yours.

To distinguish between guitar and amp cords if there aren't words on the cable to advise you, simply unscrew the barrel (shield) of the plug at one end, if you can, and take a look at the connections inside. If it's a guitar cord, you'll very clearly see one thin 'positive' wire in the center connected to the terminal from the tip of the plug, and a braided outer shield that has been twisted and connected to the ground of the plug. A genuine speaker cable, on the other hand, will have two similar-looking insulated wires inside (often the insulation on one is white, the other black, but different colors are also used), both of which come from the center of the cord, rather than one being a braided shield that encloses the other. Another way to test it is to use it as a guitar cord to connect your guitar to an amplifier. A genuine speaker cable should induce a lot of noise, since there is no shielding around the positive wire in the cable. If you can't check the cable, and have even the least suspicion at all, don't use it. Discard it, and get a genuine speaker cable. It isn't worth taking the chance to save the few dollars a decent piece of wire will cost you.

Many of the same reputable makers of guitar cables mentioned above also make quality speaker cables, but a lot of players wire up their own speaker cables. It's easy to do, if you know the basics of soldering and have the tools, and usually it's cheaper than purchasing cables while also giving you the option of customizing cable length to suit your needs. Any good quality hi-fi speaker hook-up wire will do the job, and you can often still buy this by the foot, yard, or meter at your local hardware store—or you could buy a full spool and have plenty on hand for your future needs. Very short amp-to-speaker connections within smaller combo amps can get away with 18 AWG (American Wire Gauge) wire, but I'd want to use 16 AWG for anything more than a foot or so, or 14 AWG for longer cables of two to four feet or more (this is erring toward over-caution, perhaps, but why not, since you're making these yourself?). It's also worth leaning toward heavier gauges for more powerful amps which can heat up thinner wires at high output levels. Along with the cable, you just need a pair of good quality, quarter-inch phone plugs, a soldering iron, and a little solder. Many plugs have screw-terminal connections, but I don't trust them: remove the screws entirely and make a good solder connection to the terminal so you know it will hold. With thicker wire gauges, the larger plugs with wider barrels available from some suppliers will make it easier to establish good connections and to fit the screw-on barrel over the cable. Even if you have plenty of wire, make your cables only as long as you really need them to be, and your amp will thank you for it. And while you're at it, make a spare and carry it to every gig, so you don't resort to using a guitar cord again out of desperation when your main amp connector suddenly goes missing or shorts out pre-gig.

Another good Ken Fischer tip regarding speaker cables is worth sharing. If you're looking for decent wire to make up your own cables, use a length of two-core electrical wire which has been attached to a domestic vacuum cleaner for many years. Ken's theory is that the considerable current draw of such high-amp appliances configures the molecules in the stranded wire within their AC cords so that they are efficiently directional at passing signal. While you are at it, be sure to also mark the wire before you cut it so you know which end was coming from the wall outlet and which was going into the vacuum (you will only need a portion of this length, of course) so that you use the directionality of the cable, rather than working against it— as with Ken's tip regarding guitar cables, above. Like that one, this might sound bonkers, but I know several guitarists who make their speaker cables this way and swear by the results.

Before closing this section, let me emphasize the point again: however great a guitar you've got, however rare and refined your priceless vintage or boutique tube amp, and despite the precision, high-end guitar cords you might be using in front of it, deploying a guitar cord to make the connection between amp and speaker will instantly deplete your tone. Get a quality speaker cable, or wire up your own, and you will at least know that all the goodness you are putting into the front end of your amp is making its way out the back.

GUITAR STRINGS

Chapter One of *The Tone Manual* discussed a great many elements that contribute to guitar tone, but we haven't yet examined the component with which your sound really begins: the strings. Plenty of other factors come into play simultaneously to contribute to the sound made by any guitar—wood resonance, pickup response, the density and solidity of different pieces of hardware—but without the plucked string, none of this stuff is going to make a peep. The fun thing about strings, too, is that once you develop a thorough understanding of the qualities of their different types, you can use that knowledge to tweak the sound and feel of any kind of guitar, and do so in about 15 minutes for a cost of around $5.

Many guitarists think about strings more in relation to feel than to sound, and put little consideration into elements of their strings' composition other than seeking a gauge that feels good on their fingertips and is easy to bend and fret. Some sacrifice a little finger strain for a heavier gauge that offers a punchier tone, or go heavier simply in an effort to achieve a firmer, less 'rubbery' playing feel, but still don't give much thought to the tonal properties of the strings themselves. It's important to know, however, that the steel that strings are made from, and the quality of their overall manufacture, will have a major effect on how they vibrate and therefore how they sound. Most players will be aware of these variables at some level, whether or not they know where the tonal variations are coming from, or why they are occurring.

In the jazz, blues, rock'n'roll, and classic-rock eras of the late 40s, 50s, and 60s, pure nickel-wound lower E, A, and D-strings were used (and in the early days even G-strings), with plain steel B and E-strings. Later, unwound plain-steel G-strings became the norm. A pure nickel wire wrapped around a plain steel core gave the wound strings of the previous eras a warm, full, rich tonality, and generally longer life, although nickel's lower magnetism also meant a slightly lower output from the pickups. The high cost of nickel led to a wide-scale change to nickel-plated steel windings around 1970, with a resultant tone that was brighter and somewhat thinner, if perhaps punchier, and usually saw a reduced life span for the wound strings. The significantly reduced nickel content in nickel-plated strings means a greater magnetic reaction between strings and pickups, and therefore a slightly higher output; it's worth noting that they also wear out frets

TONE TIP — String Height

String height is a key factor in any guitar's set-up, but one that newer players often approach from too narrow a perspective. Learners are understandably drawn to guitars on which the strings are as low to the fingerboard as is functionally possible—instruments which are kind to tender and unfamiliar fingers inevitably feel more comfortable. From this point on, a player's 'feel preference' is often set in stone and the 'low action-equals-great-guitar' bias is imposed on all the subsequent guitars they choose or have professionally set up.

Low action definitely makes a guitar easier to play, and for some styles it really is a necessity. But guitarists who perpetually chase 'the perfect tone,' while continually focusing on string height purely as a function of playing feel rather than as a factor of that tone, are missing a significant element in pulling it all together. The old setup rule that you 'get your strings as low as you can without buzzing' seems to make perfect sense. Set up to that criterion, however, and while your strings might not buzz noticeably, their vibrational arc will almost certainly still be inhibited by the proximity of the frets. Also, play harder than usual—which, if you're like

me, you will often find yourself doing in live situations, even if you're not initially aware of it—and that setup does also lead to a little unwanted buzzing, although your amp settings, the energy of the live gig, and any effects in the chain might help to mask it.

Just for fun, try taking this inverted approach to setting string height: instead of getting them as low as you can without inducing serious buzzing, set your strings as high as you can have them and still be able to play with some reasonable facility. Doing this correctly might also require adjusting string intonation at the bridge saddles, because their angle and distance across their speaking length is now changing slightly, too. For now, however, just try it as is, in case you choose to return your action to its starting point. As you make this adjustment, you can even note down how many turns of each saddle or bridge-height screw you make to achieve the new string height, so you can return it to normal if so desired (note that raising string height at the bridge might need to be coordinated with a tweak of neck relief at the truss rod, too; although I will leave that to your own best judgment as there is plenty of

more quickly than softer, pure nickel-wrapped strings. Other compositions introduced over the years, such as stainless steel and chrome, offer further proportional increases in overall brightness of tone compared with nickel-plated and, certainly, pure-nickel strings, and the increased hardness of these types denudes frets even more rapidly.

You can use this knowledge to fine-tune your tone as required. If you have a heavy, dark-sounding guitar that could use a little more cut and brightness, with maximum output remaining a priority, a set that some companies call 'brights'—the aforementioned chrome or stainless steel strings—might be right for you. If you want contemporary sounds and some clarity, while avoiding harsh treble and without mellowing out your tone too much, nickel-plated strings may be the best option. In the quest for authentic vintage sound and feel, pure nickel strings are likely to get you there quickest.

Nickel strings resonate differently, with more depth and richness, many would argue, and debate between the flat-neck/slight-relief lobbies, and this determination will depend upon your own preferences).

Play your guitar like this for a while and notice how much more ring, richness, and sustain you get out of it. The strings should now vibrate for close to the full potential of the instrument (which, of course, also depends upon factors such as nut and bridge type and condition, body style, neck and body woods, and so forth). Put simply, your tone is now likely to sound bigger and fuller, and to bloom with a broader voice and longer note decay than previously. If this 'as high as you can hack it' setting is a little too much for everyday playing, try backing the strings down a hair at a time, and hopefully you can find a height that offers a healthy compromise. Sure, it's also possible you preferred it the way it was before you adjusted it at all, and if your playing style involves a lot of speed riffing, hammer-ons and pull-offs, or extreme bending, you might require that low-as-possible action just to get the job done (and you will very likely mask any drawbacks with judicious high-gain amp or pedal settings). With any luck, however, you'll have discovered an easy means of achieving a fatter tone without purchasing or modifying another thing.

Higher strings can potentially induce some drawbacks that you will need to minimize. Before settling on your new action, you'll need to determine that strings don't go out of tune in any fretting positions up and down the neck. You also need to ensure that using a capo, if you play with one, doesn't throw all the strings out of pitch too badly. Also note that if this experimentation results in raising your strings considerably from their previous position—and your guitar remains playable after doing so—you might also need to adjust your pickup height slightly. Increasing the distance between pickups and strings can often also help the strings to vibrate more freely (as discussed previously), so lowering the pickups might yield a double bonus. Play with the options and see what works best for you.

Once you have established your preference, be sure to check and calibrate your intonation, as necessary. It's fine if low action floats your boat, but it's worth remembering that there's a wealth of tone hiding in that thin slice of air between string and fingerboard.

their relative softness compared to the other types can even make them feel a little easier to fret (which is also why they wear down your frets more slowly). Pure nickel strings might prove a simple means of warming up an over-bright, single-coil guitar, or even smoothing out the performance of a humbucker-carrying instrument. A loss of output and treble might seem detrimental to some players, but remember, that's what your amp's volume and tone controls are there for.

String gauge certainly affects guitar tone, but it works in conjunction with other factors such as scale length and tuning (that is, string tension), action or string height, and playing technique, specifically the lightness or heaviness of your touch and pick attack. All things being equal, heavier strings do induce a greater signal in the pickup, but that's not to say this is a universally good thing. It takes more energy to get heavier strings moving, so they need to be hit relatively harder with pick or fingertip; lighter strings will vibrate to a similar intensity with a lighter

C   H   A   P   T   E   R   5

touch, but can be overwhelmed and vibrate off-pitch in the early part of their attack when hit too hard.

In the wake of late blues legend Stevie Ray Vaughan's widely trumpeted predilection for heavy strings, thousands of players went out and increased their size by a gauge or two. Of course, Vaughan's choice suited his technique: he hit the strings like hell unchained when he wanted to really get some sound out of them—and he had to use Super Glue to seal up fissured fingertips as a result. Certainly it might be worth experimenting with strings a gauge higher than your habitual choice if you're looking for a little more oomph out of your tone and are willing to take the time to develop your technique and finger strength to compensate. Equally, going from .009s or .010s to .012s or .013s is just as likely to frustrate you by flattening out your tone.

It's also worth knowing that Stevie Ray Vaughan tuned down to E flat with these heavier strings loaded on his Strats. If you really want to adjust to heavier strings, tuning down a half step for every gauge you go up comes close to evening out the tension and giving you a feel similar to that of the gauge below at standard tuning. This might provide a means of getting familiar with a new gauge, even if you eventually return to standard pitch for the majority of your playing (which, of course, will require a little more readjustment). Also, if you have always played nickel-plated, chrome, or stainless-steel bright-style strings and want to switch to pure nickel, be aware that these strings sometimes feel soft enough to let you go up a gauge without too much effort.

Plenty of players seeking that vintage Beatles or Byrds tone of the mid 60s, or the smooth, warm jazz tones of the 40s and 50s, were frustrated in their endeavors until they rediscovered the beauty of flat-wound strings. Standard-issue on many guitars up until the mid 60s, pure nickel flat-wound strings are even warmer and, if you will, 'rounder' sounding, and help to smooth out the potential harsh highs heard in certain 'jangle' tones achieved with round-wound strings made from harder wrap materials. For the jazz player seeking vintage Wes Montgomery tones, flat-wounds can often prove a revelation and a quick trip to thick, rich sounds and smooth, finger-squeak-free changes.

Experiment with whatever strings you can get your hands on, and see what different gauges, metals, and composition types can do for you. It's a relatively affordable way to tweak your tone.

GUITAR PICKS

There's one tonal element that is entirely within every player's power to modify, with no risk to guitar, amp, or effects, without voiding any warrantees, and at very little expense. Indeed, this item is one of the most underappreciated tools in the tone arsenal. The humble pick, or plectrum—that semi-rigid sliver that sets your strings a-humming—comes in a range of different sizes, shapes, gauges, and materials, each of which induce different sounds. Unadorned fingertips offer further tone-modifying alternatives. The pick or fingertips coming into contact with the string (or strings) is where tonal considerations truly begin.

As a basic rule of thumb, if you will, thinner and more flexible picks yield a lighter, softer sound, but one that can also be effectively percussive for rhythm playing. The heavier and more rigid the material from which it is made, the less the pick gives when attacking the string, and the more energy it transfers into the string rather than into itself as it bends—which translates into a heavier sound and a more aggressive attack (this is basic science—we're talking Newton's Third Law: "For every action there is an equal and opposite reaction"). Play a set of heavy-gauge strings with a thin-gauge pick and you will mostly end up with a choked sound and a chewed-up pick. Hit them with a heavy or extra-heavy-gauge plectrum and you can really start moving some steel. Old tortoiseshell picks are the epitome of this: the rigid material offers negligible give and yields a firm attack with sparkling harmonics. Being made from an endangered material, tortoiseshell picks aren't available any more, but if you come across an old one, give it a try: the difference will probably startle you. Many man-made alternatives offer similar performance.

The shape of the attacking edge or corner of a pick also greatly influences the resultant sound. A triangular or pointed tip digs into the string sharply, inducing sparkling highs and good harmonic content thanks to its narrow but firm point of contact. A rounded edge blurs the attack slightly, yielding a warmer, smoother sound. You can use this knowledge to your advantage when seeking to alter the tone of any guitar, and don't feel you need to have to stick to a single pick type—mix it up, and find what works best for different styles of playing.

To give more bite and brightness to a Les Paul's fat, warm neck-pickup, for example, use a firmer pick with a more sharply pointed playing tip. On the flipside, warm up the cutting tone of a Tele or Strat carrying single coils with a more rounded pick, or take some of the aggression out of the high-gain pickups of your shred monster by using a thinner pick for a smoother, more compressed rhythm tone. Many jazz players use the rounded back edge of a standard-shaped pick to elicit an even smoother, more plummy tone from classic jazz boxes, and Stevie Ray Vaughan (yes, him again) was said to use the back edge of his picks to get more body out of Stratocasters. In contrast to all of this, bare thumb or fingertips yield a slightly muted, thick, warm sound, but one that can vary greatly depending upon technique. Many fingerstyle players are also capable of producing sudden, bright, attacking riffs by snapping or plucking the strings heavily, and many add fingernail tips to the attack, which brightens up the sound further.

Try out the effects of pick attack for yourself; the expense is negligible, and it's a lot easier than swapping pickups, speakers, or even strings. Procure a range of picks in different shapes, sizes, and gauges, and experiment at will to see what works for the different playing requirements you might have. After all, the more tools you have in your arsenal, the more versatile a player you're likely to be.

C H A P T E R 5

Tone Reference Guide

In the introduction to this book I said I believe that striving for your own, unique sound will ultimately prove far more rewarding than any amount of effort you make to exactly replicate the tones of great players who have gone before. Having restated that truism, however, I should emphasize that there is nothing intrinsically wrong with learning the art of tone-crafting by listening to stand-out sounds created by others. And to that end, I've compiled here a brief guide that details some tonally noteworthy recordings of the past six decades. I've also included information on the gear that was used to make them, although it is rarely possible to pinpoint this definitively.

Rather than merely paying homage once again to a much-venerated canon of guitar greats, I would like to offer a few notes here and there as addendums to 'legendary' tones that, revisited as objectively as possible, aren't always entirely stellar. I've also featured some perhaps surprising selections that I think sound truly outstanding.

I would argue that plenty of the so-called 'classic tones' that we have come to accept as exemplary have earned that status thanks to the performances of the individual players and the quality of the songs which they grace rather than their inherent sonic characteristics. Often when you analyze them with an unprejudiced ear, they can prove to be fairly grim—certainly in terms of any universal standards of 'superior tone.'

With this in mind, consider this chapter more of a listening exercise than a parade of the greatest tones or players of all time. Some entries may certainly qualify on that level, but it would be relatively easy to add dozens, hundreds, maybe even thousands of names to such a list. Instead, think of it as a brief compendium of listening suggestions, designed to illustrate how a number of tones are applied in context. In general, I'm erring away from heavily-effected tones—the spacey sounds and 1,000-pound-violin tones—and aiming more toward pure straight-in tones, with maybe a pedal or two for a little boost or shimmer.

Bear in mind that even where it is fairly certain which guitars, amps, and effects the artist used, variables such as recording environment and studio equipment, including specific microphones, preamps, desks, and outboard processing, are often unknown, or have been forgotten by those who might once have known, and that these, too, will have played a part in creating the final results that we hear on record.

Finally, one more disclaimer: in addition to the above, all of the rigs in question would undoubtedly have sounded different if you, or I, or any guitarist other than those featured here had played them. So, as ever, bear in mind that it's the head, heart, and fingers making the music that remain the biggest variables of all.

While the majority of these examples are recognized classics in the pantheon of guitar tone, there are innumerable lesser-known artists crafting outstanding tones to support beautiful music, and they are always worth seeking out.

I've listed the following tone gems in chronological order, by guitarist. The track title and, where appropriate, the name of the band follow, with the year of recording in brackets and, finally, the album on which the recording in question can be found.

C H A P T E R 6

Junior Barnard
'GOODBYE LIZA JANE'
with Bob Wills & His Texas Playboys (1945)
Available on *The King Of Western Swing: 25 Hits (1935-45)*

Putting tone aside for a moment, we've all read the debates about who recorded 'the first rock'n'roll song,' haven't we? While you might not call this song rock'n'roll, it's difficult to find another description for Junior Barnard's guitar break (starting at about 01:00).

The only reason not to credit this performance as the first rock'n'roll solo is that Barnard was peppering this stuff all over the place in the 40s, bringing his inherent understanding of the blues to the swing rhythms of Bob Wills's erstwhile 'country' outfit—and he was using heavy bends and distortion long before this cut was made.

Barnard certainly doesn't scrimp on tone. If existing films are any indication of what he used in the studio (and they very likely are), Barnard rammed his big-bodied Epiphone Emperor archtop through an Epiphone amp (to which he later added a tweed Fender Pro to play in 'stereo' after appending a second pickup to the guitar).

Rather than make do with the thick, often woolly sound of the neck pickup that such guitars then favored, however, Barnard slid his add-on DeArmond Rhythm Chief pickup right back into the bridge position for a bright, cutting tone that is still meaty and toothsome. Great stuff—and again, pure proto-rockabilly all the way, from the octave jumps to those ending licks in particular.

Jimmy Bryant
'SWINGIN' ON THE STRINGS'
with Speedy West (circa 1954)
Available on *Swingin' On The Strings*

Jimmy Bryant's tone on this early (if under-rated) Telecaster classic contains some of the archetypal bite and sting that we expect to hear from a Tele tune today, but there's also a certain round, jazzy warmth that perfectly suits Bryant's swinging, rhythmic sensibility. This otherwise hazily documented nugget is collected on an album of Bryant and West treasures, also called *Swingin' On The Strings* (Razor & Tie, 1999), alongside the likes of 'Jammin' With Jimmy,' on which Bryant deploys a similar tone, 'T-Bone Rag,' which is rather warmer and thicker, and 'Frettin' Fingers,' which leans a little more toward the kind of brightness we might expect to hear from the Telecaster—although nothing he

plays approaches the harsh tone of Speedy West's pedal-steel.

Plenty of bona fide jazz artists have used Teles, usually favoring the neck pickup, but Bryant even manages to make the bridge pickup on his early blackguard Tele sound meaty and thick. Seek out a rare piece of film footage of Bryant and West doing their thing as a 'soloing duo' (rather than backing other artists such as Tennessee Ernie Ford)—a performance of 'Flyin' High' from the *Hometown Jamboree* television show of the early 50s. In it you can clearly see Bryant's three-way switch flipped back to the bridge pickup and what looks like a TV-front Fender Pro amp behind him. And still his tone is thick, buoyant, and plummy, yet with plenty of bite and shimmer.

Hubert Sumlin
'SMOKESTACK LIGHTNING'
with Howlin' Wolf (1956)
Available on *Moanin' In The Moonlight*

Although perhaps not an example of the kind of juicy and harmonically rich sound that comes readily to mind when we consider the archetype of 'great tone' today, Sumlin's guitar sound was rarely short of chilling, always extremely dynamic, and supremely emotive (Willie Johnson and several others also played with Howlin' Wolf, but it's Sumlin's work that exhibits the most exemplary tone of all the singer's sidemen).

The best guess is that the signature riff on this track was teased from the 1955 Les Paul Goldtop with P-90 pickups that Wolf had bought Sumlin (and insisted he play with bare fingers instead of a pick to avoid obscuring his boss's vocals—as if such a feat were possible). It was probably played through a Danelectro or Valco-made combo amp, or other similar B-list model. Sumlin's mid-60s tracks often find him using a funky white guitar that was probably a Teisco Del Rey model or perhaps a similarly downgraded Selmer or Italian-made guitar, through a variety of amps, but he still sounds just as moving.

As Sumlin himself relates on the DVD *The Blues Guitar Of Hubert Sumlin* (Homespun, 2005), he last played his Les Paul for the recording of 'Going Down Slow' with Howlin' Wolf in 1962, then retired the guitar. After years of playing oddball instruments, perhaps out of necessity in an era when Les Paul models became prohibitively expensive, Sumlin later returned to Goldtops fitted with both P-90s and humbuckers, and retained his signature tone throughout every transition.

CHAPTER 6

Eric Clapton
'HIDEAWAY'
with John Mayall's Bluesbreakers (1966)
Available on *Blues Breakers With Eric Clapton*
For this renowned cut, Clapton used a 1960 Les Paul Standard (some believe it may have been a '59 model) through a cranked Marshall Model 1962 amplifier, the open-backed 2x12 combo version of the JTM45 which has forever after been known as the 'Marshall Bluesbreaker.' While his playing on 'Hideaway' is often cited as a stellar example of the sound that helped launch a blues-rock revolution (and popularized the Les Paul Standard in the process), Clapton's fills and solos on this track actually exhibit a rather jagged, buzzing, grating tone at times.

The solos on 'Double Crossin' Time,' from the same *Blues Breakers With Eric Clapton* album, might exhibit slightly better definition and dynamics, but on 'What'd I Say' and 'Key To Love' things get rather fizzy again. Push a medium-powered, open-backed combo with low-rated speakers to the tipping point and this is how it will often sound; the tone can be effective in many contexts, but might not automatically be 'the tone of God.'

Leaving to one side his stadium-rock excursions with Cream, other noteworthy Clapton cuts also exhibit guitar tones that you might do well to improve upon rather than emulate. Approached objectively, you might say his guitar on 'Layla' (Derek & The Dominoes, *Layla And Other Assorted Love Songs*, 1970), believed to have been recorded with a maple-neck Stratocaster and a tweed Fender Champ, is pinched, boxy, and constipated, while the signature riff in 'Wonderful Tonight' (*Slowhand*, 1977) is rather muted and distant. None of these comments are meant as criticism of Clapton's work, and thousands will disagree, I know, but I feel all of the above examples show how stand-out playing and musical emotion will ultimately count, irrespective of less-than-stellar tone.

Jimi Hendrix
'MANIC DEPRESSION'
with The Jimi Hendrix Experience (1967)
Available on *Are You Experienced*
We tend to remember Hendrix's recordings being heavier than they actually are. His guitar tone reveals degrees of overdrive which (the occasional heavy effect aside) are not that far removed from the sounds that the harder-hitting blues artists of the era were deploying. Sometimes, revisiting the recordings of 60s and 70s rockers reveals rather disappointingly flat, tame tones, some way from the sonic signatures of romanticized memory. But not Hendrix: his sound is always compelling, characterized by definition, clarity, and harmonic dimension even amid the impressive weight and girth of his tone.

When talk turns to early Hendrix, 'Purple Haze' is often the song that comes under awed scrutiny, but I'd rather highlight 'Manic Depression,' with its live, wiry tone that sounds very much 'in the room' and far more present than a lot of recordings by other artists of the era. Hendrix's preference for single-coil pickups in his Strats (and, occasionally, in a Tele), no doubt helped early essays like 'Manic Depression' retain tonal cut and articulation—factors that enabled his beautifully dynamic playing touch to survive the fuzz, Octavia, and wah-wah effects that were routinely slathered on these recordings.

Although we associate him with Marshalls, Hendrix also used Fenders, Valco-made Supros, and other amplifiers in the studio, so it's hard to know exactly what he is playing through here. Regardless, his tone remained as lively in the studio as it was on stage.

Jimmy Page
'COMMUNICATION BREAKDOWN'
with Led Zeppelin (1969)
Available on *Led Zeppelin*
Any discussion of Jimmy Page's early guitar tone is likely to open a fat can of worms for legions of Zeppelin fanatics to chew on in the chat rooms of cyberspace, but I am inclined to side with the view that Page recorded this one with his Telecaster and a Supro Model 24 amplifier—having owned similar amps, I can verify that it certainly sounds like it.

While we think of Led Zeppelin as one of the heaviest bands of its day, this really isn't all that weighty a tone—and you could certainly extrude heavier sounds from that rig if you wanted to. What it is, however, is pure, driving, crunchy rock'n'roll, with a meaty midrange and a crisp clarity in the highs that never teeters into harshness—all characteristics of the 6973 output tubes in this Valco-made amp, and others like it (which, although they look like tall, nine-pin EL84s, in fact sound nothing at all like them).

Elsewhere on the eponymous debut Led Zeppelin album, Page's tone occasionally gets a little heavier, but still it errs more toward blues-rock than hard-rock. You could call it plain rock'n'roll—

almost garage-rock, even, a term we don't often apply to the mighty Zep.

Fast forward to 'Whole Lotta Love' from *Led Zeppelin II* (released later in 1969), and Page's tone gets a little buzzy; by 'Black Dog,' from *Led Zeppelin IV* (1971), the buzz has increased considerably.

Listen to the 'Black Dog' with open ears, and I would suggest that most tone-conscious guitarists today wouldn't want that rig if you gave it to them, so fuzzed and fractured does it sound. (Please don't start throwing things; I know it works in the mix, but go and listen to it again carefully and see if you agree with me.) Elsewhere, of course, Page's tone is stellar, and above all else, this is undeniably powerful music.

Paul Kossoff
'ALL RIGHT NOW'
with Free (1970)
Available on *Fire And Water*

Kossoff's tone on 'All Right Now' exists in my mind's ear as a prime example of late-60s/early-70s Les Paul-meets-Marshall Brit-rock goodness: chunky, thick, with a little of that crispy EL34 crackle that helps a guitar cut through a heavy mix. Revisit the studio cut, however, and, perhaps in light of all that has come since, it sounds just a little underwhelming. As cool as the track remains, Kossoff's tone seems somewhat constricted—perhaps by a traditionally trained studio engineer persistently urging him to keep his volume levels down for the mics.

A little research reveals several invalidated claims that the artist used a late-60s Selmer Treble'N'Bass amp (another 50-watt head with a pair of EL34s) for these studio sessions, although when cranked in anger that amp can also sound far more ballsy than the sound captured here, and not far short of a Marshall Super Lead 50-watter.

Kossoff's tone on the title track of *Fire And Water*, and on another album cut, 'Mr. Big,' is similarly so-so, but free him from whatever constraints might have squelched him in the studio, and it's a different story entirely.

Check out the live sound heard on the BBC Sessions recorded by Free on June 23 1970 for a Brit-rock tone that's big, buoyant, and fat, while also lithe and lively. It seems like you can hear the pick attack clicking right out through the interaction of the speaker's voice coil and cone: "Mr Les Paul, I believe you know Mr Marshall … ."

Mark Knopfler
'SULTANS OF SWING'
with Dire Straits (1978)
Available on *Dire Straits*

Having recently landed a 'new' Technics turntable from eBay to replace the 35-year-old deck that had gradually been developing its own built-in vibrato effect, I dug out two boxes of vinyl that hadn't been spun for several years and rediscovered the glories of Dire Straits' eponymous debut album. I think Knopfler's tone on this seminal cut, not to mention the remainder of the album, and the next, *Communiqué*, had such an impact on players of the day, not so much because it was noteworthy in and of itself, but because it displayed a notable soloist riffing with a clean, straight tone in an era when the majority of guitar solos blaring from commercial radio were cranked and wailing.

Crisp, snappy, and round—in short, the archetypal tone of a clean Strat through clean-ish Fender amp—it was a strangely exciting sound, given that it was comparatively restrained. Indeed, the tone on 'Sultans Of Swing' is dynamic, infectious, perhaps not spectacular, but wonderfully effective nonetheless, and it helped Knopfler's chops stand out amid the saturated guitar sounds of the day. Listening to this again 32 years after first encountering it as an aspiring teenage guitarist, I experienced something of an epiphany: for me, this was the first thing that suggested a 'contemporary' guitarist could do something other than the overdriven Page/Hendrix/ Van Halen style that all the other guitarists were hacking away at. Perhaps ironically, it was this English guitarist's work which ultimately led me to a greater appreciation of American country twangers.

Knopfler was playing his newly acquired Fender Stratocaster at the time, allegedly through a brownface early-60s Fender 6G11 or 6G11-A Vibrolux amp—a 2x6L6 model with one 12-inch speaker. A Fender Twin Reverb and other standards were also available in the studio, however, so who really knows?

A few years later, Knopfler would register an entirely different sound in the annals of tone by cranking up a Les Paul Standard for the signature riff to the MTV hit 'Money For Nothing,' and moved over to Soldano and Trainwreck amps, among several others, finally joining the ranks of dirt-hungry rockers from which he had so vividly stood apart in the late 70s. For me, that clean-with-bite Strat sound will always be *the* Mark Knopfler tone.

Stevie Ray Vaughan
'LOVE STRUCK BABY'
with Double Trouble (1983)
Available on *Texas Flood*

For a slightly dirtier Stratocaster sound, here is SRV in early tone-god mode. This is a fat, pliant, slightly rubbery Strat tone, a little brighter and crispier than we're used to from his later work, and a joyful sound from top to bottom. Compared to the crazy multi-amp recording setups and massive Buddy Guy-meets-Hendrix tone that Vaughan would subsequently chase, this is pretty straightforward stuff. I'm not sure I'd trust one of the many rumored amp configurations used on 'Love Struck Baby' more than another, but an educated guess would point to a single amp, two at most. A blackface Fender Super Reverb or 1x15 Vibroverb combo (or both amps together) will replicate these tonal tricks.

The second cut from the *Texas Flood* album, 'Pride And Joy,' ramps it up a few notches, but still has the bite, clarity, and dynamics that make for pure, compelling blues and rock'n'roll. This is a bigger, thicker, sound for sure, but again, it's nothing that either of those amps can't do when introduced to a fatter Strat neck pickup, with perhaps a little Tube Screamer for good measure.

SRV's tone has been worshiped and analyzed so thoroughly in the 20-plus years since his death that any discussion of it today inevitably tends toward cliché—we have heard it all before.

But tune into his early work, before the Marshall-plus-Fender-plus-Dumble excess, the heavier studio reverb, the Vibratone rotary speaker, and ever more elaborate effects chains took hold, and you are reminded that at its core, this is tonally infectious stuff and the catalyst that sparked a blues renaissance.

Pete Anderson
'GUITARS, CADILLACS'
with Dwight Yoakam (1986)
Available on *Guitars, Cadillacs*

It's time for some serious twang. Pete Anderson's meaty, stinging Tele licks were one of the key ingredients that helped Dwight Yoakam reinvigorate the country genre in the mid 80s. In an era when Nashville was getting slicker, more plastic, and digitized, even succumbing to the pointy-headstock trend that was sweeping rock at the time, Anderson laid it down thick and mean with an early-60s Telecaster and a beefed-up blackface Fender Deluxe Reverb (with 6L6s and a bigger OT), and a healthy helping of fast, inventive riffs that nodded to the classic honky-tonk style while sounding entirely fresh. On this song, Anderson retains a crispness and clarity that pay homage to the sounds of Buck Owens and Don Rich, and even a little to Luther Perkins, perhaps, while offering at least a touch more bite and snarl for the new generation of pickers to sink their teeth into. If anything, it's cleaner than much of his later work, but all of Pete Anderson's early cuts with Yoakam are dexterous exemplars of pure Tele tone.

Joey Santiago
'DEBASER'
with Pixies (1989)
Available on *Doolittle*

For a lot of music fans who were growing weary of 80s spandex metal and big-hair bands, Pixies' quiet-loud, proto-grunge sound provided an exciting alternative and a conduit to filthy, but arty, guitar sounds. I always remember this lead track from the *Doolittle* album sounding huge, with Joey Santiago's guitar (or 'guitars,' given the obvious double or multi-tracking) being wildly, outrageously enormous. Live, Santiago generally went for a fairly straightforward Les Paul and Marshall outfit, with a couple of overdrive/distortion pedals to add some dirt when necessary, but it's hard to know exactly what he used on these studio tracks.

Listening back, it's really more a medium-crunch with, at times, even a rather nasal, boxy overdrive sound, but the impression of weight and menace remains, a testament to the band's dynamics and Black Francis's utterly leftfield songwriting and vocal skills. Further noise-tone thrills are found on other album cuts like 'Wave Of Mutilation,' and 'Monkey Gone To Heaven' (with its jagged, dissonant riffs and ominously hovering feedback). "Rock me, Joe!"

Kurt Cobain
'SMELLS LIKE TEEN SPIRIT'
with Nirvana (1991)
Available on *Nevermind*

For another take on that quiet-loud dynamic, this classic is just screaming for some tonal attention. Cobain's guitar on 'Smells Like Teen Spirit' always seemed utterly enormous, and listening today, it still does, in places, but it's the interplay between light and shade—the cruising clean-tone moments, with a little E-H Small Clone chorus for depth, contrasted with the fat, chewy crunch looming up to smash it to smithereens in the refrains—that really drives the song home. Cobain used all kinds of stuff in the studio, with a Fender Twin Reverb, Mesa/Boogie Studio 22, and a Fender Bassman among his amp arsenal, but he stuck with shorter-scale Fender 'student' model guitars such as Mustangs and (often modified) Jaguars and their ilk, with the occasional odd, somewhat customized C-list banger. Hit any of those amps with a bright, sharp-toned Mustang single-coil pickup via a ProCo Rat distortion pedal and you've got a big, mean sound, which Cobain's energy and attitude certainly exploited to the full.

Jonny Greenwood
'CREEP'
with Radiohead (1992)
Available on *Pablo Honey*

Here is a posse of creative Brits who toed the Pixies/Nirvana line, briefly, before moving into more adventurous soundscapes. Dirty, static-drenched, and crispy-crunchy to the max, Jonny Greenwood's tone on this breakthrough single is far removed from the sweet, overdriven lead tone many rock soloists would favor. But from his initial 'is this thing on?' *chk-ikk, chk-ikk* thwacks to the slam-chord assault that follows, this is one of the most memorable rhythm-guitar parts ever recorded in rock music—and one of the simplest. It's a classic example of using what you've got and using it well. To make all that noise, Greenwood employed a less-than-sexy rig consisting of an early-90s Fender Telecaster Plus with Lace Sensor pickups, a Marshall Shred Master distortion pedal, and a 'red-knob' solid-state Fender Deluxe 85 combo twinned with a Vox AC30. Not "so fuckin' special" after all, perhaps—but listen to what he did with it.

Jay Farrar
'CHICKEMAUGA'
with Uncle Tupelo (1993)
Available on *Anodyne*

This one is worth hearing for the way it furiously stamps the alt into alt.country. Before moving on to form Son Volt and Wilco respectively, Jay Farrar and Jeff Tweedy recorded a final album together as Uncle Tupelo, and, in places at least, this was the archetypal Americana outfit's most rocking effort. Back in the day, Farrar was the band's lead guitarist, while Tweedy hopped between bass and rhythm guitar. Farrar lets loose on this grungy, Neil Young-like excursion that staggers and struts through virtually the entire second half of the song, a full

minute and 38 seconds of frenzied riffing. His tone here is full of saturation and sag, with a crispy, sizzling edge that shouts 'cranked, small vintage amp' to my ears at least. This is way too fizzy and extreme to be a classic lead guitar tone, really, but the energy behind this performance—recorded entirely live in a studio in Austin, Texas, as was the entire album—is palpable, and the voice that conveys it is perfect for the occasion.

Farrar used a selection of Gibson SG, Les Paul Juniors and Specials, and occasionally an SG Standard. You'd think the vibrato in this piece was courtesy of a Bigsby or similar, although he performed the song live as an encore with Son Volt in later years (signaling what was usually the only solo he would take with that band) and achieved the same kind of tremulous vibrato by just giving the neck of a reissue double-cut Les Paul Special a serious throttling.

Duke Levine
'MANHOLE'
(1997)
Available on *Lava*

I wanted to draw attention to this cut not only because Duke Levine is an undersung guitar hero of our time, with serious chops in a range of styles, but because his tone on the instrumental 'Manhole' is everything that great clean-with-snarl Tele tone should be. Weaving snaky country licks around a shuffling groove, with playful nods to jazz, blues, and rock'n'roll, Levine brews up a performance that can't help but make you smile, and a tone that's a pure honeyed pleasure. In addition to his 1963 Telecaster, Duke told me that the sound came courtesy of three amps tracked: a 1966 Fender Vibrolux Reverb, 1963 Vox AC30, and late-50s tweed Fender Harvard. Crank any of those three enough—or even just the little Harvard, and blend it with the chiming clean tones of the other two—and you could imagine achieving this tone without any recourse to an overdrive pedal. Duke's unfailingly sweet touch gives plenty of drive and dynamics to the performance throughout the length of this track.

Tad Kubler
'STUCK BETWEEN STATIONS'
with The Hold Steady (2006)
Available on *Boys And Girls In America*

The Hold Steady in a book about seminal guitar tone? Damn straight, and for several reasons. They are a great modern American rock band: killer riffs,

compelling lyrics, and a real stage presence, if you have the pleasure of seeing them live—a pure celebration of what rock'n'roll should be. Live and on record, lead guitarist Tad Kubler's tone is never short of fat, juicy, and thrilling. This track opens with a warm and crunchy suspended-chord riff, segues beautifully into massive power-chord glory, and just rolls on from there through one lush riff after another. I think my favorite moment arrives, however, tone-wise at least, around 03:02 with the lead line that punctuates the Springsteen-meets-Meatloaf piano bridge.

Tad Kubler was gracious enough to provide bounteous details about the gear he was using at the time, so I will quote him at some length. Guitar-wise, although he is also fond of Les Pauls, Kubler used a Gibson ES-335 on this track; to be specific, a recent reissue of a 'block-marker' model from the early-to-mid 60s. "I'd love to tell you it was an actual 60s block 335," Kubler says, "but I didn't have a real one yet when we did this album." Although he isn't certain of the model of pickups in this guitar (most likely Gibson's '57 Classics with that Custom Shop ES-335 model), he says: "The pickups in this one are the best. They easily sound the most like PAFs."

To track 'Stuck Between Stations' he blended a combination of small low-wattage amps and large high-wattage amps for a big, thick tone. Among the selections were a 60s Silvertone 1484 with cab, an early-70s 100-watt Park head and 4x12 cab ("one of the only amps I own that I would absolutely *never* let go of"), a late-60s Fender Super Reverb with Celestion speakers, a late-60s London City head (an old Dutch clone of a Marshall Super Lead), and a Bob Amp combo (made by Bob Strakele) that has EL84 tubes.

In the studio and on tour, Kubler has also used Epiphone Blues Custom 30 amps, although he swaps their stock 6L6 output tubes for EL34s. "I've never been a fan of distortion pedals or overdrive for my regular tone," Kubler adds. "I like the sound of an amp turned up to ten. I do use a Bradshaw Boost pedal and a Crowther Audio HotCake for solos and such. But when I'm laying down rhythm tracks or anything else but solos, I just use the amp. And if I need to clean it up, I back off on the volume on the guitar."

Kubler also puts a lot of thought into mic placement and uses a wide variety of ribbon and dynamic mics to help capture the sound (confirmation of those missing links in the tone chain that we often aren't privy to), but concludes: "I've always been a pretty firm believer that it starts at the source. If you have a nice guitar and a decent amplifier—and can play guitar—things are going to sound decent."

David Grissom
'SQUAWK'
(2009)
Available on *10,000 Feet*
Not so much 'tone' as 'tangible force,' David Grissom's sound on this cut from his *10,000 Feet* solo outing is as grimy and greasy as anything you are likely to find, and it achieves its menace while sounding entirely live, lithe, and *real*. It could be Grissom's beloved Paul Reed Smith taking the call, or it could be one of several other guitars in the star's arsenal, although the one brief lick of vibrato action—a quick dive-bomb at 05:29—tips us that all this sleazy goodness could well come courtesy of his signature PRS.

For filth, however, my pal and fellow gear writer Nate 'Riverhorse' Nakadate reckons credit might have to go to a late-50s Gibson GA-40 Les Paul Amp that Grissom is known to possess, and that fat, brown, chocolatey grunge tone that this performance revels in is definitely typical of a cranked 5879 pentode preamp tube through a pair of sizzling 6V6s and an old Jensen. As thick, rich, greasy, and fattening as a deep-fried Snickers bar. Having said that, it could nevertheless be the Bad Cat Wild Cat amplifier that Grissom also endorses, and it, too, can get pretty brown and hairy when cranked in anger.

Audio Samples CD

The CD packaged with this book contains 72 short sound samples, covering a broad range of relevant tones. These are not by any means intended to be paradigms of outstanding tone, but are included more as 'listening exercises'—examples of *different* tones, provided for purposes of comparison. Some of them might sound good to you, but some will undoubtedly sound decidedly dull. They should all be useful, however, as comparative, parallel examples of the raw sound of a range of different components. As such, little effort was made to tweak or fine-tune the sounds recorded; they are all fairly raw, straightforward, and real. Also, this entire sound-sample selection is presented with the full awareness that listening to tones recorded by other hands, in a room far away, with countless unknown variables, is an exercise rife with limitations and can only ever go so far in telling you what anything truly sounds like. To really discern what works for you, it is you who needs to play the instrument and to listen in the room where the sound is created. So, just to reiterate, treat these more as comparative listening exercises than as examples of how the various ingredients might function in your own applications.

I have made an effort to mix up vintage and reissue gear here, and have thrown in a few cheap and cheerful selections too. With all of these examples—or more precisely, *sets* of examples, where different ingredients are compared in the context of specific consistencies—listen out for certain universal virtues of tone, as discussed in the introduction to this book. Does each, or any, present the kind of purity, depth, harmonic complexity, liveliness, balance, and dynamics that make you want to play or to listen to more? While recording these selections, I tended to subconsciously latch on to certain tones, and inevitably I wanted to spend more time with those setups than with others that just didn't inspire me so readily. With your own hands on the guitar, however, you might have felt differently.

All samples were recorded with minimal compression, EQ, reverb, or other processing, in order to present a 'real' sound rather than the kind of 'produced' sound that might be heard on a full-band recording. A handful of samples were borrowed from CDs that accompanied two of my previous books, *The Electric Guitar Sourcebook* and *The Guitar Pickup Handbook*, because they were extremely relevant to considerations here and simply weren't worth attempting to reproduce. The remainder was recorded toward the conclusion of the writing of this book, in a large and fairly 'lively' studio room. I used an M-S stereo recording configuration, with one mic in the 'mid' position capturing direct amp sound and a second (a figure-8 Coles 4038 ribbon mic) in 'side' position, capturing a stereo room sound (this signal split left-to-right and phase-reversed in the final mix). The mics were connected to an AEA The Ribbon Pre microphone preamp, and from there to the Digital Performer DAW on my Mac via a MOTU 828 MkII interface.

All control positions will be described on the 'o'clock scale,' with volume and tone knob settings made analogous to the time on a clock face—where 9:00 (nine o'clock) is just about a quarter rotation up from minimum (and *not* two notches short of maximum, as on Nigel Tuffnel's "this one goes to eleven" scale). Unless specifically noted, volume and tone controls on the guitars used are set to maximum.

C H A P T E R 7

Dirty Little Secret

Let's start off with a simple 'ear quiz' of sorts. Before reading further to discover what's making the heavily overdriven sounds in these first five samples, listen to each and see if you can tell which is the…

- Modern high-gain amp (using foot-switchable 'lead' channel)
- 15-watt boutique amp, cranked
- 15-watt boutique amp with overdrive pedals
- 20-watt boutique amp, cranked through an attenuator
- 35-watt vintage tweed amp, cranked

All were played with a contemporary Gibson SG Standard, set to the bridge pickup, and patched into the same 1x12 extension cab with vintage 8-ohms 1983 Celestion G12-65 speaker.

5. 1958 Fender Pro Amp (two 6L6s, two channels jumpered together). Settings: mic volume: 3:00; instrument volume: 3:00; treble: 3:00; bass: 12:30; presence: 2:00.

4. Matchless Spitfire amplifier maxed (two EL84s). Settings: volume: max; tone: max; master: 2:30 (no pedals).

3. Matchless Spitfire amplifier (two EL84s). Settings: volume: 10:00; tone: 9:00; master: 1:30; with Barber LTD overdrive pedal; settings: volume: 9:00; tone: 9:00; drive: 3:00; into an Xotic EP-3 Booster set to 11:00.

2. Orange TH30 head (four EL84s, but set to half power on two tubes, lead channel). Settings: volume: 11:00; tone shape: 2:00; drive: 2:30.

1. Dr Z Z-28 amplifier (two 6V6s, EF86 preamp tube). Settings: volume: max; bass: 11:00; treble: 5:00; through a Weber High Powered Load Dump attenuator set to approximately −9dB (reduction).

6. 1958 Fender Pro Amp (two 6L6s, two channels jumpered together). Settings: mic volume: 11:00; instrument volume: 11:00; treble: 2:00; bass: 1:00; presence: 1:30. In this one, the amp is back down to a more 'real-world' volume-setting with each channel down a little below half way. This is probably the classic tweed amp level for anything short of full-on distortion with heavy compression. Note how reducing the guitar's volume control by about 50 per cent at around 01:18 in the sound clip cleans up the amp beautifully, before it is gradually rolled back up between 01:23 and 01:27.

7. Same amp setting as example #6, but with a Hahn 228 (blackguard Fender Tele-style guitar, one-piece swamp ash body, maple neck, vintage-style Fralin single-coil T-style pickups). Guitar volume is reduced by about 30 per cent at 00:28; back up to full again by 00:34.

Speakers in Parallel and Series

The following two examples were both recorded with a Matchless Spitfire amp. Settings: volume: 12:00; tone: 11:00; master: max; through a 2x12 extension cab with Celestion G12H-30 speakers. Both played with the Hahn 228 T-style guitar, with a brief pause only to change amp output and speaker input.

8. Speakers wired in parallel, from the amp's 4-ohms output.

9. Speakers wired in series, from the amp's 16-ohms output (accessed from the 16-ohms OT tap originally capped off inside the amp's chassis).

Fat Single Coils: 25½ inches versus 24¾ inch

The amp and speaker settings for the following four are the same as example #9, above.

C H A P T E R 7

10. Koll Superior guitar (glued-in maple neck with ebony fingerboard, alder body, 25½-inch scale length) set to the bridge pickups (a TV Jones Electroflux pickup, a hybrid of a P-90 and a Telecaster bridge pickup).

11. 1953 Gibson Les Paul Goldtop with wraparound bridge, set to P-90 in the bridge position.

12. Vintage 1953 Gibson Les Paul Goldtop set to P-90 in the neck position.

13. Koll Superior set to P-90 in the neck position (Jason Lollar, '50s Wind version).

Rock'n'Roll on Single-Coil Bridge Pickups

The following examples, taken from *The Electric Guitar Sourcebook* CD, were played through a TopHat Club Royale amplifier (two EL84 output tubes) into a 2x12 cab with Celestion speakers, one G12H-30, and one Alnico Blue (the latter miked with a single Beyer-Dynamic M160 at a distance of about 12 inches and slightly off-center). Amp settings: volume: 9:30; treble: 10:30; mid: 2:00; bass: 11:00; cut: 12:00; master: max; boost: off.

14. Vintage 1964 Fender Stratocaster, bridge pickup.

15. Fender USA 1957 Stratocaster Reissue, bridge pickup.

16. Contemporary Mexican-made Fender Stratocaster, bridge pickup.

17. Fender American Vintage Reissue 62 Jazzmaster, bridge pickup.

Fat Neck Pickups, plus OD

Each of the following four examples, also from *The Electric Guitar Sourcebook* CD, were recorded on the neck pickups of the respective guitars, using the same amp and settings as 14–17 above, but with an Ibanez TS9 Tube Screamer brought in at approximately 00:16 in the sound clip. Pedal setting: drive: 12:00; tone: 12:00; level: 2:00.

18. 1961 Gibson ES-330 with P-90 in the neck position.

19. Epiphone Casino reissue with P-90 in the neck position.

20. Gibson Custom Shop ES-335 Dot reissue with '57 Classic humbucking pickup in the neck position.

21. PRS SE Soapbar with P-90 in the neck position.

Bridge Pickups: Mild Breakup

The examples in this selection, taken from *The Guitar Pickup Handbook*, were recorded through a Matchless DC-30 amplifier set to half power, into a 1x12 cab with Celestion G12H-30 speaker—the amp set for a mildly crunchy tone—with a single Coles 4038 microphone placed approximately 12 inches from the speaker.

22. Gibson Custom Shop ES-335 Dot reissue with '57 Classic humbucking pickup, bridge position.

23. Gibson Custom Shop R7 1957 Les Paul reissue with BurstBucker 2 humbucking pickup, bridge position.

24. Vintage 1961 Gibson Les Paul/SG with original PAF pickup, bridge position.

25. Vintage 1953 Gibson Les Paul Goldtop with original P-90 pickup, bridge position.

26. Grosh ElectraJet with Fralin P-90 (overwound) pickup, bridge position.

Neck Pickups: R&B Riffs, Mild Breakup

Examples 27–35 use the same amp and settings as 22–26 above. Do bear in mind that we aren't merely comparing different pickups here— the guitars themselves differ, too, and present different tones of their own, irrespective of pickup considerations. The only truly accurate 'pickup swap' test here is the transition from #28 to #29, where the amp was put on standby, and the original neck pickup in the Les Paul was removed and replaced with the vintage humbucker.

27. Gibson Custom Shop ES-335 Dot reissue with '57 Classic humbucking pickup, neck position.

28. Gibson Custom Shop R7 1957 Les Paul reissue with BurstBucker 1 humbucking pickup, neck position.

29. The same guitar as #28, now with an original 1962 Gibson 'Patent Number' humbucker, neck position.

30. Vintage 1961 Gibson Les Paul/SG with original PAF pickup, neck position.

31. Grosh ElectraJet with Fralin humbucker (medium wind), neck position.

32. Vintage 1953 Gibson Les Paul Goldtop with original P-90 pickup, neck position.

33. Vintage 1957 Fender Telecaster with a Fender Twisted Tele pickup installed in the neck position.

34. 1957 Gretsch Duo Jet reissue with reproduction DynaSonic pickup in the neck position.

35. Fender USA 1957 Stratocaster Reissue with Joe Barden S-Deluxe dual-rail pickup in the neck position.

Dude, Your Pickup's Too High

An example of what really happens when you set the neck pickup of a Stratocaster too close to the strings. The following two sound clips were recorded through the Matchless Spitfire, set to a clean tone, with the bridge pickup of the guitar selected. In the first, however, the neck pickup is set too high—very close to the strings, without touching—so that its magnetic field interferes with their natural vibration. Note how the first example sounds choked, thin, and out of tune, although the tuning was not touched between these two recordings.

36. Strat neck pickup set too high.

37. Strat neck pickup set just right.

Preamp Tube Swaps

The following selection was recorded with an original 1958 Fender Pro Amp (tweed 5E5-A model) with NOS (new old stock) RCA 'black plate' 6L6GC output tubes. The amp channels were jumpered together and the control settings were as follows: mic volume: 9:00; instrument volume: 9:00; treble, bass, and presence: all 2:00. Between takes, the amp was simply put on standby, tipped forward, and the first preamp tube was changed, as noted below. To maintain some consistency with earlier examples recorded through this amp, it was once again patched through the extension cab with a 1x12 Celestion G12-65 speaker (US made NOS Tung-Sol 12AX7 in V2 position—tone stack—and RCA 12AX7 in V3 position—phase inverter—for the following nine sound clips, and, in fact, anywhere the Pro is used). The Hahn 228 (T-style, bridge pickup) was used for examples 38–45, and #47.

38. Mullard ECC83 late-60s NOS British.

39. RCA 7025 (a 'ruggedized' 12AX7-type tube) early-60s NOS US.

40. Sovtek 12AX7WA contemporary Russian.

C H A P T E R 7

41. Phillips/JAN 5057 late-60s NOS US.

42. RCA 12AY7 late-50s NOS US (this is the tube type the amp was designed for).

43. The same setup as #42, but both amp volumes turned up to 10:30 to hear this low-gain 12AY7 pushing the RCA 6L6s a little harder.

Output Tube Swaps

The following example uses the same 1958 Pro Amp, with the same slightly hotter settings used for #43 above, but with various different output tubes to show the variations by comparison with the NOS RCA 'black plates' in #43.

44. Sovtek 5881s (a 6L6 type), contemporary Russian.

45. GE 6L6GC mid-60s NOS US.

46. The same as #45 but with the Gibson SG Standard, bridge pickup.

47. More chime, less bottom: Matchless Spitfire set to similar drive levels as the tweed Pro in the above examples, with the Hahn 228 again.

Dueling Tweeds

The following four examples compare the original 1958 Fender Pro Amp with an original 1958 Fender Super Amp, featuring the original single Jensen P12N 15-inch speaker and two Jensen P10R 10-inch speakers, respectively. The same tubes as used in examples 42 and 43 above were used in each amp, which were both recorded from the same marked-off floor positions and set to: mic volume: 10:00; instrument volume: 10:00; treble, bass, and presence: all 2:00. Other than the variables of age and a few small replacement parts (filter caps and a handful of resistors at most), the circuits in these amps are identical, other than the output transformers and speakers.

48. Tweed Pro, rock'n'roll: vintage 1964 Fender Stratocaster, bridge pickup.

49. Tweed Pro, R&B: vintage 1964 Fender Stratocaster, neck pickup.

50. Tweed Super, rock'n'roll: vintage 1964 Fender Stratocaster, bridge pickup.

51. Tweed Super, R&B: vintage 1964 Fender Stratocaster, neck pickup.

52. The tweed Super is a classic Tele amp, so here's the same amp and settings as examples 50–51, with a vintage 1957 Telecaster set to the bridge pickup.

True Bypass versus Buffer

The following three samples compare the sound of the guitar signal run through five true-bypass pedals with, firstly, no buffer, then a buffer added last in the pedal chain, and, finally, a buffer added in front of the pedal chain. In each case, a 15-foot Klotz La Grange instrument cable is run from guitar (Hahn 228, bridge pickup) to pedals and another from pedals to amp (Matchless Spitfire).

53. No buffer.

54. Buffer following pedals.

55. Buffer in front of pedals.

C H A P T E R 7

56. Examples 53–55 are edited together, in order to hear them in sequence, without pause. The transition from 'no buffer' (ending at 00:08) to 'buffer' is most noticeable, but there is even a slight difference in tone between the 'buffer before' and 'buffer after' samples.

Cable Comparisons

Listen to these three examples of different cables of similar lengths, followed by a short patch cable straight in. The Hahn 228 and Spitfire are used again (this pairing offers a lot of clarity and great harmonic 'sparkle,' characteristics that best illustrate how other ingredients in the chain might change the final tone).

57. Vintage, 'thin gray' cable, approximately 15 feet long (a cable found in the accessory pocket of the blonde Tolex case of a 1964 Fender Stratocaster, in fact).

58. A contemporary 'decent generic' 18-foot cable of moderate quality.

59. A high quality 15-foot Klotz 'La Grange' cable (no means the most expensive on the market).

60. A 2-foot Klotz patch cable.

61. Examples 57–60 have also been edited together in close succession. Can you hear the changes?

Speaker Cables

The same listening exercise performed with speaker cables patched between a Dr Z Z-28 and a 1x12 extension cab, using three different cable types, each about two feet, with the Hahn 228 in a drop-D tuning.

62. A generic speaker cable of moderate quality, approximately 16 gauge.

63. Monster cable, 14 gauge.

64. Electrical cable, 14 gauge (taken from an AC power extension cable used for outdoor power tools, directionality retained).

65. Co-axial guitar cord used as speaker cable. A no-no! (Most, perhaps not all, ears will hear some sound differences across 62–64, but *all* should hear how the guitar cord mutes and constrains the amp's tone.)

Your Thin, Cheap, Friend

What is the most affordable accessory change to affect the greatest tonal change? A different guitar pick, of course. Listen to how each of the following seven introduces a very real change in sound and feel. All are used with the 1964 Stratocaster set to the bridge pickup, through the Matchless Spitfire set clean.

66. Fender 'teardrop-shaped' pick, thin gauge.

67. Fender 'teardrop-shaped' pick, medium gauge.

68. Fender 'teardrop-shaped' pick, heavy gauge.

69. Fender 'teardrop-shaped' pick, heavy gauge, using its rounded 'back edge.'

70. Red Bear Trading synthetic tortoiseshell pick with pointed picking edge.

71. Red Bear Trading synthetic tortoiseshell pick with rounded picking edge.

72. V-Pick with pointy picking edge.

C H A P T E R   7

Glossary

Abalam Trade name for abalone laminated to thin plastic sheet, the result of a new cutting technique which yields more of the useable shell and less waste.

abalone Shellfish used for inlay material on guitars. Comes in many iridescent hues, most prized being the green heart. Becoming rare.

AC Short for "alternating current," an electric current that can change the direction in which it flows. This is the type of electricity that flows from common domestic wall outlets (commonly 120V in the US, 230-240V in the UK). See also *DC*.

acrylic Paint containing acrylic resin, widely used in guitar finishes as a more eco-friendly substitute for nitro-cellulose lacquers.

action Often used to describe only the height of the strings above the tops of the frets; thus "high action," "low action," "buzz-free action" etc. In fact, the term can refer to the entire playing feel of a given instrument; thus "good action," "easy action" etc.

active (active electronics, active circuit) Circuitry in some guitars that boosts signal and/or widens tonal range with necessary additional (usually battery) powering. Refers to a pickup or circuit that incorporates a preamp. See also *preamp*.

active powered Not necessarily amplified, but using (active) electronics to assist or improve functioning.

alder Medium weight hardwood commonly used for solid guitar bodies, for example some of those made by Fender.

alnico Magnet material used for pickups and speakers (generally of more "vintage" design). It is an alloy of aluminum, nickel, and cobalt. Also, a nickname for a single-coil Gibson pickup with flat-sided polepieces.

alternating current See *AC*.

amp(lifier) Electrical circuit designed to increase the level of a signal; but more usually, an audio system for boosting sound before transmission to a loudspeaker. The system could be a power amp, or backline instrument amplifier, or line amp.

amplification Making a signal bigger (may refer to voltage, analogous to signal level and loudness, or current). General term for amps, speakers and associated gear.

analog (UK: analogue) System which reproduces a signal by copying its original amplitude waveform. Examples include the groove of an old vinyl recording, the electrical signal on a magnetic tape recording, or the voltage levels of an analog synthesizer. As opposed to digital, where the signal is recorded as a series of numbers.

anode (plate) Part within a vacuum tube (UK: valve) which collects current.

anti-surge "Delayed" fuse (body marked "T") that withstands brief current surges without breaking. Note that it doesn't prevent current surges.

archtop Guitar with arched body top formed by carving or pressing. Usually refers to hollowbody or semi-acoustic instruments; thus "archtop jazz guitar". As opposed to the other principal type of acoustic guitar, the flat-top.

arpeggio Broken chord in which the notes are played sequentially rather than together.

ash Medium to heavy hardwood commonly used for solid guitar bodies, for example by Fender.

atonal Type of composition, usually of the 20th century, which has no allegiance to a tonal center.

attack Speed at which a sound (or filter, or envelope) reaches its maximum level. For instance, percussive sounds usually have fast attacks, while smooth, liquid sounds have slow attacks.

attenuate Reduce in strength.

attenuator Electronic circuitry that reduces level, usually in fixed steps of useful round-figure amounts, such as -10dB, -20dB. Also the knob or switch that controls such a setting.

baby blue Popular (unofficial) name for Fender's early Sonic Blue Custom Color.

backlash Any "give" in a tuner's operation where the string-post does not immediately move when the tuner button is turned.

backplate Panel fitted over a cavity in the rear of a guitar body, allowing access to pots and wiring or vibrato springs.

baffle Front panel or baseboard of a speaker cabinet onto which direct-radiating drivers and smaller horn flares are mounted.

Bakelite First plastic, invented 1909. Used for some guitars, parts and components from the 1930s to the 1950s.

ball-end Metal retainer wound onto the end of a guitar string and used to secure it to the anchor point at the bridge.

banjo tuners Rear-facing tuners found on some guitars, notably on some early Martin OM and Gibson reverse-body Firebird models.

bass pickup See *neck pickup*.

B-bender String-pulling device giving a pedal-steel effect on regular electric guitar. The best known models are by Parsons-White, and Joe Glaser.

bias For a tube (valve) guitar amp, a critical "tune-up" setting (and also of a tape machine or other piece of equipment), generally involving some auxiliary voltage or current that helps the circuitry to work properly.

Bigsby Simple single-spring non-recessed vibrato device developed by Paul Bigsby. Now sometimes used as a generic term for similar designs by other makers.

binding Protective and decorative strip(s) added to edges of the body and/or fingerboard and/or headstock of some guitars.

birdseye Type of maple with small circular figure.

blade pickup (bar pickup) Pickup (humbucker or single-coil) that uses a long single blade polepiece for each coil, rather than the more usual individual polepieces for each string.

block markers Square-shape or rectangular-shape position markers in the fingerboard.

blond (blonde) Natural finish, usually enhancing plain wood color; or (on some Fenders) a slightly yellowed finish.

Bluesbreaker Nickname for the Marshall 2x12 combo used by Eric Clapton on the John Mayall album of the same name. Originals are highly sought after, and the model was re-issued by Marshall in the late 1980s.

board (UK: desk) Mixer, mixing console, mixdown unit.

boat neck Alternative name for V-neck (describes shape). See *V-neck*.

bobbin Frame around which pickup coils are wound.

body Main portion of the guitar, onto which are (usually) mounted the bridge, pickups, controls etc. Can be solid, hollow, or a combination of the two.

bolt-on neck Describes a (usually solidbody) guitar with neck bolted rather than glued to the body. Typified by most Fender electric guitars. In fact, such a neck is most often secured by screws.

bookmatched Wood split into two thin sheets and joined together to present symmetrically matching grain/figure patterns.

bottleneck Style of guitar playing using a metal or glass object to slide up and down the guitar strings instead of fretting individual notes. The broken-off neck of a bottle was originally used, hence the name.

bound See *binding*.

bout Looking at a guitar standing upright, the bouts are the outward curves of the body above (upper bout) and below (lower bout) the instrument's "waist."

boutique amp High-end, generally hand-built and hand-wired guitar amplifier produced usually in limited numbers by an independent craftsman.

box Slang term for (usually hollowbody "jazz") guitar.

BPM Beats per minute – the tempo of the music.

Brazilian rosewood Hardwood derived from the tropical evergreen Dalbergia nigra and used in the making of some guitar bodies, necks and fingerboards. Now a protected species, meaning further exportation from Brazil is banned.

bridge Unit on guitar body that holds the saddle(s). Sometimes also incorporates the anchor point for the strings.

bridge block On acoustic guitars, this refers to the drilled section of a bridge through which the strings are threaded.

bridge pickup Pickup placed nearest the bridge. At one time known as the lead or treble pickup.

bridgeplate On electric guitars, this is the baseplate on to which bridge components are mounted; on acoustic guitars, the reinforcing hardwood plate under the bridge.

bullet Describes the appearance of the truss-rod adjustment nut visible at the headstock on some Fender and Fender-style guitars.

burst Abbreviation of sunburst (finish), but often used specifically to refer to one of the original sunburst-finish Gibson Les Paul Standard models made between 1958 and 1960.

button Knob used to turn tuners (machine heads).

cable Another name for a cord (lead) to supply mains power, or to connect amps and speakers, or to connect instruments and amplifiers. Can also be used generally for the sheathed connecting wires, with or without connectors.

camber See *radius*.

cans Slang term for headphones.

capacitor (cap) Frequency-dependent electrical component. Within an electric guitar tone control, for example, it's used to filter high frequencies to ground (earth) making the sound progressively darker as the control is turned down. Used similarly in guitar amplifiers, as well as for filtering noise from power supplies by passing AC signal to ground.

capo (from capo tasto or capo dastro) Movable device which can be fitted over the fingerboard behind any fret. It shortens the strings' length and therefore raises their pitch. Used to play in different keys but with familiar chord shapes.

carbon graphite Strong, stable, man-made material used by some modern electric guitar makers. Has a very high resonant frequency.

cathode biased In a tube amp, an output stage which is biased according to the voltage drop across a resistor connected to the cathode of the power tube(s). Often considered a source of "vintage" tone, it is a feature of the tweed Fender Deluxe, the Vox AC-30 and others. See also *fixed bias*.

cavity Hollowed-out area in solidbody guitar for controls and switches: thus "control cavity."

cedar Evergreen conifer of the Mediterranean; the timber is used particularly in the making of classical guitar necks. In flat-top and other building the term often refers to "western red cedar," which is not a cedar at all but a North American thuya or arbor vitae.

cellulose See *nitro-cellulose*.

center block Solid wooden block running

through the inside of a semi-acoustic guitar's body.

chamfer Bevel or slope to the edges of a guitar's body.

chassis Steel or aluminum casing that houses the electronics of an amp or an effects unit.

checkerboard binding Binding made up of small alternate black and white blocks running around the circumference of a guitar body. Normally associated with high-end Rickenbacker guitars.

cherry Shade of red stain used in translucent guitar finishes and most commonly associated with Gibson who used it extensively from the 1950s onwards. Hence often referred to as Gibson Cherry Red.

choke Small transformer within some guitar amps which helps to filter AC noise from the circuit.

choking String colliding with a higher fret as the string is played and/or bent.

class A Amplifier with output tubes set to operate throughout the full 360-degree cycle of the signal. Class A is sometimes considered "sweeter" sounding harmonically, but is less efficient power-wise than class AB. (The term is often incorrectly used to describe guitar amps which are in fact cathode-biased class AB circuits with no negative feedback, and therefore share some sonic characteristics with class A amps.) See *class AB*.

class AB Amplifier with output tubes set to cut off alternately for a portion of the signal's 360-degree cycle, thereby sharing the load and increasing output efficiency. (In reality, this is the operating class of the majority of guitar amps, and certainly of many classics by Marshall, Fender, Mesa/Boogie and others.) See *class A*.

clay dot Refers to the material used for the dot inlays on Fender guitars from circa 1959 to mid 1964.

coil(s) Insulated wire wound around bobbin(s) in a pickup.

coil-split Usually describes a method to cut out one coil of a humbucking pickup, giving a slightly lower output and cleaner, more single-coil-like sound. Also known, incorrectly, as coil-tap.

coil-tap (tapped pickup) Pickup coil which has two or more live leads exiting at different percentages of the total wind, in order to provide multiple output levels and tones. Not to be confused with coil-split.

comping Playing style, usually associated with jazz, which sustains the tempo and rhythm of a piece while simultaneously stating its chord changes.

compound radius See *radius*.

compressor Sound processor that can be set to smooth dynamic range and thus minimize sudden leaps in volume. Overall perceived loudness is in this way increased without "clipping."

conductor wires Wires attached to the start

and finish of a pickup coil which take the output signal to the controls. A four-conductor humbucker, for example, actually has five output wires: four conductor wires and a fifth (bare) wire which comes from the pickup's grounding plate and/or cover and must always be connected to ground (earth).

conical radius See *radius*.

contoured body Gentle curving of the front and/or back of a solid guitar body, and usually designed to aid player comfort.

control(s) Knobs and switch levers on outside of guitar activating the function of electric components that are usually mounted below the pickguard or in back of the body.

control cavity See *cavity*.

cord (cable, UK: lead) Cable to supply unit with power, or to connect amplifiers and speakers, or to connect instruments and amplifiers.

counterpoint Music that consists of two or more independent melody lines.

coupling Exchange of mechanical energy between an instrument's string(s) and soundboard.

cross-head screw Screw that has two slots in a "cross" shape in its head. (Also "Phillips-head".)

crossover Circuit, sometimes built into amps and/or speakers, that splits a signal into two or more complementary frequency ranges.

current Flow of electrons in an electrical circuit, measured in amps.

cutaway Curve into body near neck joint, aiding player's access to high frets. A guitar can have two ("double," "equal," "offset," "twin") cutaways or one ("single") cutaway. Sharp ("florentine") or round ("venetian") describe the shape of the horn formed by the cutaway.

cypress Conifer native to southern Europe, east Asia and North America and widely planted for decorative purposes and for wood. Used in the 19th century for the bodies of cheaper guitars taken up by the flamencos.

damping Deadening of a sound, especially by stopping the vibration of a string with, for example, the palm of the hand.

DC Short for "direct current." Electric current flowing only in one direction. Tube (valve) amps utilize DC voltages for the vast portion of their internal operation.

DC resistance "Direct current" resistance: a measurement (in ohms) that is often quoted in pickup specs to give an indication of relative output.

dead string length Portion of the string beyond the nut and behind the saddle.

desk See *board*.

digital System of recording or processing which stores and processes analog information by converting it into a series of numbers (binary 1s and 0s).

digital modeling See *modeling amp*.

diode Electronic component used within some guitar amps as a solid-state rectifier to convert AC current to DC. Also occasionally used in solid-state overdrive circuits. See also *rectifier*.

dissonance Perceived sonic clash between two or more notes that are sounded together.

distortion Signal degradation caused by the overloading or intentional manipulation of audio systems (such as guitar amplifier). Often used deliberately to create a harsher and grittier or sweeter and more compressed sound.

dive-bomb See *down-bend*.

dog-ear Nickname for some P-90 pickups, derived from the shape of the mounting lugs on the cover. See also *soap-bar*.

dot markers Dot-shape position markers in fingerboard.

dot-neck Fingerboard with dot-shape position markers; nickname for Gibson ES-335 of 1958-62 (and reissues) with such markers.

double-locking vibrato See *locking vibrato*.

double-neck (twin-neck) Large guitar specially made with two necks, usually combining six-string and 12-string, or six-string and bass.

down-bend Downward shift in the strings' pitch using a vibrato. In extreme cases this is known as dive-bombing.

down-market See *low-end*.

DPDT switch Double-pole double-throw switch, usually miniature or sub-miniature variety used for guitar coil-tap or other such switching.

dynamics Expression in music using a range of volume (intensity) shifts.

earth (UK term; also known as ground, especially in US) Connection between an electrical circuit or device and the ground. A common neutral reference point in an electrical circuit. All electrical components (and shielding) within a guitar (and amplifiers, signal processors, etc) must be linked to earth as the guitar's pickups and electrics are susceptible to noise interference. See also *shielding*.

ebonized Wood darkened to look like ebony.

ebony Dense, black hardwood used for fingerboards and bridges.

effects (effects units, FX) Generic term for audio processing devices such as distortions, delays, reverbs, flangers, phasers, harmonizers and so on.

effects loop Patch between the preamp and power amp (or sometimes within preamp stages) of guitar amp, processing unit or mixer for inserting effects that will operate on selected sound signals.

electron tube See *tube*.

electronic tuner Typically battery-powered unit that displays and enables accurate tuning to standard concert pitch.

end-block Thick wooden block used to join sides of guitar at the lower bout.

EQ See *equalization*.

equalization (EQ) Active tone control that works by emphasizing or de-emphasizing specific frequency bands. General term for tone control.

European spruce Sometimes called German spruce, picea abies tends to come from the Balkans. Spruce originally meant "from Prussia." Used for soundboards.

face See *plate*, *soundboard*.

Farad Measure of electrical capacitance, and usually (for electric guitar capacitors) quoted in microfarads (μF) or picofarads (pF).

feedback Howling noise produced by leakage of the output of an amplification system back into its input, typically a guitar's pickup(s).

f-hole Soundhole of approximately "f" shape on some hollowbody and semi-acoustic guitars.

figure Natural pattern on surface of wood; thus "figured maple".

fingerboard (fretboard, board) Playing surface of the guitar that holds the frets. It can be simply the front of the neck itself, or a separate thin board glued to the neck.

finish Protective and decorative covering on wood parts, typically the guitar's body, back of neck, and headstock.

five-position switch See *five-way switch*.

five-way switch (five-position switch) Selector switch that offers five options, for example the five pickup combinations on a Strat-style guitar.

fixed bias In guitar amps, a technique for biasing output tubes using a pot to adjust negative voltage on the tube's grid as compared to its cathode. (Note that the name is somewhat misleading as "fixed-bias" amps generally have a bias which is adjustable, whereas cathode-biased amps are set and non-adjustable.) See *cathode biased*.

fixed bridge Non-vibrato bridge.

fixed neck See *glued neck*.

flame Dramatic figure, usually on maple.

flame-top Guitar, often specifically a Gibson Les Paul Standard, with sunburst maple top.

flat-top Acoustic guitar with flat top (as opposed to arched) and usually with a round soundhole.

floating bridge Bridge not fixed permanently to the guitar's top, but held in place by string tension (usually on older or old-style hollowbody guitars).

floating pickup Pickup not fixed permanently to the guitar's top, but mounted on a separate pickguard or to the end of the fingerboard (on some hollowbody electric guitars).

floating vibrato Vibrato unit (such as the Floyd Rose or Wilkinson type) that "floats" above the surface of the body.

flowerpot inlay Describes an inlay depicting a stylized vase and foliage used by Gibson on, notably, its L-5 model.

14-fret/12-fret Refers to the point at which a flat-top acoustic guitar's neck joins the body.

frequency Number of cycles of a vibration occurring per unit of time; the perceived pitch of a sound. See also *Hertz*.

fretboard See *fingerboard*.

fretless Guitar fingerboard without frets; usually bass, but sometimes (very rarely) guitar.

frets Metal strips positioned on the fingerboard of a guitar (or sometimes directly into the face of a solid neck) to enable the player to stop the strings and produce specific notes.

fretwire Wire from which individual frets are cut.

FX Abbreviation for effects. Also known more formally as signal processors – boxes that can be used to alter sound in a creative and/or artistic manner.

gain Amount of increase or change in signal level. When dBs are used, increased gain is shown as +dB; reduction is shown -dB; and no change as 0dB.

gauge Outer diameter of a string, always measured in thousandths of an inch (.009", .042" etc). Strings are supplied in particular gauges and/or in sets of matched gauges. Fretwire is also offered in different gauges, or sizes.

gig Live musical event.

glued neck (glued-in neck, set neck, fixed neck) Type of neck/body joint popularized by Gibson which permanently glues the two main components together.

greenback Describes a particularly desirable Celestion 12" guitar speaker that had a green magnet-cover, also known as the model G12M.

ground (also known as earth, particularly in the UK) Connection between an electrical circuit or device and the ground. A common neutral reference point in an electrical circuit. All electrical components (and shielding) within a guitar (and amplifiers, signal processors, etc) must be linked to earth as the guitar's pickups and electrics are susceptible to noise interference.

ground wire Wire connected from vibrato, bridge, tailpiece, switch, pickup cover, grounding plate etc to ground (earth).

grounding plate Metal baseplate of pickup that is connected to ground (earth).

grunge tuning Tuning all strings down one half step (one semitone) for a fatter sound.

hardtail Guitar with non-vibrato bridge (originally used primarily to distinguish non-vibrato Fender Stratocasters from the more common vibrato-loaded models).

hardware Separate components (non-electrical) fitted to the guitar: the bridge, tuners, strap buttons, and so on.

harmonic Usually refers to a ringing, high-pitched note produced by touching (rather than fretting) strategic points on the string while it is plucked, most noticeably at the fifth, seventh and 12th fret. In fact, "harmonics" also occur naturally during the playing of the acoustic or electric guitar (or any stringed instrument) and are part of any guitar's overall voice.

harmonic distortion "Ordinary" distortion occurring in analog (audio) electronics, speakers and mikes, involving the generation of harmonics.

headstock Portion at the end of the neck where the strings attach to the tuners. "Six-a-

side" type (Fender-style) has all six tuners on one side of the headstock. "Three-a-side" type (Gibson-style) has three tuners on one side, three the other.

heel Curved deepening of the neck for strength near body joint.

herringbone Describes a black-and-white decorative inlay for acoustic guitars, as popularized by the Martin company.

Hertz (Hz) Unit of frequency measurement. One Hertz equals one cycle per second. See *frequency*.

hex pickup Provides suitable signal for an external synthesizer.

hook-up wire Connecting wire (live or ground) from pickup to pots, switches etc.

horn Pointed body shape formed by cutaway: thus "left horn," "sharp horn," etc. See also *cutaway*.

hot In electrical connections, means live. Also used generally to mean powerful, as in "hot pickup."

hot-rodding Making modifications to a guitar, usually its pickups and/or electronics.

HT Symbol denoting high voltage in amplifier circuits (short for High Tension) and particularly used in the UK. See *B+*.

humbucker (humbucking) Noise-canceling twin-coil pickup. Typically the two coils have opposite magnetic polarity and are wired together electrically out-of-phase to produce a sound that we call in-phase. See also *phase*.

impedance Electrical resistance to the flow of alternating current, measured in Ohms (Ω). A few electric guitars have low-impedance circuits or pickups to match the inputs of recording equipment; the vast majority are high impedance. Impedance matching is important to avoid loss of signal and tone. Also commonly encountered with speakers, where it is important to match a speaker's (or speaker cab's) impedance to that of the amplifier's speaker output (commonly 4Ω, 8Ω or 16Ω).

Indian rosewood Hardwood from tropical evergreen tree, known as East Indian rosewood or Dalbergia latifolia. Used for acoustic guitar bodies, fingerboards or necks, especially now that Brazilian rosewood is not freely available.

inertia block See *sustain block*.

inlay Decorative material cut and fitted into body, fingerboard, headstock etc.

insulation Plastic, cloth or tape wrap, or sheath (non-conductive), around an electrical wire, designed to prevent wire(s) coming into contact with other components and thus shorting the circuit.

intonation State of a guitar so that it is as in-tune with itself as physically possible. This is usually dependent on setting each string's speaking length by adjusting the point at which the strings cross the bridge saddle, known as intonation adjustment. Some bridges allow more adjustment, and therefore greater possibilities for accurate intonation, than others.

jack (UK: jack socket) Mono or stereo connecting socket, usually ¼" (6.5mm), used to feed guitar's output signal to amplification.

jackplate Mounting plate for output jack (jack socket), usually screwed on to body.

jack socket See *jack*.

jewel light Fender-style pilot light with faceted cut-glass "jewel" screwed on over a small bulb.

Kluson Brand of tuner, originally used on old Fender, Gibson and other guitars, and now reissued.

lacquer See *nitro-cellulose*.

laminated Joined together in layers; usually wood (bodies, necks) or plastic (pickguards).

lead Shorthand for lead guitar: the main guitar within a group; the one that plays most of the solos and/or riffs. Also (UK) term for cord; see also *cable*, *cord*.

lead pickup See *bridge pickup*.

leaf switch See *toggle switch*.

LED Abbreviation of light emitting diode, a small light often used as an "on" indicator in footswitches, effects and amplifier control panels. Sometimes also used as a component within circuits.

ligado Left-hand technique involving hammering-on and pulling-off. Especially important in flamenco playing.

linear taper See *taper*.

locking trem See *locking vibrato*.

logarithmic taper See *taper*.

logo Brandname and/or trademark, usually on the headstock.

lower bout See *bout*.

lug Protruding part or surface. On electrical components, a lug (sometimes called a tag) allows a connection to be made.

machine head See *tuner*.

magnetic pickup Transducer using coils of wire wound around a magnet. It converts string vibrations into electrical signals.

mahogany Very stable, medium weight hardwood favored by most guitar makers for necks, and by many for solid bodies.

mains Term for high AC voltage (particularly in the UK) as supplied by domestic wall socket – that is, the "main" domestic supply.

maple Hard, heavy wood, often displaying extreme figure patterns prized by guitar makers. Varying kinds of figure give rise to visual nicknames such as quilted, tigerstripe, curly, flame.

master volume/tone Control that affects all pickups equally. In amplification, a master volume control governs the output level – or operating level of the power section – when partnered with a gain, drive or volume control that governs the level of the individual preamp(s).

microfarad See *Farad*.

MIDI Abbreviation of Musical Instrument Digital Interface. The industry-standard control system for electronic instruments. Data for notes, performance effects, patch changes, voice and sample data, tempo and other information can be transmitted and received.

mod Abbreviation for modification. Any change or after-market customization made to a guitar, amplifier or effects pedal.

modeling amp Guitar amplifier using digital technology (though occasionally analog solid-state circuitry) to emulate, or model, the sounds of classic tube amps.

mother-of-pearl Shell of some molluscs, for example abalone, used for inlays in decoration of rosettes, fingerboards, headstocks, tuning pegs etc.

mounting ring Usually plastic unit within which Gibson-style pickups are fitted to the guitar body.

mustache bridge Describes the shape of a flat-top acoustic guitar bridge plate, typically found on the Gibson J-200 model.

neck Part of the guitar supporting the fingerboard and strings; glued or bolted to the body, or on "through-neck" types forming a support spine on to which "wings" are usually glued to form the body.

neck block In acoustic guitars, the end of the neck inside the body where it is built up to meet the top and back of the guitar.

neck pickup Pickup placed nearest the neck. At one time known as the rhythm or bass pickup.

neck pitch Angle of a guitar's neck relative to the body face.

neckplate Single metal plate through which screws pass to achieve a bolt-on neck fixing (Fender-style). Some bolt-on neck-to-body joints use separate washers for each screw.

neck pocket Rout, or recess, into which the neck fits on the body of a bolt-on-neck guitar.

neck relief Small amount of concave bow in a neck (dipping in the middle) that can help to create a relatively buzz-free action.

neck-tilt Device on some Fender (and other) neck-to-body joints that allows easier adjustment of the neck pitch.

nickel Major component of most metal guitar strings.

nitro-cellulose (US: lacquer) Type of finish used commonly in the '50s and '60s but now rarely seen on production guitars.

noise Any undesirable sound, such as mains hum or interference.

noise-canceling Type of pickup with two coils wired together to cancel noise, often called humbucking. Any arrangement of pickups or pickup coils that achieves this.

nut Bone, metal or (now usually) synthetic slotted guide bar over which the strings pass to reach the tuners and which determines string height and spacing at the headstock end of neck.

nut lock See *locking nut*.

Offset Contour Body Fender trademark used to describe the distortion of a conventional solidbody shape to aid the player's comfort and present the neck at a more comfortable angle. Fender's Jazzmaster and Jaguar models were the first with this design.

offshore Made overseas; more specifically and often used to mean outside the US.

ohm Unit of electrical resistance.

open tuning Tuning the guitar to a chord or altered chord, often for slide playing.

out of phase Audible result of the electrical linking of two coils or two pickups in either series or parallel in such a way as to provide at least partial cancellation of the signal. Usually the low frequencies are cancelled so that the resulting sound is thin, lacking in warmth, and often quite brittle. To create an audible result that is in-phase (for example of two coils within a humbucker) the coils must be linked electrically out-of-phase. Phase relationship also depends on polarity of magnets. See also *humbucker*.

output attenuator An attenuator connected between guitar amplifier and speaker. Also see attenuator.

oxblood Describes the color of the woven grille cloth used on Fender amps in the early 1960s.

PAF Gibson pickup with Patent Applied For decal (sticker) on base – as was the first, vintage version of the Gibson humbucker.

parallel Electrical circuit that has all the positive points joined together and all the negative points joined together. If we consider that a single-coil pickup has a positive (live, hot) and negative (ground, earth) output, when two single-coil pickups on a Stratocaster (position two and four on a five-way switch), for example, are selected together, they are linked in parallel. Can also apply to the parallel linking of resistors or capacitors in a circuit, etc. See also *series*.

passive Normal, unboosted circuit.

PCB Abbreviation for printed circuit board, a mass-produced fiber board with copper "tracks" making connections between components. It is now the most common circuit board in modern consumer electronics, and is employed in the majority of guitar amplifiers, other than those that use expensive hand-wired designs.

pearl See *mother-of-pearl*.

pearloid Fake pearl, made of plastic and pearl dust.

pentode Tube (valve) containing five functional elements. Most output tubes in guitar amplifiers are pentodes. Also see *triode*.

phase Relationship of two waveforms with respect to time. See also *out of phase*.

Phillips screw or screwdriver See *cross-head screwdriver*.

pick (plectrum, flat pick) Small piece of (usually) plastic or metal – and in olden times tortoiseshell – that is used to pluck or strum a guitar's strings.

pickguard (UK: scratchplate) Protective panel raised above body or fitted flush on to guitar body.

pickup Any unit mounted on a guitar (or other stringed instrument) which transforms string vibration to an electrical signal to be passed along to an amplifier. See *magnetic pickup, piezo pickup, transducer*.

pickup switch Selector switch that specifically selects pickups individually or in combination.

pin bridge Acoustic guitar bridge that secures the strings by pins rather than by tying.

pitch Frequency of a note: the perceived "lowness" or "highness" of a sound. See also *neck pitch*.

plain strings Plain steel guitar strings with no outer windings. See *wound strings*.

plectrum See *pick*.

plexi Nickname for Marshall amplifiers of the mid to late 1960s that used gold-painted "plexiglas" plastic control panels. Also used to refer to the sound produced by Marshall amps of this era, or the reproduction of such a tone.

P-90 Model name for early Gibson single-coil pickup.

point-to-point Method of constructing hand-wired amplifier circuits where individual components are connected directly to each other, without the use of a circuit board.

polarity Relationship of positive and negative electrical currents (or north and south magnetic poles) to each other. The magnetic polarity of a pickup refers to the north or south orientation of the magnetic field as presented to the strings.

pole Simultaneously-switched circuit within an electrical switch; thus "two-pole."

polepieces Non-magnetic (but magnetically conductive) polepieces are used to control, concentrate and/or shape a pickup's magnetic field. Can be either adjustable (screw) or non-adjustable (slug) as in an original Gibson humbucker. Magnetic polepieces are those where the magnet itself is aimed directly at the strings, as in an original Stratocaster single-coil.

polyester Type of modern plastic finish used on some guitars.

polyphonic Music made up of several independent lines, each of which is known as a voice.

polyurethane (urethane) Type of modern plastic finish that is used on some guitars.

position markers Fingerboard inlays of various designs; visual clues to the player of fret positions.

pot (potentiometer) Variable electrical resistor that alters voltage by a spindle turning on an electrically resistive track. Used for volume and tone controls, etc.

power amp Output stage of a guitar amplifier that converts the preamp signal to the signal capable of driving a speaker. In a tube (valve) amp, this is where the big tubes live.

preamp (pre-amplifier) Circuit designed to boost low-level signals to a standard level and EQ them before they're sent toward the power amp (hence "pre-amplifier") for full amplification. Guitar circuit usually powered by battery that converts the pickup's output from high to low impedance (preamp/buffer) and can increase the output signal and boost or cut specific frequencies for tonal effect. Also, the first gain stage in a guitar amp, which generally also includes the EQ circuitry and any overdrive-generating stages.

pre-CBS Fender guitars and amps made before CBS takeover in 1965.

pressed top Arched top (usually laminated) of hollowbody guitar made by machine-pressing rather than hand-carving.

purfling Usually synonymous with binding, but more accurately refers to the decorative inlays around the perimeter of a guitar alongside the binding.

push-pull Power amplifier in which output tubes (valves) operate on alternate cycles of the signal. (This is the most common power amp format in guitar amps that contain more than one output tube.) Also as "push-pull switch," a switch contained on a potentiometer on a guitar or amplifier, which can be pulled to engage a switching function in addition to the potentiometer's standard rotary function.

pyramid bridge Flat-top acoustic guitar bridge having pyramid shaped "bumps" at each side. Common to early Martins.

quarter-sawn Wood cut on radius of tree so that "rings" are perpendicular to the surface of the plank. Structurally preferable to flat-sawn wood for guitar building.

quilted Undulating figure seen on surface of wood, usually maple.

rectifier Component within a guitar amplifier which converts electrical current from AC to DC; can comprise solid-state diodes or a tube (valve) rectifier.

reissue Instrument or amp based on an earlier and usually classic model, reintroduced at a later date.

relief See *neck relief*.

resistor Electrical component which introduces a known value of resistance (measured in ohms) to the electrical flow in a circuit.

resonant frequency Frequency at which any object vibrates most with the least stimulation.

reverb (reverberation) Ambience effect combining many short echoes; can be imitated electronically, generally by the installation of a spring unit in guitar amps, or digitally in pedals and studio effects units.

rhythm pickup See *neck pickup*.

rosewood Variegated hardwood traditionally used for acoustic guitar backs, sides and fingerboards. Brazilian or Rio is the most highly prized; Indian is more common.

rout Hole or cavity cut into a guitar, usually into the body. Cavities of this kind are thus said to be routed (rhymes with "shouted") into the body.

saddle(s) Part(s) of a bridge where the strings make contact; the start of the speaking length of the string; effectively the opposite of the (top) nut.

sag Slight drop in power supply of a guitar amplifier (particularly noticeable in designs comprising tube rectifiers) when a powerful note or chord is played, producing a compression-like softening and squeezing of the signal.

scale length (string length) Theoretical length of the vibrating string from nut to saddle; actually twice the distance from nut to 12th fret. The actual scale length (the distance from the nut to saddle after intonation adjustment) is slightly longer. See *intonation*, *compensation*.

scratchplate See *pickguard*.

scratch test To verify if a pickup on a guitar plugged into an amp is working by gently rubbing ("scratching") the tip of a screwdriver on the pickup's polepieces and listening for sound.

selector Control that selects from options, usually of pickups.

semi See *semi-acoustic*.

semi-acoustic (semi-solid, semi) Electric guitar with wholly or partly hollow thin body. Originally referred specifically to an electric guitar with a solid wooden block running down the center of thinline body, such as Gibson's ES-335.

semi-solid See *semi-acoustic*.

serial number Added by maker for own purposes; sometimes useful for determining the period of the instrument's construction.

series Electrical linkage of positive and negative points within an electrical circuit with additive effect – for example, the two pickup coils within a series-wired humbucker. In this instance, the total resistance of a series-wired humbucker is the sum of the resistance of each coil. Parallel linkage of the same two coils results in the resistance being one quarter of the sum total. Generally, the higher the resistance the "darker" the resulting tone. Also applies to method of linkage of capacitors or resistors within an amplifier or other electrical circuit. See *parallel*.

set neck (glued neck, glued-in neck, fixed neck) Type of neck/body joint popularized by Gibson which permanently "sets" the two main components together, usually by gluing.

set-up General term including but not restricted to a broad and complex combination of factors (string height, saddle height, intonation adjustments, fret condition, neck relief, etc) required to get the guitar playing to its optimum level.

shellac Natural thermoplastic resin made from secretions of lac insect, which lives on trees in India and Thailand. Dissolved in alcohol, it creates a finish that is applied to guitars by French polishing.

shielding (screening) Barrier to any outside electrical interference. Special paint or conductive foil in the control or pickup cavity to reduce electrical interference. See also *ground*.

signal Transmitted electrical information – for example between control circuits, or guitar

and amplifier, etc – usually by means of a connecting wire or cord (lead).

single-coil Original pickup type with a single coil of wire wrapped around (a) magnet(s).

single-ended Amplifier in which the power tube (valve) – usually just one – operates through the entire cycle of the signal. Such amps are necessarily, therefore, class A. Classic examples include the Fender Champ and Vox AC-4.

skunk-stripe Walnut strip inserted in back of one-piece Fender maple necks after truss-rod is inserted.

slab board (slab fingerboard) Fender type (circa 1959-62) in which the joint between the top of the neck and the base of the fingerboard is flat. Later this joint was curved.

slot-head screw Type with a single slot in its head.

slush lever See *vibrato*.

snakehead Headstock shape that is narrower at the top than the bottom. Usually refers to early Gibson type.

snot green See *mint green*.

soapbar Nickname for P-90 pickup with a cover that has no mounting "ears". See *dog-ear*.

solid General term for any solidbody guitar.

solid-state Circuitry using transistorized components rather than tubes (valves).

soundboard Vibrating top of a guitar body. See *top*, *plate*.

SPDT switch Single-pole double-throw miniature switch.

speaker (loudspeaker, driver) Component consisting of a ceramic or alnico magnet, voice coil, and paper cone, driven by an amplified signal to reproduce sound waves in moving air.

speaking length Sounding length of a guitar's string: the part running from the nut down to the bridge saddle.

splice-joint One method of fixing a guitar head to its neck when each has been carved from a different section of wood.

splined Grooved surface of potentiometer shaft that assists tight fitting of a control knob.

spring claw Anchor point for vibrato springs in body-rear vibrato cavity. Adjusting the spring claw's two screws will affect the position and potential travel of the vibrato.

spruce Soft, light hardwood used for the soundboard on many acoustic guitars.

stop-tail Slang for the style of wrapover bridge fitted to low and mid-priced Gibson solidbodies. See *wrapover bridge*.

stop tailpiece See *stud tailpiece*.

strap button Fixing point on body to attach a guitar-strap; usually two, on sides (or side and back) of guitar body.

Strat Abbreviation of Fender Stratocaster, so universally used that Fender have trademarked it and use it themselves.

string block In classical-guitar terminology, this is the drilled section of a bridge through which the strings are threaded.

string length Sounding length of string, measured from nut to bridge saddle (see also *scale length*).

string post Metal shaft on tuner with a hole or slot to receive the string and around which the string is wound.

string winder Device to assist in the speedy winding of a string onto the tuner's string-post.

stud tailpiece (stop tailpiece) Type of tailpiece fixed to solid or semi-acoustic guitar top, either as a single combined bridge/tailpiece unit, or else as a unit separate from the bridge.

sunburst Decorative paint finish in which (usually) pale-colored center graduates to darker edges.

sustain Length of time a string vibrates. Purposeful elongation of a musical sound, either by playing technique or electronic processing.

sustain block (inertia block) Metal block under the bridgeplate of a floating vibrato (vintage-style Fender, for example) which, because the vibrato is not permanently fixed to the body, replaces the body mass necessary for sufficient string sustain.

sympathetic resonances Sounds produced by open strings that are not struck.

syncopation Displacement of the normal beat.

synth access Guitar type with a built-in pickup to enable connection to an external synthesizer unit.

system vibrato See *vibrato system*.

table See *plate, soundboard, top*.

tailpiece Unit on body separate from bridge that anchors strings. See also *trapeze tailpiece*, *stud tailpiece*.

taper Of a potentiometer: determines how smoothly the resistance is applied as the control is turned down. Most modern pots use a logarithmic taper as opposed to a linear taper.

tapped pickup See *coil-tap*.

thinline Hollowbody electric guitar with especially narrow body depth; term coined originally by Gibson for its Byrdland model introduced in 1955.

three-position switch See *three-way switch*.

three-way switch (three-position switch) Selector switch that offers three options.

through-neck (thru-neck) Neck that travels the complete length of a guitar, "through" the body, and usually with "wings" added to complete the body shape.

tigerstripe Dramatic figure, usually on maple. See *flame*.

timbre Tone quality or "color" or "flavor" of a sound.

tin To apply solder to a wire before making the soldered joint.

toggle switch Type of selector switch that "toggles" between a small number of options. It is sometimes called a leaf switch.

Tolex Trade name of vinyl covering manufactured by DuPont corporation and commonly used by Fender (and some others) on guitar amps and hardshell cases. (Often generically – if incorrectly – used to refer to any vinyl amp covering.)

top Vibrating face of the guitar. See *soundboard, plate*.

top nut See *nut*.

tranny Short for "transistorized." Nickname given to solid-state circuitry or equipment.

transducer Unit that converts one form of energy to another; the term is sometimes used generically for piezo-electric pickups, but technically applies to any type of pickup or loudspeaker, etc. See *magnetic pickup, piezo pickup*.

trapeze tailpiece Simple tailpiece of trapezoidal shape.

treble-bleed cap Simple circuit where capacitor (sometimes with an additional resistor) is attached to volume control potentiometer and thus retains high frequencies when the volume control is turned down.

treble pickup See *bridge pickup*.

tremolo (tremolo arm, tremolo system, trem) Erroneous but much-used term for vibrato device/system. The musical definition of tremolo is the rapid repetition of a note or notes. Perhaps this is why Fender applied the name to its amplifier effect, which is a regular variation in the sound's volume.

triode Tube (valve) containing three functional elements, and most common in the preamp circuits of guitar amplifiers in the form of "dual triodes" – tubes which contain two triodes in a single glass bottle.

truss-rod Metal rod fitted inside the neck, almost always adjustable and which can be used to control neck relief.

truss-rod cover Decorative plate covering truss-rod access hole, usually on headstock.

tube US term for the electrical component that the British call a valve; an abbreviation of electron(ic) vacuum tube. In a guitar amp, a tube amplifies the input signal by regulating the flow of electrons.

Tune-o-matic Gibson-originated bridge adjustable for overall string height as well as for individual string intonation.

tuner Device almost always fitted to the headstock, one per string, that alters a string's tension and pitch. Also called machine head or (archaically) tuning peg. See also *electronic tuner*.

tuner button Knob that the player moves to turn the tuner mechanism in order to raise or lower a string's pitch.

12-fret/14-fret Refers to the point at which a flat-top acoustic guitar's neck joins the body.

twin-neck See *double-neck*.

two-pole See *pole*.

unwound string See *wound string and/or plain string*.

up-bend Upward shift in the strings' pitch brought about by using a vibrato.

up-market See *high-end*.

upper bout See *bout*.

upscale See *high-end*.

valve Short for "thermionic valve;" the British term for electron tube. See *tube*.

vibrato (slush lever, trem, tremolo, tremolo arm, vibrato bridge, vibrato system, wang bar, whammy) Bridge and/or tailpiece which alters the pitch of the strings when the attached arm is moved. Vibrato is the technically correct term because it means a regular variation in pitch. Also used to define this effect when

contained within a guitar amp.

virtuoso Instrumental performer with excellent technical abilities.

V-joint One method of fixing head to neck, or neck to body. More complex than normal splice-joint.

V-neck Describes shape of cross-section of neck on, typically, some older Strats, Teles, and Martins.

waist In-curved shape near the middle of the guitar body, usually its narrowest point.

wang bar See *vibrato*.

Watt Unit of electrical power, commonly used to define the output of guitar amps, the power-handling capabilities of speakers, etc. Technically, the rate that energy is transferred (or work is done) over time, equal to a certain amount of horse-power, or joules per second. Named for James Watt, British pioneer of steam power.

whammy See *vibrato*.

wolf note (wolf tone, dead note) Note with a sound unpleasantly different from or less resonant than those around it. The phenomenon is much affected by instrument construction, and can be indicative of a minor flaw in a guitar.

wrapover bridge Unit where strings are secured by wrapping them around a curved bar.

zero fret Extra fret placed in front of the nut. It provides the start of the string's speaking length and creates the string height at the headstock end of the fingerboard. In this instance the nut is simply used to determine string spacing. Used by some manufacturers to make the tone of the open string and the fretted string more similar.

Index

A P P E N D I X

Author's thanks

The author wishes to thank his publishers Nigel Osborne and Tony Bacon, his editor David Sheppard, and the book's designer Paul Cooper. Thanks to Duke Levine and Tad Kubler for prompt and detailed replies about their recording rigs; to Andrew Russell, Zach Field, and Bruce Derr for helping to keep the music flowing; and to Florence, Fred, and Jess Hunter … just for being there.

A P P E N D I X